**Physical and Creative Activities
for the Mentally Handicapped**

Physical and Creative Activities for the Mentally Handicapped

EDITED BY GRAHAM UPTON

Lecturer in Education, University College, Cardiff

CAMBRIDGE UNIVERSITY PRESS

Cambridge

London · New York · Melbourne

Published by the Syndics of the Cambridge University Press
The Pitt Building, Trumpington Street, Cambridge CB2 1RP
Bentley House, 200 Euston Road, London NW1 2DB
32 East 57th Street, New York, NY 10022, USA
296 Beaconsfield Parade, Middle Park, Melbourne 3206, Australia

First published 1979

Printed in Great Britain at the University Press, Cambridge

Library of Congress Cataloguing in Publication Data
Main entry under title:
Physical and creative activities for the mentally handicapped.
Includes bibliographies and index
1. Mentally handicapped children – Education.
2. Creative activities and seat work.
3. Physical education for the mentally handicapped.
4. Drama in education. 5. Music in education.
I. Upton, Graham, 1944 –
LC4611.P48   371.9'28   77-82519
ISBN 0 521 21778 4 hard covers
ISBN 0 521 29279 4 paperback

CONTENTS

Contributors   vi
Foreword   ix
Preface   xi
Acknowledgements   xiii
Introduction   1

Section I: **Movement and Physical Education**
                 Veronica Sherborne

   1 The significance of movement experiences in the
     development of mentally handicapped children   15
   2 Content of a developmental movement programme   25
   3 The physical education programme   35

Section II: **Music**
                 Ann Hunt

   4 The importance and value of music   57
   5 Planning the programme   66
   6 Activities, songs, instruments and booklists   80

Section III: **Drama**
                 Muriel Judd

   7 Drama in the school curriculum: its aims, purposes and
     objectives   107
   8 Some dramatic activities   116

Section IV: **Art and Craft**
                 Maureen Reynolds

   9 Prerequisites for successful art and craft   135
  10 Some specific activities   151

Index   177

CONTRIBUTORS

Ann Hunt

Freelance lecturer on Music in Education for the mentally handicapped. Formerly headteacher of Gulworthy School for Autistic Children and lecturer on the Bristol N.A.M.H. course for teachers of the mentally handicapped. Trained as an infant/ junior teacher and taught in ordinary and special schools. Has recently been involved in a research project on music for the mentally handicapped and is the author of *Listen, Let's Make Music.*

Muriel Judd

Until 1977 Head of the Department of Drama, West London Institute of Higher Education (formerly Maria Grey College of Education). Trained at the Central School of Speech and Drama and is a qualified speech therapist as well as a teacher. Currently involved in research into drama for the mentally handicapped.

Maureen Reynolds

Headteacher, Springwater School (E.S.N.(S)), Harrogate. Formerly in charge of the education section at Oulton Hall subnormality hospital. Trained as a teacher of the mentally handicapped on the N.A.M.H. course at Manchester and has taught mentally handicapped adults and children for over twenty years. Recently awarded the Open University Course Certificate 'The Handicapped Person in the Community'.

Veronica Sherborne

Senior Lecturer in the School of Special Education in Bristol Polytechnic (formerly Redland College of Education). Trained in Bedford College of Physical Education and at the Art of Movement Studio with Rudolf Laban. Has been training teachers of mentally handicapped children for 20 years and has worked for many years in Canada, America, Norway and other countries. She is the author of chapters in a number of books and has made three films (which are available all over the world).

Graham Upton

Lecturer in Education, University College, Cardiff. Formerly Lecturer in Special Education at Leeds Polytechnic where he was involved in training teachers of the mentally handicapped. Trained and taught in Australia in ordinary and special schools. Author of a number of articles on various aspects of special education and currently involved in research on language development with the mentally handicapped.

FOREWORD

At the simplest level of description, mentally handicapped children are those who, by reason of some impairment, have difficulty in accumulating knowledge of the world they inhabit, the world of people, objects, events and ideas. This disability has behavioural consequences, on which the diagnosis of mental handicap is largely based. Knowing what is an expected and acceptable response to the approaches of unfamiliar adults, or how to manage cutlery, avoid danger or express joy or sorrow, we are all aware, does not come easily to handicapped children.

Some behaviour can be taught by following the procedures usually associated with training, but two essential components of skill are often missing, the elements of adaptation and propriety. Knowing how to do something does not necessarily imply knowing when to and when not to. For this reason, structured programmes, necessary and valuable as they may be, are not enough. Good habits are clearly better than bad habits, but it is not only habits but skills we need to inculcate. These include the skill of thinking, to develop which is one of our aims even when we doubt whether some of our most disabled children may ever be capable of more than very, very simple pre-verbal, non-representational thought.

What *is* thinking? This is a very large question but we can say, in Bruner's words, that it is one of the 'subtle events that may occur between the input of a physical stimulus and the emission of an observable response'. Thus, when a child tries to make sense of his environment by sorting it into classes of objects and events, in other words when he sets out to categorise, he is taking to the road of thought and understanding.

If he travels far enough he will meet occasions which utilise the behaviour we call productive thinking, for he will have practised the skill of generalising previous experience to present demands. Moreover, predictive ability, which is an inherent aspect of perception, becomes part of the process of conceptualising. Imaging the road he has traversed, the child can now imagine what may be round the next bend.

Whenever we wish to help children to develop skills of thinking we have to include in the curriculum experiences which encourage decision-making, categorisation and generalisation. This is where this book comes in. The activities we customarily call creative not only provide opportunities for expression, but also have a contribution to make to reception. It is by engaging with the sights, sounds, spaces, people and materials of the 'outside' that we furnish the 'inside'.

The first steps in this engagement are noticing and attending. Attention comes about both because of factors in the environment which arrest and grip and because the organism is motivated to turn to and be hooked by the alerting circumstances. Idiomatic ways of describing this include having an eye to, lending an ear to, and giving the mind to the matter in hand. And what illuminating idioms these are.

The activities so ably dealt with by the authors engage the eyes, ears, minds and hands. More than that, they involve the whole body in activity and enterprise. Moreover, many of the tasks demand the co-operation of child and teacher, and of children with each other. They provide so many opportunities for children to come to understand, at whatever depth they can, the nature of the information that reaches them through their senses.

It is not only mentally handicapped children who have limitations. Many teachers feel that the children's weaknesses are sometimes matched by their own inability to help them; they are often frustrated in their attempts to understand whatever their pupils are trying to communicate. By using their eyes and ears to observe the children moving, making music, acting, drawing and modelling, teachers give themselves a chance to get to know their charges better. Thus a virtuous circle is formed: the more the teachers understand the children, the better the children comprehend the world they live in.

One can write of the fun and enjoyment of physical and creative activities and all the contributors to this book have rightly done so. Bringing laughter to a child is no mean thing. Nor is even the simplest knowledge to be despised. The pages that follow present a wealth of ideas for teachers who wish to give their pupils happiness and appreciation of some of the many good things the world is full of. It has, consequently, been a privilege to read each of the sections and the able introduction. Most teachers will find much of use in them and will undoubtedly wish to keep referring to them for their sound principles and exciting practices.

To return to the travelling metaphor: this is a guide-book we have been waiting for.

Kathleen Devereux
Cambridge

PREFACE

There is a great deal of knowledge about the education of severely mentally handicapped children but it is locked away at the moment within the minds of those who have been teaching them. What we have to do is seek it out and share it.

(Stevens, 1972, p.46)

Teachers of the mentally handicapped seem to have been reluctant to write about their work or about the educational needs of the children they teach. Relative to the number of children in schools for the mentally handicapped, there is surprisingly little published material available which deals directly with their education. There is no general shortage of literature about mental handicap, but most of this focusses on medical and psychological issues. The importance of medical and psychological research to the understanding of mental handicap cannot be overestimated, and the value of this information to the teacher is obvious. However, the dangers of an inadequate supply of literature on specifically educational issues such as teaching methods and techniques are equally obvious. The dangers are particularly apparent at present because of the recent entry of the mentally handicapped into the education system and the entry of many new teachers into the field of mental handicap. Limited dissemination of ideas can only mean limited guidance for these teachers and ultimately restricted development for the children. While there is undoubtedly much good practice in the education of the mentally handicapped, it is vital that this is shared.

The reasons for this lack of published information are not clear, but must reflect the fact that education for the mentally handicapped has only recently been given official recognition. In Britain, it was not until 1971 that mentally handicapped children were included in the education spectrum. The Education (Handicapped Children) Act of 1970 provided for the education of all mentally handicapped children, and on 1 April 1971 the responsibility for the education of these children passed from the Department of Health and Social Security to the Department of Education and Science. While the 1944 Education Act represents a landmark in special education, it excluded the mentally handicapped from its provisions and declared them to be 'ineducable'. The 1959 Mental Health Act brought some hope for these children by ensuring the provision of training centres. Some recognition of the importance of the work carried out in these centres came in 1964 with the establishment of a Training Council to provide training courses for the staff of these centres. However, these centres were not part of the education system, nor were the staff accorded full teacher status. As second-class citizens in a medically dominated Health Service, it is perhaps little wonder that few teachers felt confident enough to write.

Teachers of the mentally handicapped have now been accorded full professional status, and symbolic of their own gradually developing professionalism is the emergence of a steadily developing literature. The importance of this developing literature must rest primarily on the effect it has on the quality of education the children receive. At the same time a developing literature serves broader ends. It focusses attention on the importance of education for the mentally handicapped and emphasises the central role of the teacher. As Simpson (1970) states, 'up until now teachers have been mainly on the receiving end of advice from research workers. Now is the time to reverse the situation' (p.17). It is hoped that this book will help redress the balance. It is written by educators for educators and is firmly grounded in the business of the classroom.

In this book the minds of four teachers with real knowledge of the mentally handicapped are unlocked. All that remains is, in Mildred Stevens' words, 'to share it'.

References

Simpson, P.F. (1970). Facing the new challenge. *Special Education,* 59(4), 15–17.
Stevens, M. (1972). Teaching young mentally handicapped children. In *Educating Mentally Handicapped Children,* ed. A.F. Laing. Faculty of Education, University College of Swansea.

Graham Upton,
Department of Education,
University College, Cardiff

ACKNOWLEDGEMENTS

Particular thanks go to Mr Harry Hoyle, Senior Lecturer in Special Education, Leeds Polytechnic, for the part he played in planning and preparing the original outline for this book. Without his help it is unlikely that the book would ever have been produced.

Thanks are also extended to Dr John Barrat for the assistance he gave to Veronica Sherborne in preparing her manuscript. Also to Mr C.E. Dearden for the photographs in chapter 10 and to Ms Jacqueline Cobb for the artwork in chapter 6. Bedford Square Press have also been generous in giving permission for four songs originally published in *Listen, Let's Make Music* to be reprinted in chapter 6.

xiii

INTRODUCTION

John is fourteen and has an assessed I.Q. of 35. He is small for his age and slightly overweight. He has little effective language. His co-ordination and motor control are poor. He cannot read and has little concept of number. He can feed, dress and wash himself but still has occasional toilet problems. His vision is good but he has slight hearing loss. He has recurrent respiratory ailments and has been diagnosed as brain damaged. In spite of his difficulties John is a happy child. He is affectionate and loving.

This book is written about children like John, children who for a variety of reasons are not able to function intellectually at the level of the majority of people in our society. Children like John have been variously described as idiots, imbeciles, feeble minded, mentally defective, oligophrenic, mentally retarded, educationally subnormal, mentally handicapped and, more recently, children with severe general learning difficulties. In this book the term 'mentally handicapped' has been used, not because it is regarded as more descriptive or helpful than any other term, but because it is arguably the least emotionally loaded term.

Labelling children such as John is important in that it is a prerequisite for obtaining special educational treatment and other support. However, it is a process which has inherent difficulties and dangers. Some authors (e.g. Goldberg and Rooke, 1967; Kirk, 1972; Dunn, 1973; Hobbs, 1975) have undertaken extensive discussions of the problems of terminology and the nature of the conditions to which it refers. For the teacher, much of this sort of discussion is academic and of little value in the classroom. Also Brown (1973) draws attention to the fact that no matter how important such discussions may be, they can have a negative influence by placing the locus of responsibility on the child. That is, it is the child who is mentally handicapped, the child who is the idiot, the child who is subnormal. Brown suggests that it would be more productive and more relevant for the teacher for the locus of responsibility and interest to be placed outside the child and on the teacher and the environment of the classroom. As he notes, the teacher can do nothing about defective genes or brain damage, but he is in control of the environment of the classroom. He therefore suggests that we might profitably think in terms of 'students who present teachers with severe instructional problems' (p.104). While this might appear to be another attempt at labelling, it is more than that. It draws attention to the need for a change in orientation of the study of these children and

1

their education. There is an urgent need for greater emphasis on the development of teaching methods and techniques. An understanding of terminology is undoubtedly helpful for the teacher, but the terms themselves have little instructional relevance.

Applying a label to a group of children can also disguise the fact that these children are all individuals with their own strengths and weaknesses. A single class of mentally handicapped children can, and generally does, 'include a wide range of behaviour patterns, mental abilities, physical conditions, and social competencies' (Goldberg and Rooke, 1967, p.113). While mentally handicapped children constitute a homogeneous group by virtue of their intellectual limitations, the heterogeneity of such a group is usually apparent even to the casual observer. Some may be grossly deformed and immobile, while others may be physically as capable as otherwise 'normal' children. Emotionally some may be disturbed and disruptive while others will be mature and co-operative. Some may be doubly incontinent and unable to feed themselves, others may be able to travel on public transport. Furthermore the range of aetiological conditions, i.e. those that cause the handicap, is likely to be as great as the number of children in the group. The label of 'mentally handicapped' can serve to obscure these differences and the concomitant need for individualised instruction.

EFFICACY OF SPECIAL EDUCATION

While there is undoubtedly much good practice in special schools for the mentally handicapped, there is at the same time little room for complacency. A number of reports and research projects have been concerned with the quality and effectiveness of special education for the mentally handicapped, with generally disquieting results. Goldberg and Rooke (1967), for example, conclude from their review of research in this area that the 'children in special classes did not make important amounts of progress in socialisation, intellectual development, or self care over and above children who remained at home' (p.119). Unfortunately most of the research studies have been of American origin and conducted in situations where special education for the mentally handicapped was either not compulsory or in the early stages of development and organisation. In this situation, as Blackman and Heintz (1966) point out, 'the variables are so complex and ill defined' (p.28) that the conclusions that can be drawn are limited. However, they do raise questions which must be considered carefully if special classes are to fulfil their purposes and live up to their promise.

On the British front, studies of the efficacy of special education for the mentally handicapped have been limited. Marshall (1967) carried out what is probably the most thorough and best-known study. She carried out a detailed study of some 164 children in nineteen Junior Training Centres during their last two years at school. A variety of assessments were made of social and educational development. While the results reveal progress in social development, the development of language and communication skills was found to be considerably below the levels which might be considered desirable. This discrepancy between social and intellectual development undoubtedly reflects the emphasis that was placed on the development of social skills in the Training Centres. But while self-help skills are basic to independence and ease the task of those who care for the child, the importance of language and communication skills is arguably as great, if not greater. It could be that the development of language skills is inherently more difficult for the mentally handicapped child than the development of social skills. However, Gulliford (1971) contends that the 'lower communication scores are partly due to insufficient attention to language, to uncertainty about methods of promoting language as well as the inherent difficulties of the children' (p.83).

Simpson (1967) comments on a survey and many visits he carried out to Junior Training Centres over a five-year period. He sums up the results of his experience as follows: 'I have seen much to encourage the belief that the best training centres equate in their aims and methods with the best schools for normal children. On the other hand I have seen a lot which I believe must be challenged as "inessential". Unfortunately far too many training centres would appear to function almost wholly at this "inessential level".' (p.4)

The significance of Marshall's and Simpson's findings has been complicated by the transfer of responsibility for the education of the mentally handicapped from the Health to the Education service. There is some evidence, however, which suggests that there is still cause for concern. Hughes (1975) reports a more recent survey of the educational needs of the mentally handicapped. While a number of positive points emerge from his study, his conclusions about the effectiveness and quality of the education are somewhat disquieting. Unlike Marshall, Hughes found significant weaknesses in the development of social skills as well as communication and language skills. Is it possible that the situation is deteriorating? Hughes apparently thinks not as he concludes that 'the results of the investigation highlight the effects of these schools being in the "educational wilderness" until April 1st, 1971'. Similarly McMaster (1973) implies that all is not well when he suggests the need for a 'framework which will allow a holistic view of a fragmented, unstructured and largely chaotic field' (p.12).

To some extent the negative nature of many of these studies may be due to the inadequacy of the parameters that were used. Furthermore there is a highly subjective element involved in their assessments. The studies of Hughes and Simpson are both based on the authors' expectations of what should be happening rather than an objective analysis of what is appropriate or feasible. The other more objective studies all assessed the progress of the children with instruments that were not directly linked to the teaching procedures or content. In fact two studies which have evaluated the effectiveness of special education programmes in terms of their own goals (Peck and Sexton, 1961; Harvey, Yep and Sellin, 1966) both found positive results. Hughes in fact admits that 'the teachers may be satisfied with what has been achieved' (pp.232–3). Dissatisfaction with results may therefore be a dissatisfaction with aims and philosophies, not only with teaching methods and techniques.

It is clear, however, that there are doubts and questions which must be examined and answered. There would seem to be reason to question whether present methods and techniques are fulfilling the expectations which are held for them. There is an obvious need, perhaps long overdue in some people's minds, for a 'realistic appraisal of what education for the mentally handicapped is all about' (McMaster, 1973, p.viii).

THE PLACE OF PHYSICAL AND CREATIVE ACTIVITIES IN THE EDUCATION OF THE MENTALLY HANDICAPPED

The need for a reassessment of education for the mentally handicapped was taken up with some enthusiasm in the mid-1960s by many educationalists in the United States. Generally they concluded that there was a need for greater structure in approach. Lindsley (1964), for example, suggested the need for a 'synthetic environment' with 'prosthetic devices' designed to cater for the needs of the mentally handicapped in the same way that a therapist might use artificial limbs, ramps and elevators for the physically handicapped. Within this frame of reference, behaviour modification techniques were seen to have value and their use subsequently burgeoned at an un-paralleled rate. In a wide variety of situations they have been demonstrated to be extremely potent tools for modifying the behaviour and encouraging the development of mentally handicapped children and adults. Unfortunately this interest in behaviour modification has tended to dominate both research and thinking in this reappraisal of the meaning and nature of education for the mentally handicapped. There is still an urgent need for a re-examination of the value of specific curriculum areas for the mentally handicapped. This is particularly true of areas such as art, music, drama, and movement, which have traditionally been considered to be basic in any educational programme for the mentally handicapped.

Many writers on the education of the mentally handicapped have placed consider-able emphasis on physical and creative activities. Lloyd (1953), for example, suggests a time-table for junior-age children based on a sixty minute activity session involv-ing reading and number work, a fifty-five minute session of directed physical edu-cation and music and movement, with the rest of the day devoted to free play and creative activity. In practice such an allocation of time to physical and creative activi-ties would be unbalanced and it is unlikely that this figure was ever reached. In fact more recent writers tend to complain of the lack of emphasis given to physical and creative activities. Stevens (1971), for example, suggests that the need for move-ment 'is the need least recognised and encouraged by the teachers of these children' (p.15). An assessment of the time actually allocated to physical and creative areas is provided by Hudson (1961), who undertook a content analysis of a large number of lessons in schools for the mentally handicapped in the United States. Over the range of these classes, art and craft, music, drama and physical activities accounted for approximately one-quarter of all lesson time. While changes in educational provisions since 1961 may have affected the amount of time spent on these activities, the proportion tends to agree with this writer's experience.

The value of physical and creative activities for the mentally handicapped has similarly been frequently elaborated upon. Neale and Campbell (1963) stress the potential contribution which physical and creative activities can make towards the development of adjustment and fulfilment. They suggest that these activities 'provide special opportunities for the youngster to come to terms with himself in his own way and at his own rate . . . [and offer] more freedom than other aspects of the usual curriculum for the expression of one's feelings and imagination and for the achievement of fuller self-realisation' (pp.45—6). Hughes (1975) suggests that the poor progress made by the children in his survey was largely the result of limited free play and creative activities. He notes that the reasons for the poor progress must lie in a combination of factors but instances the 'lack of facilities in domestic arts, handwork, gardening and P.E. and less time devoted to manipulatory skills and muscular co-ordination; lack of opportunities to exercise socialisation skills; "over-protectiveness"; a general lack of learning by doing, and a lack of appropriate teaching methods' (p.232). While factors such as the lack of appropriate teaching methods may be of significantly greater import than some of the others, physical and creative activities are obviously seen by him as being of considerable value to educational development.

The claims advanced for the value of physical and creative activities have been supported to some extent by research findings. One of the best-known studies in the field of mental handicap, the Brooklands project (see Lyle, 1960; Tizard 1964), indirectly underlines the value of physical and creative activities. In this study, a group of sixteen five- to ten-year-old children was removed from a large subnormality hospital and placed in a small hostel, Brooklands. This was run on family lines and during the day 'nursery'-type education was provided for the children. They were encouraged to climb, ride cycles, experiment with manipulative toys, undertake constructive and dramatic play and physical activities, and generally to engage in social play. At the end of three years this group was found to have made significant gains in verbal and emotional development in comparison with a matched group that had remained in the hospital. Obviously many factors connected with the hospital and home situations were involved in producing this differential pattern of development. However, the project also underscores the value and importance of the physically and creatively oriented teaching programme.

A number of studies have been undertaken to evaluate more directly the value of physical and creative activities with the mentally handicapped. Mann, Burger and Proger (1974) have undertaken a comprehensive review of studies carried out to investigate the value of physical activities with various groups of exceptional children. A large number of these studies concerned the mentally handicapped, and of these they conclude that physical education 'seems to have a sharpening effect on fine-motor, cognitive and academic performances' (p.245). Michielutte (1974) has undertaken a similar review of research on the use of music and concludes that 'these reports strongly indicate that music can be of considerable value in the areas of physical, emotional and social development' (p.266). Unfortunately many of these studies have been based on inadequate research designs so it is difficult to know how much confidence to place in the results. Nevertheless, they are sufficient in both quantity and quality to justify the conclusion that mentally handicapped children profit from physical and creative experiences.

A RATIONALE FOR A SENSORY-MOTOR APPROACH TO LEARNING

It is well established that mentally handicapped children tend to experience a delay in sensory-motor development and have marked difficulty with perceptual-motor tasks. Rutter, Tizard and Whitmore (1970), for example, found that mentally handi-capped children performed at a markedly inferior level to their 'normal' peers in terms of their co-ordination, constructional ability, motor impersistence and chore-iform (jerky, uncontrolled) movements. Activities such as physical and creative activities, which involve a large sensory-motor component, must therefore be an integral part of the curriculum.

Beyond this need for sensory-motor experiences for their own sake, educators have long attached importance to the relationship of sensory-motor learning to other learning. Lerner (1971) notes links which go back to Plato and Aristotle, and Spinoza advised 'teach the body to do many things; this will help you to perfect the mind and come to the intellectual level of thought' (Lerner, p.60). Similarly in special education, the pioneer work of Itard and Seguin in the eighteenth and nine-teenth centuries involved a heavy emphasis on sensory-motor activities. Itard based his work with Victor, the wild boy of Aveyron, on sensory-motor training. His justification for this was that, so great was 'the intimate relation which unites physical with intellectual man that, although their respective provinces appear and are in fact very distinct . . . the borderline between the two different sorts of func-tion is very confused. Their development is simultaneous and their influence re-ciprocal' (Itard, 1962, p.67).

A number of theoretical frameworks have been advanced upon which an emphasis on sensory-motor training can be justified. Piaget's concept of developmental stages is perhaps the best known of these. Piaget has suggested that there are specific stages in intellectual growth which differ in type or quality of thought involved and through which each child passes. The initial stage in Piaget's model is the sensory-motor period, which for most children occupies approximately the first two years of life. This period is succeeded by the conceptual period which lasts usually until approxi-mately age eleven and which is concerned with the development of symbolic thought. Two sub-stages are delineated with this phase, the intuitive and the concrete oper-ational. In the intuitive stage there is an increased precision in the use of symbols but this is often limited, while in the concrete-operational stage a more rigorous examination of the world begins and reality is more carefully defined. This period in turn gives way to the period of formal operations, when the child is able to cope with hypothetical and abstract thinking. The significance of Piaget's stages for the mentally handicapped has been explored by a number of writers, although actual research has been limited. Inhelder, however, has suggested that the 'severely and profoundly mentally retarded adult can be viewed as fixated at the level of sensori-motor intelligence; [and] the retarded adult should be seen as not capable of surpassing the pre-operational intuitive period' (quoted by Robinson and Robinson, 1976, p.255). Physical and creative activities which are primarily sensory-motor based would thus seem highly appropriate for the mentally handicapped child's learning style and capabilities.

Kephart (1960) has proposed a similar hierarchical system of development which has direct and obvious implications for teaching the mentally handicapped. In his model Kephart postulates a series of increasingly efficient strategies for processing information from the environment. The model is strictly hierarchical and the stages must be passed through sequentially. If learning at one level is incomplete, learning at higher levels will be affected. The earliest stages in this model are motorically and perceptually based and thus this early perceptual motor learning is the final arbiter of all future learning. Ball (1971) notes that 'Kephart's theory rests on the assumption that perception and cognition . . . ultimately develop from a motor base' and that 'without the necessary motor elaborations, and generalisations, intellectual growth will be impaired and distorted' (p.125).

Similar models have been developed by Getman (1965) and Barsch (1967) and both of these systems similarly suggest the importance of sensory-motor based learning for all later learning and development.

If, as has been suggested by some of the Piagetian research, many mentally handicapped children function at the perceptual-motor levels of learning, then it would seem that education for these children should have a sound foundation in perceptual-motor activities. Lerner (1971), writing about the needs of children with learning difficulties, notes that perceptual-motor training is frequently ignored and that many treatment programmes build upon assumed perceptual-motor competencies. However, as she notes, 'for many children such assumptions cannot be made, for these children have not had the necessary experience to internalise a comprehensive and consistent scheme of the world. These children have been unable to adequately organise their information-processing systems to the degree necessary to benefit from such a curriculum. As a consequence they are disorganised, motorically, perceptually and cognitively' (p.95). Mentally handicapped children would seem to be one such group for whom such assumptions cannot be made.

There are a number of programmes available for teaching perceptual-motor skills in a highly structured fashion (e.g. Kephart, 1960; Frostig and Horne, 1964). Currently there is much debate about the effectiveness of these programmes (see Goodman and Hammill, 1973; Hammill and Wiederholt, 1973; Mosher, 1974).

In this situation, the importance of the 'natural' training which is involved in physical and creative activities cannot be underestimated.

A number of writers have suggested that the value of physical and creative activities stems from their multi-sensory nature. Price and Williams (1974), for example, talk of the multi-sensory nature of dance and suggest that there are kinaesthetic, social and rhythmic channels through which mentally handicapped children can learn, whereas approaches which rely on cognitive processes are less likely to succeed because of the children's primary cognitive deficit. Lerner (1971) also comments on the value of the multi-disciplinary nature of physical and creative activities. She writes:

In the motor learning process, several input channels of sensation or perception are integrated with each other and correlated with motor activity, which in turn provides feedback information to correct the perceptions. Thus in performing a motor activity such as a somersault, the child *feels* the surface of the floor; has a body *awareness* of space, changing body positions and balance; *sees* the floor and other objects in relation to his changing positions; *hears* the thump of his body on the floor; and *moves* in a certain fashion. (p.90)

AN INTEGRATED APPROACH TO PHYSICAL AND CREATIVE ACTIVITIES

In this book, art and craft, drama, music, and physical education have been presented and written about as separate activities. These activities are independently viable and can stand as separate subject areas but strict division into subject areas is essentially artificial. On many occasions a lesson may be solely a music or a drama lesson, but more frequently it will contain elements from more than one area. More particularly, many lessons will contain elements of drama, movement and music for it is difficult, particularly at a basic level with mentally handicapped children, to define strict dividing lines between the three. Neale and Campbell (1963) note that 'the distinction between music, drama and movement is an arbitrary one. At best the distinction is possible according to the aims and emphasis that the teacher gives to a session of activities. All three grow naturally out of a child's delight in rhythm, pleasure in expression, and love of movement' (p.51). Art and craft is perhaps more frequently taken as a distinct lesson, although the relationship of art and craft to other creative activities is generally close.

A valuable way in which teaching in different areas can be integrated is by working to themes, or using a project approach. Not only is the project method a means of bringing together diverse subjects but it also allows the children to contribute at their own level towards a co-operative effort. With mentally handicapped children project work seems to be widely used although little has been written about methods and techniques. Fellows (1965) provides a useful outline to basic techniques but these need adaptation for working with mentally handi-

capped children. Three distinct types of projects seem relevant and valuable —
specific, fixed term, and recurrent.

Specific
Projects can be related to a specific event scheduled for a particular date which can
be planned for and worked towards. Examples are the Olympic games, a military
tattoo, or a fair.

Fixed term
A fixed term project is explored in some depth over a fixed period of time which
could be anything from a week to a whole term. Amongst the most common themes
used for this purpose are animal themes; environmental themes such as 'the farm',
'shops', 'houses'; service themes such as 'railways', 'firemen', and 'the garage'; and
interests and hobbies such as 'sport' or 'holidays'.

Recurrent
Seasonal themes are perhaps the most common recurrent themes but other popular
themes include festive events such as Christmas, Easter and Harvest.

Physical and creative activities can play an important role in any project, for
central to the ethos of the project method is an emphasis on exploration and discovery, factors inherent in physical and creative activities. The diagram illustrates
how physical and creative activities could be integrated into a project on transport.

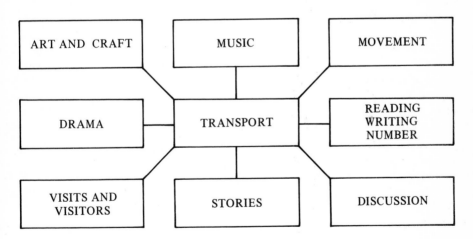

Themes which could be pursued in art and craft are many, and much of the end
product of the project could involve art and craft display work. Scrapbooks could
be made, displays assembled, friezes constructed, models made of various forms
of transport, landscapes built, and towns, countries and cities planned out.

In drama, transport could be acted out. Trains, buses, bicycles, planes, boats, and even steamrollers can be formed; imaginary drivers, passengers and ticket collectors chosen, and imaginary trips to imaginary places undertaken. Roads can be built, ships can be loaded, emergencies can happen and people can be rushed to hospital by ambulance or rescued by helicopter. Horses and carts and old cars can appear, and historical themes can be examined.

In physical education, wheelbarrows might have to be pushed and horses ridden. The balance beam can become a gangplank, a warm-up run around the hall, a car race. Hoops can become wheels. Cars can suddenly have to stop, and then move away again as the lights turn green.

In music we can sing, 'Down by the station', 'Listen to the car horns', 'The wheels of the bus go round and round' or 'I'd like to be a boatman'. Sounds of trains, cars and planes can be recorded, listened to and identified, and then used in a music-making session. There are also many records available which include the sounds and names of ships, cars and planes.

This book is essentially a practical one. It is written by teachers for teachers, and should be equally valuable to the experienced, the inexperienced and those in training. Parents and others involved in the care of the mentally handicapped may also find much of value. The contributors are experts in their area of specialisation, and have all had extensive practical experience with the mentally handicapped. They have produced suggestions and ideas for working with the mentally handicapped based on theoretical knowledge and practical expertise. Some of the ideas will be familiar to experienced teachers; many will be new, and many are innovative and challenging. All have been tried and found to be practical and valuable in fostering the development of the mentally handicapped child.

In section I, Veronica Sherborne outlines her own highly original and innovative approach to physical education. While some teachers may be familiar with her work already, this represents the most detailed exposition of her ideas that is available. In chapter 1 she discusses the theoretical basis of her approach and outlines the benefits she believes this approach can have on the intellectual, social and physical development of mentally handicapped children. She also provides an outline of the stages through which she considers movement skills develop. In chapters 2 and 3 the application of her techniques is elaborated and specific teaching methods are enumerated. She stresses the need for a balanced physical education programme and, a surprise perhaps for some people, will be the importance that she attaches to physical skills as well as the more creative movement for which she has become so well known. Chapter 2 is concerned principally with developmental movement, for which she provides a valuable framework for the progression of activities and elaborates on teaching techniques that are relevant at particular stages of development. Chapter 3 considers general problems of organisation and time-tabling, and then looks in detail at teaching methods for the more traditional physical education activities involving apparatus. In this chapter some particularly interesting ideas are advanced for dealing with children with special difficulties. The ideas on dealing with hyperactive and multi-handicapped children are especially innovative.

In section II, Ann Hunt provides a detailed and insightful introduction to teaching music with the mentally handicapped. In chapter 4 she provides what is undoubtedly the most carefully considered and detailed analysis of the potential value of music for mentally handicapped children that is yet available. She outlines specific areas where music may be of most value and illustrates most of these with relevant case study material. In chapter 5 she presents a detailed framework for teaching in which she outlines various stages through which teaching might progress and provides some specific examples of teaching programmes. Chapter 6 provides a detailed statement of specific teaching techniques, activities, and materials. Of particular interest are the sections on home-made instruments and the lists of songs, records and books which are provided. The ideas that are presented here are exceptionally easy to follow and require little prior musical knowledge. At the same time there is much here that the teacher with specialist musical knowledge will find of great value. And the result is undoubtedly music.

In section III, Muriel Judd outlines an exciting and imaginative approach to teaching drama. Basing her ideas on the concept of 'drama in education' rather than 'drama as theatre' she expounds a convincing argument about the value of drama for the mentally handicapped and at the same time spells out some very practical teaching suggestions. In chapter 7 she writes on the nature of dramatic activity and of the elements of drama that seem to have most relevance for the mentally handicapped. She follows this through into chapter 8 with an elaboration of the specific teaching methods and dramatic activities that can be utilised to achieve the aims that she establishes for drama with the mentally handicapped. She also provides a most valuable framework against which the children's progress can be evaluated. The significance and importance of many of her points are illustrated vividly, and often beautifully, with examples of dramatic work.

In the final section Maureen Reynolds provides the reader with detailed and extensive suggestions for teaching art and craft. In chapter 9 she discusses the pure enjoyment which art and craft can bring, but outlines also the many secondary benefits which can accrue from well-taught art and craft. She discusses what she considers to be the prerequisites of successful art and craft: organisation and preparation. There are some particularly important comments on display and an interesting idea for a mobile art and craft cupboard. The final chapter consists of a detailed list of suggested activities with comments on their relevance for particular age and ability groups. The section concludes with a most useful annotated list of further reading for teachers who wish to pursue specific topics in greater depth.

All of the ideas presented in this book are aimed primarily at the teacher and the classroom. All are based on experience and of proven worth. At the same time all are breaking new ground in that they are amongst the first detailed expressions of ideas in this sphere of work with the mentally handicapped. As such they will, it is hoped, serve to stimulate discussion and research as much as they serve to provide answers to pressing classroom problems. There is still much to be learnt about the education of the mentally handicapped. The authors of this book are presenting their ideas for examination and evaluation. Others must follow their example, for it is only on the basis of a rich and varied literature that informed discussion can take place; and it is only from informed discussion that education will come to serve the best interests of the children with whom we are all concerned.

Further reading

Ball, T.S. (1971). *Itard, Seguin and Kephart: Sensory Education – A Learning Interpretation.* Charles E. Merrill, Ohio.
Barsch, R.H. (1967). *Achieving Perceptual-Motor Efficiency.* Special Child Publications, Seattle.
Blackman, L.S. & Heintz, P. (1966). The mentally retarded. *Review of Educational Research,* **36,** 5–36.
Brown, L. (1973). Instructional programs for trainable-level retarded students. In *The First Review of Special Education,* vol. 2, ed. L. Mann & D.A. Sabatino, pp.103–36. JSE Press, Philadelphia.
Dunn, L.M. (1973). *Exceptional Children in the Schools.* Holt, Rinehart & Winston, New York.
Fellows, M.S. (1965). *Projects for Schools.* Museum Press, London.
Frostig, M. & Horne, D. (1964). *The Frostig Program for the Development of Visual Perception.* Follett Publication Co., Chicago.
Getman, G.N. (1965). The visuomotor complex in the acquisition of learning skills. In *Learning Disorders,* vol. 1, ed. J. Hellmuth, pp.49–76. Special Child Publications, Seattle.
Goldberg, I.I. & Rooke, M.L. (1967). Research and educational practices with mentally deficient children. In *Methods in Special Education,* ed. N.G. Haring & R.L. Schiefelbusch, pp.112–36. McGraw-Hill, New York.
Goodman, L. & Hammill, D. (1973). The effectiveness of the Kephart–Getman activities in developing perceptual-motor and cognitive skills. *Focus on Exceptional Children,* **4**(9), 1–10.
Gulliford, R. (1971). *Special Educational Needs.* Routledge & Kegan Paul, London.
Hammill, D. & Wiederholt, J.L. (1973). Review of the Frostig visual perception test and the related training program. In *The First Review of Special Education,* vol. 1, ed. L. Mann & D.A. Sabatino, pp.33–48. JSE Press, Philadelphia.
Harvey, A., Yep, B. & Sellin, D. (1966). Developmental achievement of trainable mentally retarded children. *Training School Bulletin,* **63,**100–8.
Hobbs, N. (1975). *Issues in the Classification of Children,* vols. 1 and 2. Jossey-Bass, San Francisco.
Hudson, M. (1961). *Identification and Evaluation of Methods for Teaching Mentally Retarded (Trainable) Children.* George Peabody College for Teachers, Tennessee.
Hughes, J.M. (1975). The educational needs of the mentally handicapped. *Educational Research,* **17**(3), 228–33.
Itard, J.M.G. (1962). *The Wild Boy of Aveyron.* Prentice-Hall, Englewood Cliffs, New Jersey.
Kephart, N.C. (1960). *The Slow Learner in the Classroom.* Charles E. Merrill, Ohio.
Kirk, S.A. (1972). *Educating Exceptional Children.* Houghton Mifflin, Boston.
Lerner, J.W. (1971). *Children with Learning Disabilities.* Houghton Mifflin, Boston.

Lindsley, O.R. (1964). Direct measurement and prosthesis of retarded behaviour. *Journal of Education*, **147**, 62–81.

Lloyd, F. (1953). *Educating the Sub-normal Child*. Methuen & Co., London.

Lyle, J.G. (1960). The effect of an institutionalised environment upon the verbal development of imbecile children. III. The Brooklands Residential family unit. *Journal of Mental Deficiency Research*, 4(14), 14–22.

Mann, L., Burger, R.M. & Proger, B.B. (1974). Physical education intervention with the exceptional child. In *The Second Review of Special Education*, ed. L. Mann & D.A. Sabatino, pp.193–250. JSE Press, Philadelphia.

Marshall, A. (1967). *The Abilities and Attainments of Children Leaving Junior Training Centres*. National Association for Mental Health, London.

McMaster, J. McG. (1973). *Toward an Educational Theory for the Mentally Handicapped*. Edward Arnold, London.

Michielutte, R. (1974). The use of music with exceptional children. In *The Second Review of Special Education*, ed. L. Mann & D.A. Sabatino, pp.251–71. JSE Press, Philadelphia.

Mosher, R. (1974). Effectiveness of perceptual-motor programs. *Journal of Leisurability*, 1(4), 10–17.

Neale, M.D. & Campbell, W. (1963). *The Education of the Intellectually Limited Child and Adolescent*. Novak, Sydney.

Peck, J.R. & Sexton, C.L. (1961). Effect of various settings on trainable children's progress. *American Journal of Mental Deficiency*, **66**, 62–8.

Price, D. & Williams, M. (1974). *Modern Educational Dance with the Mentally Handicapped Child*. City of Cardiff College of Education, Cardiff.

Robinson, N.M. & Robinson, H.B. (1976). *The Mentally Retarded Child*. McGraw-Hill, New York.

Rutter, M., Tizard, J. & Whitmore, K. (1970). *Education, Health and Behaviour*. Longman, Harlow.

Simpson, P.F. (1967). Training centres – a challenge. *Special Education*, **56**, 4–8.

Stevens, M. (1971). *The Educational Needs of Severely Subnormal Children*. Edward Arnold, London.

Tizard, J. (1964). *Community Services for the Mentally Handicapped*. Oxford University Press, London.

Section I : Movement and Physical Education

1 THE SIGNIFICANCE OF MOVEMENT EXPERIENCES IN THE DEVELOPMENT OF MENTALLY HANDICAPPED CHILDREN

SENSORY-MOTOR DEVELOPMENT

Mentally handicapped children are developmentally retarded; that is, they may function in some ways at the level of development of a six-month-old baby or a three-year-old child when they are chronologically much older. The highest level of intellectual development that some mentally handicapped children achieve is about that of a five-year-old child. A child may develop physically and motorically, emotionally, socially and intellectually at different rates, and the mentally handicapped child shows a wider discrepancy in this than the normal child. For instance, a mentally handicapped adolescent may reach a level of development emotionally and socially which is in many ways similar to that of a normal adolescent while achieving the intellectual development of a normal four-year-old.

The earliest learning experiences of all children arise from sensory-motor information. The child first becomes aware of sensations within his body, and as he becomes more active he then becomes aware of the movements of his body. Sensory-motor experiences are fundamental to the child's development. The earliest experiences of every baby involve those of being carried, supported, contained, fed, bathed and generally handled. The baby also experiences being rocked, patted, warmly held and cared for. He receives these physical sensations in a relatively passive way, but these early bodily experiences give the child his first information about himself and about the people around him. The baby becomes aware of his own body moving when he kicks, plays with his fingers, lifts his head when lying on his stomach, or rolls over. These experiences help to give the child the confidence to control his body and explore his world.

The very young child develops emotional and physical security through physical contact with the adult. The child responds intuitively and sensitively to the quality of support and care he receives from the care-giver who looks after him, and his emotional development may be affected by his early experiences. The child's confidence is built up on the physical trust established between him and his parents. Although the development of a baby's relationship with his parents is often created through physical contact, the baby also relates to his parents through looking at the adult's face, particularly the eyes. The adult must be especially responsive to the child's gaze, so that the child is rewarded by sounds and smiles for his efforts

15

to engage in eye contact. This is one of the most important ways of helping the young child to focus his attention and strengthen his developing relationship with the adult. The young child's desire to communicate and to relate to others is stimulated by the security he experiences, and the enjoyment he obtains from playing with a responsive adult. A sense of his identity slowly develops, partly through his growing awareness of his body and his growing awareness of other people.

Much of the development which the young child will go through is founded on these experiences of physical awareness of his own body, and of its increasing capacity to move, as well as on his physical and emotional interaction with other people. The child's growing concept of his body and sense of identity are influenced by the child's sensory and motor development.

It is helpful to understand the developmental processes of the normal baby, so that we can assess which experiences have been missed by the retarded child. It is possible to 'feed in' many essential experiences to the young mentally handicapped child which can help to prevent further retardation and which can help the child make the best use of his resources, however limited these may be. The mentally handicapped child needs the stimulus of movement and of relationship play for much longer than the normal child because he is slower to respond and to benefit from it.

In the normal baby early physical development and interaction with his parents are achieved because he is both demanding and responsive; he wants to extend his physical capacities and to explore. The mentally handicapped child is usually not motivated to extend himself and he suffers unless the adults concerned with him realise the need to stimulate the child through physical play. It is understandable if the parents of a mentally handicapped baby give up trying to play with him because of his lack of response, but it is important that the parents give the baby as much help as possible in developing an awareness of his body and of its movement, as well as of helping him to relate to others. The education of the mentally handicapped child begins at birth and it is through giving him enjoyable and rewarding experiences that we can make a most important contribution to his development. Movement experiences should be given in the form of play which the child enjoys so much that he wants to respond and to be active, and feels motivated to continue activity.

I worked recently with two Down's syndrome boys, one of eighteen months and the other of two years, and their respective parents. The two-year-old child had been played with by his parents from birth and was treated like their older child. His father picked him up and swung him and handled him in vigorous movement play which the boy enjoyed. The father was a farmer and took his son to work with him. The child was running and climbing and exploring everything and making contact with many people. He knew the meaning of the words 'tummy', 'nose', 'toes', among many others. He was functioning physically, emotionally and intellectually like a normal two-year-old. The parents of the eighteen-month child had concealed him for a year, and his mother suffered from severe depression. His parents had not played with him. He was played with by one of my students and sat impassively on her stomach as she lay on the ground. He showed no interest in the activities of other children and did not respond to gentle rocking and bouncing or to the student's voice. He avoided eye contact, but finally reacted by smiling when his fringe was lightly blown upwards, and he looked down at the student, and tried to touch her nose. He made no effort to crawl or stand.

Parents of mentally handicapped children experience pressures which are difficult sometimes for teachers to appreciate, and they are in great need of help and support, particularly in the pre-school years. Thus it can be especially beneficial, both for the parents and the child, if the child can attend a pre-school play group. This should preferably be a play group for both normal and handicapped children, called opportunity groups in some areas, as it is a great help to the handicapped child if he can play with normal children. It is also a valuable experience for student teachers if they can take part in a 'family link' scheme in which a student is attached to a family with a handicapped child for a year, or sometimes longer. This can also benefit the child and the family, as the student is often willing and able to play with the child and take him out. This in turn can be instructive for the family and provide them with a much-needed relief from the pressure which having a handicapped child inevitably entails. The provision of education from the age of three in some areas also has obvious benefits for the child and the family.

THE NEEDS OF THE MENTALLY HANDICAPPED CHILD

When a mentally handicapped child first comes to school, he may be functioning at the level of intellectual development of a one- or two-year-old normal child, although it is impossible to generalise about mentally handicapped children because each child is so different. Some children may be multiply handicapped, with a very limited range of movement, while others will be as physically able as normal children. Some children will not advance beyond the level of intelligence of a one-year-old child, while others may be quite intelligent but severely disturbed. Although extremely varied, mentally handicapped children tend to be more like children of their own age in terms of movement than in any other aspect of their make-up. They can consequently experience success and satisfaction from taking part in many forms of activity, such as movement classes, swimming, work on large apparatus and movement to music. Children who have experienced success in movement which involves the body as a whole, and who have directed their often excessive energy in a purposeful way, tend to settle down more readily to classroom tasks which demand fine motor control. As the child becomes more competent in his physical ability, he is more confident about tackling other areas of learning which he finds more difficult. However, because the young mentally handicapped child has often missed out on so much in terms of developing body awareness, motor control and the capacity to make relationships, he needs movement opportunities which will help him to catch up with these aspects of his development.

Like so many normal children, mentally handicapped children need particular help in focussing attention on what they are doing so that they become more able to 'listen to' their bodies and learn from experiences happening inside them. The teacher will have to find ways of 'feeding in' bodily experiences to children who have become used to inactivity and who are deprived of sensory-motor stimulation. When physical activities are well taught most children find them rewarding and enjoyable, and they are then motivated to persevere in them. A child who is motivated is involved and involuntarily focusses his attention on the activity. Through enjoyable and rewarding movement we can help mentally handicapped children to concentrate and be absorbed in what they are doing. In this way we can help them with one of their biggest problems, the inability to focus attention and to learn from experience.

Mentally handicapped children need opportunities to extend their range of movement and acquire a wider movement vocabulary which will give them increased self-confidence and self-esteem. They also need help in controlling and organising their energy, which in some cases is excessive and in others is minimal. Mentally handicapped children need help as well in relating to other people. Some of the earliest forms of communication are developed through movement play between child and adults, and later between child and child. The child who is physically confident and responsive to others, who has imitated voice sounds and has experimented with his own sounds, will be ready for the next step which is verbal communication; all these activities and experiences are a preparation for the development of language.

The author's experience suggests that a comprehensive developmental movement programme helps the mentally handicapped child not only physically and motorically but socially, emotionally and intellectually as well. The aim of such a programme is to help each child make the best use of all his resources, and he will benefit from a developmental movement programme throughout his time at school. In the author's experience, on the whole it is education through physical experiences which is most neglected in the school programme. This is mainly because teachers generally have not been helped to understand the fundamental contribution that movement experiences can make to the retarded child's growth and development.

TEACHING THROUGH BUILDING RELATIONSHIPS

Mentally handicapped children vary enormously in their range of abilities and disabilities, and one of the main problems in teaching them is creating a flexible programme which encourages each child to make progress in his own particular way within the framework of the class. Some children may reject all human contact, others may demand attention, while some will be sociable. A few children may be overactive, and perhaps aggressive and destructive, while others will be withdrawn and timid. The teacher's task is to gain the confidence of each child, because it is only through developing a relationship with each child that she will be able to teach him. Mentally handicapped children are quick to assess the dependability and genuineness of the adult, but it may take at least a month before they accept a new teacher.

When children first come to school the teacher can find many ways of relating physically to each child. She can help to establish physical trust by supporting the child's weight in different ways, such as by taking him on her lap, holding the child under the arms and giving him a swing, helping him jump, or, sitting on the floor, helping the child to somersault over her shoulder. Anxious, nervous children will not often allow the weight of their body to be supported and it may take them a long time before they trust themselves to another person. What they are showing is a basic lack of trust in themselves, and as they begin to find it safe to commit their weight to an adult they gain confidence and are less defensive.

Anxious children whose bodies feel tense and resistant, and who dare not give their weight to an adult, will also not give their weight to the ground or to any supportive surface. The teacher has to 'feed in' situations to the child in which he finds it is safe to commit himself. One can feel a child begin to relax his body when he is being rocked and sung to, and one can see a child develop self-trust in the way he will let his body rest, roll and slide on the floor.

Fig. 1. A relationship has been established between adult and child. The child is willing to make contact when the adult is behind and supporting him.

There are many activities which children enjoy and many of them involve the free flow of the weight of the body, such as in swinging, sliding, bouncing, rolling and rocking. Severely disturbed children who live in a world of their own and feel threatened by human contact nevertheless often tolerate adult support in order to experience the pleasant sensation of being swung or rocked. Children who are physically confident and secure can rest their weight on the floor in a relaxed way. They can roll fluently, land easily from a height, and fall without hurting themselves. Down's syndrome children are often particularly able in these activities.

The mentally handicapped child can benefit from relationship play with an adult in two ways. One is that it helps him to relate to another person in terms of building up trust in the adult and within himself, and helps him to communicate in a physical and social way. The second is that through play the child develops a greater awareness of himself. He experiences the hardness, the solidity, and the weight of his body against the adult's body. The adult can 'feed in' to the child that he has a stomach, back, hips and shoulders, knees, elbows, hands, feet and head, through movement play. This kind of play is similar to that which many parents give their children at home. It is physically and emotionally satisfying to the child and makes an important contribution to the child's development. Most children are hungry for physical closeness, for a game of rough and tumble, for the fun and humour, and for the sharing of experiences with the adult.

When playing with developmentally retarded children the adult needs to realise consciously that it is a learning experience for the child. The type of play is indicated by the stage the child has reached developmentally, and the adult, whether teacher, friend, or parent, needs to have some understanding of the ways in which play can contribute to the child's development. Many teachers have the help of an assistant in the classroom, who is often a married woman with experience in handling young children. She can give invaluable help in working physically with children.

It is possible to organise movement sessions once or twice a week in which the teacher and her assistant, and any other assistants who can be freed, can work with a class of children. The teacher and the assistant can do a great deal to help a whole class but it is a great advantage to young children if they can also have a weekly session of one-to-one movement play.

One way of achieving a higher ratio of adults to children is to ask for volunteers from a local secondary school to come and work with the children. An education authority drama adviser has organised 150 boys and girls from sixth forms in several schools to work once a week in seven special schools for the mentally handicapped. The adviser prepares the sixth formers in each school in two practical movement sessions before they commit themselves to work in the special schools. The adviser begins by directing the relationship play with the children himself, and later hands over the sessions to the teachers involved in the scheme. When movement classes have been developed through a school some of the senior children can partner the younger children. Young mentally handicapped children respond very well to adolescents, whether they are normal or handicapped. An adolescent boy in a hospital school was able to help a severely physically and mentally handicapped child to walk when teachers and physiotherapists had failed.

STAGES OF DEVELOPMENT

Movement play between adult and child is often natural and spontaneous but there are various stages of development which it is helpful to understand when planning movement work.

The child as passive recipient

It is important to keep the early part of the session at floor level, both to 'anchor' the children and to help them find the security which the floor gives and the freedom of movement which it allows. At first the adult provides physical security for the child through different ways of supporting and containing him. The child uses the adult's body as a base, and not only experiences physical support but also gains confidence from being accepted by, and having the attention of, one person.

The child as equal partner

The profoundly mentally handicapped child may receive movement play in a passive way and may not respond actively or initiate any activity. It is a step forward when a child who has passively accepted movement play begins to respond actively and starts to share in the play with the adult.

In the early stages of relationship play, the child can use the adult's body as apparatus in a variety of ways — to sit on, slide over, or wriggle through. The adult can devise different ways of rocking the child or of bouncing him gently. Movements in which the child feels the flow of his weight have a harmonising effect because the child experiences the wholeness of his body and fluency of its movement.

The type of play between adult and child must be adjusted to the child's needs, and the adult can develop sensitivity in anticipating what these are and in responding to the varying signals which indicate how the child is feeling and what he needs. The adult should encourage every sign of initiative on the part of the child.

At some point, the adult will have to feed in strength to the child so that he experiences his energy by exerting it against the adult. The child can be encouraged to focus his strength and organise his energy against the resistance of the adult. The adult has to judge how much resistance to provide so that the child works hard and finally succeeds in such games as struggling to get free when tightly held by the adult, or in wriggling through a tunnel made by the adult's body. Pushing back to back is much enjoyed by children.

Fig. 2. Sixth formers and staff join in a movement group. Later the mentally handicapped children were able to make bridges and tunnels for younger children in the school.

The child as initiator

When the child is able to relate to the adult on a reciprocal basis he is ready for the next step, which is to be responsible for moving the adult. This may be very brief but it is a positive sign that the child is prepared to be actively involved. Children are more ready to move the adult if the adult is lower than themselves and therefore not physically threatening. Mentally handicapped children enjoy rolling adults over the floor, and they often do this most easily by using their feet. A group of children working together can roll their teacher, or they can pull her along the floor. Children become so interested in moving the adult that they concentrate and often work together as a group for the first time.

  In building relationships with children it is important for the teacher to give children the experience of looking after her. Sometimes teachers expect to give physical experiences to their children but find it less acceptable to let children take care of them. Children will trust the teacher much more readily if she has shown trust in them. It is probably a strange idea to some teachers to suggest that they offer themselves as living apparatus to their children. I was working for the third morning with nine- to fifteen-year-old children from a hospital school and we had reached the point of working together to carry one of the

Fig. 3. Balancing weight in a sharing relationship. Note the mentally handicapped boy's concentration on his partner.

children. A child then suggested that they should carry me. I lay down and hoped for the best. The children lifted, carried and put me down with reasonable care. It is often true that if you expect a lot from children you will usually get it, but the teacher will sometimes have to take calculated risks. It is not easy for a teacher to be at a lower level than children, or to let them be the active partners in the relationship. But in doing this she will not lose authority and control over the children (and children accept and appreciate an adult who is willing to play with them and trust them). Many teachers have said that they have come to know their children better through movement and drama sessions because they are physically involved with the children.

Children working with each other

Young mentally handicapped children find it relatively easy to relate to an adult because the adult can adjust the relationship play to suit the child. When young children have had considerable practice in relationship play with an adult they may be ready to partner another child. The child's capacity to concentrate on another child tends at first to be very brief, but, on the other hand, the ability to relate can be surprising. Children enjoy rolling a partner and pulling a partner along the floor by his ankles. One child is trusting and the other is caring.

When working with older children it is possible to help them to work with a partner from the start, beginning with simple, safe situations, such as sliding and rolling. In sliding, the child can be pulled by the ankles, the hands, or an ankle and a wrist. Children seem particularly to enjoy being slid. They find it a pleasant, free-flowing feeling. A child can roll his partner by using his hands, feet, back, or even his head. Children also enjoy pushing back to back and one child can push another along the floor giving him a 'ride'. There are some disturbed children who will only tolerate contact with someone if that person is behind them. As long as there are two children in a class able to work together, the other children will observe them and will learn from them. The teacher, and assistant if there is one, will need to help the less responsive children. As older children become more skilled they will be able to work together in threes and fours. They enjoy holding hands in a ring and by threading under their arms and stepping over their arms, tying themselves into a knot. The knot can then move over the floor, or the children can sit down together, stand up together, and then untie the knot. Three children kneeling on all fours side by side can carry a fourth child on their backs.

Children find relationship play enjoyable and rewarding. They become involved in it, they learn to concentrate and they benefit from the experience. They show initiative and inventiveness; they make decisions; and they learn about themselves through physical interactions with other people.

If the teacher has had personal practical experience of building relationships through movement and if she is convinced of its value, she will be able to help children to make relationships with other people and become more aware of themselves. She can help the mentally handicapped child catch up in areas of his own development where he has difficulties. A high standard of co-operation can be achieved between children and teacher, and between children, which can make for good relationships in the classroom and in the school generally.

2 CONTENT OF A DEVELOPMENTAL MOVEMENT PROGRAMME

The main emphasis of physical education in many special schools is on helping the children to develop physical skills in relation to apparatus of different kinds. But when a child climbs a frame or plays with a ball, his attention is on the apparatus or the object in his hand; his attention is not on his body. However, it is easier to encourage children to play on and with apparatus than it is to help them to focus attention on their own bodies. Also teachers generally feel better equipped for and more confident about taking lessons involving the development of physical skills using apparatus than in taking movement sessions where the children learn to relate to their own bodies and discover the great variety of ways they can move. Ideally the acquisition of physical skills should be based on movement experiences related to the development of self-awareness, and a balanced physical education programme should include developmental movement and physical skills training. This chapter is concerned with developmental movement and the next chapter is concerned with physical skills in relation to apparatus.

The need for the child to develop self-awareness and the contribution that this makes to the child's overall development is not always recognised or understood. It is therefore necessary to describe in some detail how the teacher can strengthen the mentally handicapped child's awareness of his body and of its movements. In order to teach body awareness the teacher may need to go back and discover the movement of her own body as if she were a very young child. The movement of the adult is generally automatic and sophisticated, so that it is difficult for adults to recall what the early learning experiences of movement were like.

The teacher may find it is best to start by taking movement sessions in the classroom as it is often easier to develop a good working relationship in the more restricted space of the classroom than in a large hall. A high standard of work can, in fact, be developed in a school without a hall or large apparatus. The staff of one hospital school I know open up and clear two adjoining classrooms one day a week. The whole school has movement classes; all the staff, both teachers and teachers' assistants, take part, and sixth formers from a local school also join in. Senior children in the school also work with younger children and over several years the children have developed a high standard of strength, control, agility, co-operativeness and sensitivity. As the school has no apparatus, the staff and senior children have had to be their own apparatus.

In the beginning it may be difficult to sustain the children's interest in what they are doing because they may not be used to finding out about and depending on their own physical resources. The teacher should be content if the session only lasts ten minutes to start with. If the teacher perseveres the session can be gradually lengthened as the children's capacity to concentrate, and become involved, increases. It would not be unusual for a class ultimately to continue for an hour, and the experienced teacher will find that the children take increasing responsibility for the content of the session. In the hospital school I have referred to, the senior children can take their own movement sessions, mostly based on partner work.

AWARENESS OF THE GROUND

The floor provides a surface against which children can feel the solidity, the hardness and the heaviness of their bodies. This is a reinforcement of their experience as babies when they felt their weight against the body of the adult who supported them. It is particularly important to help the mentally handicapped child to become aware of the solid central part of his body. Through lying, rolling and creeping along the floor the child becomes more aware of his trunk. It is interesting to compare the drawings by normal children of four and five years of themselves standing up and lying down. In the drawings of the children standing, the legs tend to be long and thin and the trunk relatively unimportant. In the drawings where they are lying down the children usually depict a large trunk and relatively small limbs.

The floor plays an important part in movement classes, and ideally it should be clean, free of splinters etc., slightly slippery and not too cold to the touch. When I have had to teach on concrete or asphalt or on very dirty floors I have felt like a pianist with all the notes below middle C missing. One cannot give children the security, the anchoring and earthing experiences which they need without a reasonable surface to work on. Carpeting does not allow the sliding, spinning, slithering activities which children enjoy and which they need in order to obtain greater freedom of movement. It is useful to work on grass occasionally, and to use gymnastic mats to help children gain confidence in falling and rolling activities.

Rolling over the floor is beneficial for many reasons; it involves a continuous letting go of the weight of the body and provides the smallest degree of falling that the body can experience. Confident children roll easily, while anxious children resist letting their weight go, and tend to hold their heads away from the floor. It is a significant moment when an anxious child lets his head rest on the ground. Rolling can help to feed into the child the idea that he has a back and stomach, hips and shoulders, as he feels these parts against the floor. Some children may roll in a flexible way with a shoulder or knee initiating the movement, the rest of the body following. Movement through the body is successive, with one part moving continuously after another with some degree of twist in the waist. Tense children tend to roll all in one piece, like a bar, but one can help a tense child to develop greater flexibility in the middle of the body by holding him by the ankles as he lies on his back, pulling him gently, swaying him from side to side, until the waist begins to melt, and a fluent snake-like movement begins to flow through his body. If a child has a rigid trunk he will find it difficult to take in new movement experiences. If there is no movement in the centre of the body it is likely that the child is experiencing very little, or benefiting only superficially from physical experiences. Sometimes the only way to help a child experience the centre of his body is to tickle him.

Mentally handicapped children can gain physical confidence from learning to fall in easy and safe ways, and they will stand, run and jump more confidently if they are familiar with managing their weight close to the floor first. After experiencing different ways of rolling (which represent the safest way in which to let the body fall), the child can sit on the floor and roll backwards onto his shoulders and then up onto his hips again. At a more advanced stage children are able to roll sideways in a curled-up position. A rounded, curled-up body falls more comfortably than an open, stiff one, because weight is transferred smoothly from one part of the body to the next. Learning to transfer weight smoothly from one part of the body to another helps the child develop increased body awareness.

Children enjoy sitting on the floor and spinning round on their hips, followed by a fall. This helps the child learn to adjust his body to new situations, and to prepare his body for subsequent movements, and is a sign of increasing body mastery and maturity. Children can become agile and inventive in discovering how to fall in a variety of ways. They can try falling from all fours, letting the body melt into the floor, roll and come up on all fours again, or they can fall sideways from kneeling, keeping slightly curled up so that they roll easily. Children can progress to falling from standing, and can then do a little jump, fall and roll and stand up, which involves joining four different actions. This is a good preparation for jumping and landing from heights when the children come to work on large apparatus. Through rolling, falling, tumbling and somersaulting, children can develop self-mastery and self-confidence and get a satisfying experience from being in a good relationship with their bodies. These activities involve the body as a whole, emphasise fluency of body weight, and have an integrating effect on the child. It is important to develop and maintain the agility, liveliness and flexibility of the mentally handicapped child. If the child is confident about being able to fall easily he will be more confident in tackling everyday skills such as going up and down stairs, or playing on uneven ground.

AWARENESS OF THE CENTRE OF THE BODY

Physical education programmes often emphasise the need for children to relate to the space around them, to extend into different directions in space, and to understand the concepts of high and low, under and over, and in front and behind. Before a mentally handicapped child can appreciate the possibilities of space he needs to have a base from which he can operate, and that is himself. It is important therefore to help children to establish as far as possible a sense of the centre of the body. If a child has a lively, mobile middle to his body, his extremities will be connected to the centre and his lower half will feel connected to his upper half through the centre. He will, consequently, be more co-ordinated and feel more of a whole. As he increases his awareness of his body, and gains self-confidence, he will be ready to explore directions in space all round him and to extend himself far from his centre into space. It is not uncommon to see children moving about rather emptily and mechanically in space. If they can develop a good base and a good centre from which to move, their movement will belong to them, however far from the centre they move.

Mentally handicapped children need a great deal of help with developing awareness of the centre of the body. They enjoy spinning on their stomachs on the floor, and creeping and sliding on their stomachs. If a child can curl up into a ball it indicates that he has some concept of the centre of his body, a centre towards which he can curl up. Most young children of school age are able to curl up tight, but many mentally handicapped children are unable to do this without help. Sometimes the adult may have to curl the child up inside her own body and rock the child so that he enjoys the sensation of being close to himself. The child can experience being curled up when he brings all the parts together by hugging his knees. Body awareness is strengthened through physical contact. The teacher can ask the child to make himself into a knot or parcel. She can pretend to undo the knot so the child has to maintain the closed position against slight resistance. The teacher can pull the child over the floor while he remains curled up. An older child can lift his partner, who is tightly curled up, off the ground. The teacher can curl up herself, and ask the children to pull her open; she should let them succeed bit by bit so that they slowly open her out.

The teacher can also help the child feel the middle of his body by helping him to do a somersault over her shoulder while she sits on the floor. The child should stand behind her, lean over her shoulder and put both hands on the floor between her legs, if he can reach. The teacher should then pull the child's head and shoulders down and towards her and help the child unroll his body either onto the floor or on her legs. The teacher can mould the child's body over her shoulder and on her body as if he were made of clay; tucking in the head and neck and rounding the back helps to soften a stiff body. Children enjoy rolling over an adult's shoulder and being upside down. Because they cannot see what they are doing they are likely to be more aware of sensations coming from inside their bodies. The more children can trust their bodies, the more confident they become.

Disturbed, anxious children often have stiff necks and shoulders and continually look about them. When they allow their heads to be tucked in and shut their eyes they are showing signs of trust and self-confidence. Helping children to feel more earthed on the floor and more centred in their bodies gives them a sense of physical security.

Children can experience movement extending from the centre of the body into the limbs more easily when the whole body is supported on the ground than when they are standing. They can move more flexibly and fluently when their bodies are supported on the ground than when they stand on the narrow base provided by two feet. When children stand, their movement is restricted because they have difficulty maintaining balance.

LOCOMOTION

The floor provides a supportive surface similar to that provided by water and is an invaluable piece of apparatus for helping the child to discover a great variety of ways of moving. The child can travel over the floor by pulling himself along on his stomach, or lying on his back he can push himself along head first with his feet, he can travel by spreading out and then closing up his body; he can roll, wriggle, slither and crawl in a great variety of ways. It is important to encourage children to move backwards as well as forwards. This means that the child has to control parts of his body which he cannot see in an area of space which is out of his sight. I have seen a normal child do this at eight months when he was crawling backwards downstairs and reaching behind him for the next step.

In exploring different kinds of locomotion over the floor, the teacher can help the child by suggesting that he moves on his back, or his front, uses his knees, elbows, feet and hands to push with, and by encouraging the child to use different directions, forward, backwards and sideways. It can also help to describe the child's movement and link it with the movement of different creatures. The child will become more at home in his body through being more at home on the floor.

AWARENESS OF KNEES

In order to help mentally handicapped children to gain control of their weight, the teacher will have to help them to develop awareness of the weight-bearing parts of the body. To this end it is important that they develop muscular strength and control over the knee joints in order to maintain an upright stance, to balance, to be stable and to absorb weight in a fluent resilient way. Mentally handicapped children often walk with stiff knees and a wide gait to obtain a broader base. They are not sure of their ability to control their weight. Children who are aware of their knees will use them with appropriate strength and resilience and this will help them to walk with a more normal gait.

The simplest way to start is for the children to sit with their knees bent up in front of them, perhaps seated in a circle. Children enjoy hammering on their knees with their fists, smacking them, patting them, rubbing them. They enjoy the different sounds they can make, and the different sensations help the children feel the

boniness of their knees. The children can press their knees until they flatten and
'disappear' and then pull them back into a bent position again. Children can bang
their knees together, pull them apart, they can beat them with their elbows, cross
over and beat opposite elbow on knee and touch their knees with their chin. Children enjoy sliding on their knees using their hands to pull them along; their knees
can separate and close as they slide. They can also spin and walk on their knees in
different directions. In all these activities they feel their knees against the floor.
The children can try hopping or walking with their knees completely bent so that
the knees are close to their shoulders in a squatting position. They can 'grow legs'
and gradually come up into a standing position with knees slightly bent. They can
smack their knees, grasp them and walk holding on to them, stepping in different
directions, and seeing how high their knees can be lifted. The children can stick
their knees together and try walking and hopping in this position; they can stick
their knees sideways, wide apart, and try walking. They can press their knees back
until they 'disappear' and walk with stiff legs and they can let their knees 'melt' so
they move with wobbly 'jelly' legs. Knees are very expressive, as every comedian
knows, and mentally handicapped children enjoy exploring the many ways their
legs can move.

Children need to experience the stability which comes from strong control of
the knee joints. The child has most control over the weight of his body when he
bends his knees slightly; his centre of gravity is then lowered and he has a fairly
wide base. The children can make their knees so strong that when the teacher
tests them she cannot push them over. When the children have experienced steadiness and stability, they can try jumping, galloping and skipping to find out how
their knees can lift them off the ground. It is important to stress that a knee can
take the child backwards as well as forwards, and can turn the child round. If
mentally handicapped children have control over their knee joints they will be
better able to control their weight in standing and walking. In my experience a
child who is physically stable is more likely to be emotionally stable as well.

AWARENESS OF HIPS

The hips are also a part of the body which supports weight. It is difficult for mentally handicapped children to be aware of their hips because they are the central
as well as the heaviest part of the body. They can become aware of their hips by
spinning in a sitting position. This is free-flow movement which all children enjoy.
If one of the children spins and falls over it is a good idea to take this as an example
and encourage all the children to make the sequence of spinning, falling over, and
sitting up again. Children can then try bumping their hips on the floor, by lifting
their hips a little way off the ground, supported on hands and feet, and then dropping them down on to the floor. They can slide over the floor on their hips, pro-
pelling themselves with hands and feet in different directions. The children can

hold their hips up while supported on hands and feet and turn over, hips still high, onto all fours. This can lead into making 'bridges' for other children and the teacher to crawl under, or to clambering over partners. Children can also balance on their hips, fall back on to their shoulders and rock back on to their hips again.

AWARENESS OF OTHER PARTS OF THE BODY

I have described ways of developing awareness of the centre and of the weight-bearing parts of the body in some detail, but it is also necessary for the children to become aware of their hands, feet, elbows, shoulders and faces. Children discover parts of their bodies more readily if physical contact is used to feed in body sensations such as stamping feet on the floor, knocking elbows on knees, and feeling faces with hands. The teacher can emphasise the learning experience by describing the activities and the children's vocabulary can similarly be developed by using words to reinforce the movement experiences.

STABILITY

Stability is best built up from experiencing steadiness close to the ground. Children can be helped in several ways to make use of the floor as a firm and stable base. They can be on their stomachs or backs with their legs and arms spread out like a star and 'stick' to the floor with as much determination as they can muster. They can try to hold on to the floor so that the teacher or their partner cannot push or pull them off their base. It is important not to destroy a child's feeling of stability by succeeding in shifting him off his base, but he should be tested in such a way that he has to use all his strength and determination to maintain it. One partner can also attempt to turn the other over. These energetic games are not competitive but are a way of testing a child's capacity for holding on.

   A child can also learn how to hold the floor in a kneeling position, with one leg bent out sideways and his foot holding the floor to give him a wider base. The child can also experience being a 'rock', by sitting and holding on to the floor with his feet and hands spread out on a four-square base. In both these stable positions the child can be tested for steadiness from the front and back and from the sides. Partners can sit back to back and use their feet and hands to grip the floor firmly. They can then push against each other and see if they can stand up together keeping their backs in contact.

   The next stage is to stand with a broad base and bent knees and to try either to push or pull a partner off his base. Partners can push hip to hip, back to back, or shoulder to shoulder. These games are much enjoyed by children and in my experience do not encourage aggression. Mentally handicapped children need a great deal of help to develop strength and determination. In pushing and pulling against a partner a child learns to exert his energy in one direction only, and by so doing he learns to focus his energy, to concentrate. Children with excess energy can be helped to come to terms with it and learn to organise it. The combination of experiencing steadiness, stability and strength, with the focussing of attention, is very important for children whose concentration is limited. The amount of energy and determination of which each child is capable must be sensitively judged by the teacher. A child must feel that he has succeeded however small the amount of strength he can muster. A child's capacity to concentrate may be very slight to begin with but will increase as he becomes more able to direct his strength and energy.

It is interesting to compare a child's relaxed fluency in rolling with his firmness in resisting force when he is trying to be immovable. The child who has good all-round movement development will be able to be both relaxed and strong. Some Down's syndrome children are successful in both ways of moving.

QUALITY OF MOVEMENT

I have described ways in which the teacher can help the child let go of the weight of his body and let gravity and the fluency of movement move him (free-flow movement), and also ways in which the child can experience firmness and stability, where he learns to establish himself (strength). When children have enjoyed vigorous, lively movement, either towards the end of a movement class or perhaps after several weeks of work, they will be ready to move with care and sensitivity. This quality of lightness is the opposite way of using energy from that of strength but it is just as important. Down's syndrome children often have a natural lightness and delicacy in the way they use their hands, and I have seen these qualities in quite a heavy child as she ran and skipped. A teacher can help children achieve lightness and fine touch by using suitable music to inspire them, but perhaps the easiest way of developing caring and gentleness comes through looking after a partner. For example the teacher can sit down and shut her eyes. The class can then help her to stand up, lead her round the room, sit her down and rock her gently, and finally lay her down on the floor. The teacher can subsequently follow this sequence with a child and then the children can try to partner each other. Children enjoy leading a 'blind' partner, and where children cannot shut their eyes they can cover them with a hand. In my experience it is usually the older children who have the care and sensitivity to look after another person, as this quality of movement seems to demand a degree of emotional maturity.

On the whole, mentally handicapped children are not able to be either very strong or very gentle, but as they develop their capacity for being strong, they usually then begin to develop their capacity for being gentle. I have seen adolescent boys achieve a high standard of controlled strength in the movement classes as well as great sensitivity in looking after young multiply handicapped children.

PROGRESSION

In the film 'A sense of movement' I compare the movement ability of a class of five-to eight-year-old mentally handicapped children with a class of mentally handicapped adolescents. The younger children can work with the teacher, assistants and mentally handicapped adolescents on a one-to-one basis. They are able to relate to their partners both in terms of receiving movement experiences and in being able to look after the adult; they can also work as a group when sitting in a circle on the floor. They move freely and confidently close to the floor and are learning how to fall. Some can jump. They are all beginning to become aware of their feet, knees and elbows.

The senior class progresses from partner work to groups of three or four, and the whole group of twelve children can work together. There is a wide range of ability but most of the children have achieved a good degree of body awareness and are confident in jumping, turning and landing. Some have developed strength well and are also able to be gentle with each other. They are inventive and much of the material for the lesson comes from the children. The more advanced children can link up several movements in a sequence. They have difficulties with speech, but there is a lot of verbalising.

The main difference between the younger and older children is that the older children have developed their resources. After three or four years of movement teaching they have developed in two areas: increasing body awareness, and increasing capacity to make relationships with other people. The older children are mostly able to concentrate on what they are doing and have achieved a good degree of self-mastery. There is a happy working atmosphere in both classes but the seniors work particularly well together.

NOTES ON TEACHING

It is important that the movements I have described are seen as bodily experiences and not mechanical exercises. Children need help to become as deeply involved as possible in what they are doing, otherwise the activities will be superficial and have little meaning or value. Unfortunately it is easy to train mentally handicapped children to move in a mechanical and superficial way. To teach in a way which contributes to the development of self-awareness the teacher needs to know from personal experience what movement feels like as an inner sensation. When she teaches she should also be involved in, and enjoy, the activity herself in order to enhance the children's enjoyment of movement.

In the beginning the teacher should participate in the movement lesson, for the children will learn from her by observation. She may have to give the children an idea of what she means, but must not give a demonstration which could indicate that there is only one right way of moving. She should encourage the children to develop their own variations of the movement she has suggested. As the children show more initiative and become more confident the teacher can be less physically involved in the lesson and spend more time observing. Some children will understand what she says, others may interpret her tone of voice. Even though some children understand quite well, they have difficulty in speaking themselves. For these children movement lessons can provide a good way of encouraging non-verbal communication.

At first the teacher can take activities in a sequence which she finds the children enjoy and are accustomed to. As she gains experience, she will find that a lesson develops through a combination of her ideas and those which the children give her, so that although she may start off with a set plan she may change it completely and follow a lead from one or two of the children. With practice she can develop most of her lesson from the children's ideas. As she becomes more skilled at observing children's movement she will be able to choose activities which she sees the children enjoy, as well as those which the children need in order to extend them further. Many of the learning experiences will come from the children observing each other. It is difficult taking movement classes with severely handicapped children because of the very wide range of abilities. It is tempting to go at the speed of the most able children, but the teacher needs to value every child and suggest activities which each child will benefit from in his own way.

If the teacher understands the purpose and value of what she is teaching and can present it as enjoyable play and discovery, children will be happy to repeat movement activities which they need to re-experience. Children generally only become bored with activities if the teacher is not enthusiastic and inspiring. Teachers teach well when they are convinced about the value of what they are teaching and when they are confident about putting it over to the children.

Movement classes develop the expressiveness of the human body and there is a natural tendency for the movement class to lead to drama. The different methods of travelling over the floor may remind the children of creatures in water and on land and dramatic situations will emerge from working with partners or in groups. The teacher can also link the increasing physical confidence that the children develop to their work on large apparatus. Children who have a rich movement vocabulary also move imaginatively to music, and their social dancing will be greatly helped if they have gained sensitivity and awareness of others.

The aim of a developmental movement programme with mentally handicapped children is primarily to foster sensory-motor development, but it can contribute to all aspects of children's growth. From it children can acquire a foundation of body-knowledge which will affect their capacity to develop in many directions.

3 THE PHYSICAL EDUCATION PROGRAMME

ACTIVITIES

The physical education programme for mentally handicapped children should include as wide a variety of activities as possible, so that the children can extend their range of skills and learn to cope with the world around them. Most schools can provide opportunity for work on conventional gymnastic apparatus as well as with small apparatus, but they should also have facilities for children to play simplified forms of outdoor games adapted to their skills and interests. The children should have the opportunity to run, explore and climb in fields, woods and hills, and by the sea if possible. Outings to farms and places of interest, camping and riding are also valuable experiences and within the ability range of most children. Some mentally handicapped children are physically almost as capable as normal children and can enjoy roller skating, ice skating, badminton, trampolining (under specialist supervision) and competitive swimming. Swimming can be particularly valuable, and one of the most important activities for mentally handicapped children is to play and develop skills in water.

It is sometimes difficult to provide suitable activities for the more able children who, because they are in classes with children who may have multiple handicaps, are often not sufficiently stretched. One association of parents I know has organised riding for the children at weekends, and many parents take their children swimming, but on the whole it is the school which will have to provide activities which will extend the children and give them a variety of experiences. Often the success of these activities though, still depends on facilities being available outside the school.

TIME-TABLING

There are difficulties in organising a varied programme of physical activities. Schools may have poor facilities indoors with limited space and equipment. The outdoor play area may be inadequate and there may be no access to a swimming pool. Sometimes the school hall is used for morning assemblies and music sessions, as well as physical activities. The hall is often the school dining room, and stacking away the tables and putting them out again takes time and can limit lesson time. Each class may be limited to one hall session and perhaps one swimming session a week. However if the head is convinced of the necessity for physical education, greater priority may be given to the children's needs. The programme of physical activity in the school in which I made the film 'A Sense of Movement' gives each class a session in the swimming pool and a movement class in the dining area each week (both of these are taken by a teacher with special responsibility for physical education), and three sessions per week in the gymnasium which are supervised by the class teacher. The sessions in the gymnasium include work on large and small apparatus. In this school the children therefore have to change daily into shorts and tee-shirt, or a swimming costume, but as a result of regular practice they have learned to be quick at dressing and undressing. This is an important part of the children's training, and they certainly look and probably feel different in clothing designed for activity. The children work in bare feet as the floors are clean and not splintery. Feet are inspected before every swimming session for verrucas. In one school, after a practical class, the senior children put their kit into the school's washing machine and then dry and iron it.

STAFFING

Teachers without specialist training often feel inadequately prepared to take physical education classes. They may lack confidence and perhaps interest, and as a result practical classes sometimes disappear. In some schools a member of staff may have special responsibility for physical acitivity throughout the school. Others have the services of a physical education specialist who may teach one or two days a week, but it is difficult for a part-time specialist to make the kind of contact with the children which is necessary for them to make significant progress. It is therefore important that the specialist teacher is backed up by the co-operation and involvement of the class teacher. Also the class teacher may then feel able to carry on the specialist teacher's programme in other sessions during the week and thus provide continuity and reinforcement for the children.

   The class teacher is really the best person to take physical activity because she knows the children better than anyone else. A short course, and observation of other teachers, may help to develop the skills and confidence to work in this area. However, if a teacher feels that activities are becoming repetitive and mechanical and are no longer learning experiences for the children, then specialist help should be requested. It may be that the specialist involved has not had any experience with mentally handicapped children, but if the specialist and the teacher work together then the children can only benefit as will the teachers themselves.

THE PHYSICAL NEEDS OF THE ADOLESCENT

When mentally handicapped children are young they are often lively and exuberant and may have difficulty in channelling their excess energy. As they grow older, and especially in adolescence, many of them become less physically confident, less energetic, and some of them put on a great deal of weight. Loss of energy is seen in some normal adolescents, but in the case of mentally handicapped children the loss of vitality can be serious. These children are at a disadvantage because of their mental handicap and unless they are encouraged to be vigorous, lively and responsive to all kinds of activities and new experiences they will be doubly handicapped and suffer from secondary retardation. If senior children do not have an enjoyable physical education programme they may gradually become less and less willing to exert themselves and begin to settle into a state of minimal activity. Older children tend to spend much of their day sitting. They may sit in a coach on what is often a long journey to and from school; they may spend most of their day sitting in class; and then may sit in front of the television at home. It is sad to see children lose their spontaneity and sense of humour, but this can happen as part of the process of learning to behave in socially acceptable ways. However these two aspects of human behaviour are not mutually exclusive. Many children and adults do not lose their capacity to play and yet can behave with dignity on social and public occasions.

One important aspect of physical activity is the element of play that is involved and the opportunity it gives to children to be inventive and to show initiative. Children deprived of opportunities for physical activity can lose their capacity to play and explore. Mentally handicapped adolescents, like normal adolescents, are sometimes scornful of activities they regard as childish. If they have had a limited experience of movement they are likely to find it easier to learn objective skills using apparatus than to focus on developing awareness of their own bodies. They will probably not feel comfortable about movement at ground level. In this they may be reflecting the attitudes of some of their teachers. As a rule though, adolescents enjoy partner work and respond to relationship play. A partner is an object which the adolescent can focus on and work with. Many adolescents enjoy and gain a great deal from partnering and working with younger, smaller children. It is important for mentally handicapped children to feel needed, and valuable for them to be in a position of giving to others.

Some adolescents are physically nervous. It is difficult, although not impossible, to help these children gain confidence, but obviously the best time to have helped them was when they were younger. If anxious adolescents are going to enjoy activities which are new and a bit threatening, it is essential for the teacher to be convinced of the need for a stimulating physical activity programme. Furthermore the teacher must have the confidence of her children and should be willing to join in the activities herself. I have seen adolescents who have had movement teaching throughout school in which all the members of the staff in the school have been involved. These adolescents are self-reliant, responsible, communicative, creative, and physically confident and able. They have picked up all these qualities from, and through, their teachers and teachers' aides. Self-respect and self-confidence are acquired more naturally through bodily experiences than through other aspects of the child's education. The physical education programme is often the most neglected part of the education of mentally handicapped adolescents, and yet it has so much to offer.

WORK ON LARGE APPARATUS

Most schools have a hall or dining area in which gymnastic apparatus can be put out. However, since the age range in most special schools extends from five (or younger) to sixteen (or older), it is extremely difficult to provide apparatus which is appropriate for younger children and at the same time sufficiently challenging to the older group. If it can be arranged, a sensible solution is for the older children to work in the gymnasium of a local secondary school. This is not only beneficial for the handicapped children but also helps generally in the acceptance and understanding of mental handicap by normal children.

There are a number of bodily sensations which gymnastic apparatus can provide which are especially beneficial for mentally handicapped children.

Activities involving free flow of the weight of the body

Free-flow bodily experiences have a harmonising, integrating effect on children which can be experienced in swinging, sliding and bouncing. Free flow of the weight of the body is also felt in jumping from a height and landing with a roll on a crash mat. Children should learn to fall first from standing, and later from a height, in such a way that on landing they roll and transfer the weight of the body quickly and easily. I encourage children to land slightly sideways so that they roll and tumble in a more flexible way than they would if they rolled in the straight line of the normal forward roll or somersault. It is safer to land almost on all fours and tumble sideways with the body lightly curled up. Children can hurt themselves in a forward roll if instead of curling up they balance on their heads and land on a straight flat back. When I am certain that a child can do a forward roll in the way described in the previous chapter (p.26) I then help the child to use this as a method of landing. However I believe that the more flexible method of landing and rolling teaches children more about managing the weight of their bodies. The children also become more skilful and agile at landing in a variety of ways.

Many mentally handicapped children can jump off a high vaulting box, land with a sideways roll, and stand up. In doing this, they have made the transition from flight through the air to absorption of the weight of the body into the ground to standing up again, against the pull of gravity. They are playing with gravity, and this activity is enjoyed as much by the mentally handicapped as by normal young children. The teacher can see the children become more skilful in making smooth transitions from one part of the sequence of movement to the next. A boy I worked with recently extended his jump off the box until he was landing on a crash mat over four feet away, and still he could land with a fluent roll.

A crash mat is a most valuable piece of equipment. In one school I know the senior children enjoy experimenting with falling and rolling more than working on any other apparatus. Another school, which has no facilities for work on apparatus, comes weekly to work in a college gymnasium. Several adolescent girls will not attempt any activity which involves their feet leaving the ground, but they will fall and roll on the crash mat quite happily. They have tried this because they have seen their student partners doing it. They would not have done this had they not built up a good relationship with the students. Tense, nervous children begin to lose their anxiety and rigidity through learning to fall in safe and pleasant ways, and as they begin to enjoy the experience. Crash mats are very useful in helping children to experience falling in a safe way.

Bouncing on a trampoline has some similarity to landing on a crash mat. I have seen an extremely aggressive boy become much calmer and an overweight adolescent girl change from being stubborn and bad-tempered to cheerful and responsive after sitting on trampettes and finding they could bounce on them. An extremely disturbed adolescent girl who refused not only any physical contact but

Fig. 4. An overweight boy from a hospital school has gained enough confidence to enjoy bouncing and landing on a mat.

would not allow anyone near her, allowed two students, one on each side, to support her under the elbows so that she could bounce standing on a trampette. She would probably not have accepted help from an adult standing in front of her and holding her hands, but her desire to bounce and to swing on ropes was so strong that she accepted physical contact. On the other hand I have seen a very young boy in a hospital class bounce obsessionally on a small trampette until he was introduced to more interesting activities and coaxed to give up his monotonous bouncing.

Trampettes and trampolines have a great deal to offer mentally handicapped children by helping them to experience the weight of their body and use their weight positively. However, trampettes and trampolines can be dangerous and must be very carefully supervised. They are in fact banned from schools in some areas of England. Bouncing is such a valuable activity that it would be very helpful if a 'safe' trampette could be designed especially for handicapped children.

All children enjoy sliding. The best kind of slide is one built into the side of a hill, but short slides can be made with a bench hooked on to a supporting frame or a bar. Children can be encouraged to be inventive in finding a variety of ways of sliding; feet first, head first, on backs, on stomachs, lying and sitting. Sliding on the back and stomach helps the child develop awareness of his body, and this may be an effective way of 'earthing' a highly disturbed child.

Swinging is popular with most children and swings are often provided in school playgrounds. It may be difficult for a mentally handicapped child to swing holding on to a gymnasium rope as his arms may not be strong enough to bear his weight for long, and when two ropes are tied together for a child to sit on, his feet may not be able to reach the floor. Children who are disturbed and hyperactive may want to swing dangerously high and will have to be persuaded to try activities which are not as exhilarating and bring the child into contact with the ground or other supportive surface such as a slide. Very nervous children may have to be coaxed on to a swing and moved gently because they might find the instability of the swing very frightening. The best way to help a nervous child is for the adult to sit on the swing with the child on her lap, both holding the ropes.

Apparatus especially designed for physically and mentally handicapped children includes a swing with a chair-like seat with a bar in front which can be closed to hold the child safely in, and a 'baby bouncer' in which a child can be safely strapped, with the head supported if necessary. The child can push off the floor with his feet and thus strengthen leg muscles which are not strong enough to take his full weight when standing. Both these pieces of apparatus are suspended from the ceiling and are adjustable for children of different heights. (This material is available from H. Hunt Ltd, Liverpool.)

Children enjoy bouncing, falling and sliding on big inflatable mattresses, but these take up a lot of room indoors, are liable to puncture and are expensive.

Some mentally handicapped children seem to enjoy using apparatus in unconventional ways. They like creeping into large boxes with holes in them. They like hiding in small places. Many enjoy crawling through tunnels, and I have seen many children who enjoy being rolled up in gymnastic mats. Young children who are functioning at about the level of a two-year-old will often use apparatus to play hide and seek and seem to prefer and benefit from this sort of activity, rather than using apparatus in the conventional way.

Clinging and climbing

It is interesting to see if a child can cling on to an adult. This can often give an indication of his previous physical and emotional experiences. An emotionally disturbed child is often able to cling with his arms but not with his legs. Severely disturbed children seem to find this kind of close involvement with an adult very threatening. Frequently, though, they will accept being contained with their back towards the adult. It would also seem that the adult's back is not as threatening as her front, and I have seen many disturbed children who will not make any greater physical contact initially than to sit astride an adult's back when she was on all fours.

To test the child's physical response and capacity to cling, the adult can get on all fours with the child on her back, his arms around her neck and his legs gripping her waist. The adult can move a little, pretending to shake off the child who has to grip more strongly. Alternatively the adult can kneel and sit back on her heels and the child can sit astride her thighs facing her with his arms around her neck and gripping her waist with his legs. The adult can then slowly tip forward on to two knees and one hand with the other hand and arm supporting the child's body. This should not be continued for too long though as it is hard work clinging against gravity. More able, older children can be asked to run and leap on to a standing adult, putting their arms around her neck and legs around her waist. The adult should embrace the child and hold him safely and then spin around with the momentum of the leap. The adult can always tell if the child's grasp is strong enough and if he needs support or not. For the sake of the adult who is the willing horse in these activities, it is best to cover this work before the children grow too big and heavy.

Children also enjoy climbing under, over, and round, an adult's body. For example. the adult can make a 'tree' by kneeling on one knee with the other leg bent but with foot firmly on the ground to make a stable base. Arms are held out, bent at the elbows. Children can gain confidence from clinging to and clambering on adults who can adjust to the child and help and encourage him. Later this experience will help them to tackle other kinds of climbing.

Most schools have some kind of large climbing apparatus, either in or out of doors. The simplest designs are the best and I have noticed that children are not attracted to apparatus where the bars are placed at acute angles and are too close together. The bars of the frame should be easy for the children to grasp, but this can present problems as the size of a child's hands varies so much between the ages of five and sixteen.

Most children enjoy climbing and gain a great deal from the experience in terms of learning to manage the weight of their body and co-ordinate all four limbs. In this way they gain confidence in their physical ability and become more courageous. Some children will only dare to climb a foot or so from the ground, but this can be a great achievement for them. Other children, particularly the disturbed ones, may climb as high as they can with no awareness of how they are going to get down.

Climbing apparatus is normally rigid, but children enjoy climbing a rope ladder or clambering on rope netting (like the rigging of a ship) which is hung over a high bar and stretched out on each side at an angle of about 45°. Rope and wood are much pleasanter materials to hold on to than metal or cement, but they need careful maintenance, particularly if they are out of doors.

Most children enjoy being upside down and will somersault over a bar even though they may need help in keeping the body curled up. Children also enjoy walking along a bench, or other broad surface, especially if it is raised a few feet from the ground. Some children may need to travel along the bench first on all fours. I do not ask children to walk along narrow balance beams because retarded children need a secure broad base, and balancing on a narrow bar makes them far less stable. However, if more skilful children want to balance on a narrow surface I encourage them to try.

Safety

It is essential for a teacher with a new class to develop a good relationship with the children and to take activities at floor level before embarking on large apparatus. When children have learned to control the weight of their bodies in tumbling, rolling, falling, sliding and crawling activities, and have developed some degree of body awareness and mastery, they will be prepared to tackle the challenge of large apparatus sensibly. Similarly, if children have developed a sensitivity to and awareness of others, they will be co-operative in the way they use the apparatus. When the teacher knows her children well, she will be able to anticipate their reactions and take particular care of the high climbers. Often the children who benefit most from energetic physical activity are the hyperactive, unpredictable children who give the teacher the most problems in ensuring their safety.

The teacher must check the stability and security of all apparatus, and must arrange activities so that children on one piece of equipment cannot knock over or land on top of children working on another. There must be adequate room for landings, anticipating that some children may travel further than expected. As there are normally not more than ten children in a class the teacher can keep an eye on everyone, but the help of a teacher's aide is invaluable.

Organisation

At first children should play on and explore one piece of apparatus. Later the teacher can link up two pieces of apparatus, or a sequence of activities like an obstacle track can be arranged; the only problem here is that hold-ups occur where certain pieces of apparatus take longer to negotiate. When mentally handicapped children link up activities they have to learn to make transitions from one activity to the next. They also have to learn to adapt to different circumstances, to anticipate a different way of moving, and to enjoy solving the problems of different challenges.

When children are time-tabled to have physical activity in a hall for half an hour the whole of this time should be used and the children encouraged to be as energetic as possible. This means that undressing and dressing should take place in the classroom before and after the session so that children can get as much benefit as possible from the short time they have. The teacher should also change into trousers or track suit for this session. She may start the session feeling weary, but will often feel invigorated by the end. Both children and teacher can benefit from physical activity.

Even the most physically handicapped children can join in in some way. Children in wheel chairs should be helped to get on to the floor and to do what they can. They can roll and fall sideways on a crash mat, they may be able to slide down a bench, and might be able to enjoy the fun of swinging. In all these activities they may need the support of one or two people, but the more physically handicapped children are, the more they need physical experiences. The school physiotherapist can and should be asked for advice about suitable activities.

A well-equipped gymnasium gives children a chance to climb, explore, and become more agile in ways that country children often experience naturally and freely. A gymnasium should be like an adventure playground, full of enjoyable activities. Student teachers and experienced teachers often need a few sessions on apparatus themselves before they begin to enjoy it. They have often experienced failure in school themselves, in that they may not have been able to vault, or climb ropes. Instead of thinking of a gymnasium as a place for acquiring certain skills I encourage students to experience activities as bodily sensations, and to help in this I ask them to slide, swing, turn upside down, with their eyes shut, so that they 'listen' with better concentration to information coming from their bodies.

Gymnastic equipment makes a unique contribution to mentally handicapped children in that it extends their range of movement experiences; it encourages the children to show initiative and to be inventive, to become self-sufficient and to solve problems, to be courageous, and perhaps most important of all, to be successful.

SMALL APPARATUS

Mentally handicapped children, like normal young children, need help with learning to catch and throw. They often have difficulty in co-ordinating the movement of their hands with watching the flight of a ball, and they find it difficult to let go of a ball at the right moment. In the early stages a mentally handicapped child needs individual help from an adult, but as he becomes more skilful he can work with another child.

The adult can begin by sitting on the floor facing a child a few feet away and rolling a ball along the floor to the child. The child will probably push it back with both hands. Still sitting, the adult can throw a bean bag, or large woolly ball, and show the child how to gather it in both hands and hold it against his chest. When the child is ready to catch and throw standing up, and from further away, it is interesting to note how he throws. If the ball is small enough to hold in one hand he will probably imitate the adult and throw underarm. When children become more skilful they can try throwing bean bags into a fairly wide container, or rolling a ball to knock down skittles. The teacher has to adapt the skill that is being taught to the child's capabilities. As he becomes more proficient the skill can be made more challenging. The child's attention span is likely to be limited, but will probably be longer if his efforts are rewarded by success.

Children can progress to using racquets to hit a ball or shuttlecock. I have seen senior boys using tennis racquets and balls in a playground, and some older children can play badminton.

Hoops can be used in a variety of ways. They can be placed on the floor to form 'stepping stones'. It is then interesting to observe when a child who steps into and out of the hoops becomes able to jump over this small obstacle. Hoops can be used to skip with; they can be crawled through when held vertically; and they can be bowled between partners. Mentally handicapped children can have fun learning to skip with a rope, but this is a skill which requires quite complex co-ordination. High jumps can be made by supporting a long cane at each end on low blocks; if kicked the cane falls off and does not trip the child.

Mentally handicapped children can be taught to kick a ball but this is best done outside. Physically able children should be encouraged to run and kick a ball to each other, and to learn to catch and throw while moving. Most mentally handicapped children have little idea of playing in a team against another team, but these activities can be done for the fun of playing together.

Some teachers like to organise indoor team games with teams standing in lines. The physical education programme should help each child develop his personal skills as far as is possible, and help children to relate to each other. Such team games, which can be rather static, frequently do little to further either of these aims and are not meaningful to children who are functioning at the very most at the level of a normal five-year-old.

WATER SKILLS

An essential part of the physical education of all mentally handicapped children should be the experience of being in water and, if possible, of learning to swim. Children gain confidence from learning to move in a new medium. Some children will be nervous of the water at first, but for most children the experience is stimulating and highly enjoyable and is particularly therapeutic for hyperactive children.

If possible the swimming pool should have a ramp by which to enter the water. Nervous children can begin by sitting in a few inches of water before they go in any further. The pool should have a shallow end in which the children can stand, and it should be big enough so that the more able children have the challenge of a fairly long distance to swim. The water should be warm, especially for multiply handicapped children whose movements are limited.

As a rule children should swim once a week but more intensive periods may be helpful. One school I know found it beneficial to arrange swimming classes every day for two weeks. The children made much greater progress by swimming daily and after the block period of daily swimming they returned to weekly sessions with a much higher degree of confidence and skill.

It is essential for adults to be in the water with the children, particularly with the younger and less able ones. It may be possible to organise help locally from mothers or senior school children. A high standard of swimming can be achieved if an experienced swimming teacher can show the helpers the best way to support children and how to plan progression for individual children. If the water is made enjoyable with the use of buoyancy aids and brightly coloured floating toys, and there are capable adults to help, the children may make a lot of progress.

As in other activities, mentally handicapped children show a wide range of ability in the water. The more able children may be able to dive in off the side of the pool, and some may be able to swim under water. A tall microcephalic boy of sixteen I know can swim faster than many normal children in a city swimming club. For those children who can swim well it can be stimulating and satisfying to take part in competitive swimming.

Some parents may refuse permission for their children to swim, but unless there is clear contra-indication the school should try to persuade the parents of the value of swimming.

RIDING

All children benefit from contact with animals. There are in fact some children who have difficulty relating to people but are attracted to animals. Riding is particularly beneficial to these children. Besides the close contact with an animal the child feels and responds to the regular rhythm of the pony's walk and this may have a harmonising effect on a child who is normally tense and jerky. The child also acquires a new skill and with practice can gain confidence and feel like a horseman who is at one with his pony. Riding is particularly beneficial to children with physical disability of the legs; children who cannot walk, or find walking difficult, can often sit astride a pony and experience a normal way of moving. Riding has a lot to offer the physically handicapped and the emotionally disturbed child. However, riding is expensive, and can be difficult to organise as two people are usually required for each pony, one leading the pony while the other walks beside the child. Furthermore the ponies must be docile and quiet. In spite of these difficulties more and more schools are sending children riding.

MOVEMENT TO MUSIC

Most mentally handicapped children respond to and enjoy music whether it is singing, playing percussion, or recorded music. If children have been sung to from babyhood and gently bounced and rocked to nursery rhymes and cradle songs, they will probably be used to movement and music combining to make an enjoyable experience and will respond readily to this combination in school. If musical accompaniment for movement is used discriminatingly it can help the children in many ways. Music can create a mood which involves the whole class and it can help heighten a dramatic situation. Rhythmic music with a clear and lively beat can be used for dance-like movement and lead to simple dance patterns. Some children move instinctively to a beat while others are unable to adjust their personal rhythms to the music they hear. Music can stimulate children to greater activity and involvement, and there may be one or two children who only take part in a movement class when there is musical accompaniment. Other children may be fascinated by watching the record going round.

I have seen ten-year-old handicapped children moving to Saint-Saëns' 'Carnival of the Animals', and older children enjoying 'being strong' to 'Mars' from the Planet Suite of Holst. Children also enjoy moving to familiar popular music and to music from television programmes.

A teacher may decide that she and her children need a fresh stimulus, and experiment with using music to accompany movement. If the children have acquired a rich movement vocabulary and are accustomed to using their own resources, they will relate to the music as if it were a 'partner'; older children in particular will enjoy dancing. Social dancing will develop easily if the children have learned to relate to each other.

However if the children always move and dance to music they will not be free to use their personal rhythms or to discover new ways of moving, and they will come to depend on music and be unable to move without it. If a teacher feels more confident in taking movement classes with music than without, she should continue to use music as this will give her security. But she should realise that continual use of music may limit the range and variety of the children's movement and bring about a certain conformity and dependence.

PLAYGROUNDS

Children may spend quite a large part of each day in the school playground. To use this time constructively they should have plenty of activities of different kinds available to them. Ideally a playground should have a paved and a grassy area, a small hill, and a 'wild' area of trees and bushes. A slide can be built into the hill, and a grassy slope is ideal for rolling down. Many playgrounds have one or more climbing frames, normally made of metal. Wood is much pleasanter to the touch than metal or cement, but it must be regularly weatherproofed. One of the difficulties of climbing on frames or constructions out of doors is that the children have outdoor shoes on which are not suitable for getting a good grip on apparatus. Another problem is to decide what is the best surface to have under the frames so that if a child fell he would not be severely hurt. Sand may be used but this also presents problems.

Some schools have swings, but these should be fenced off and supervised as they can be dangerous. Swing seats which are like a small rubber tyre are much safer than wooden seats.

Like most children, mentally handicapped children enjoy riding tricycles and playing with wheeled toys big enough for them to sit in, but they do need to be taught how to play with them and be given plenty of opportunity for play.

Children should get out to play every day, if possible, because this may be the only time in the day that they are out of doors. It is unlikely that severely handicapped children will have the chance to play outside with other children when they are at home. Conditions at home and in school are often cramped and children benefit from having space to run and play in, as well as from the fresh air. From the teacher's point of view it is also possible to get to know individual children far better during playtime than in the classroom.

CHILDREN WITH SPECIAL DIFFICULTIES

The hyperactive child

A few children in a special school may be hyperactive. By definition these children find it difficult to concentrate; they often flit from one object or activity to another, becoming more and more frustrated and increasingly lost. They seem to run away from, and avoid, learning experiences which are considered to be important to development. These children suffer from excessive and uncontrolled energy, and need a great deal of help in channelling this energy in constructive ways. Often there are not enough outlets at school or at home where the child can expend his energy in safe and socially acceptable ways. He can become increasingly frustrated and, having no emotional control or stability, can become destructive towards other children and objects in the classroom. Many hyperactive children express their excess energy not only physically but also vocally by shouting loudly, often deafeningly, which can be extremely disturbing to other children and the teacher.

Hyperactive children seem driven to escape from involvement and commitment of all kinds. They will not trust their bodies to the support of the floor, and they

will not let an adult support them. They may avoid relationships in a number of
ways; they may escape literally by running away; they may cut themselves off by
being obsessionally involved with one object or activity; they may avoid physical
and eye contact. They seem particularly to like being as high and as far from the
ground as possible, and will climb as high as furniture or gymnastic apparatus will
allow. They appear to feel threatened by being low down and often refuse to sit
or lie down on the floor. They seem to prefer all kinds of free-flowing movement
and crave the exhilarating sensation of flying through space on a swing. They will
swing for long periods; this can act like a drug and the children may become calmer,
but on the whole the swinging seems to take them further and further from reality.

Hyperactive children are often as skilful and as competent at activities such as
running, climbing and swinging as normal children of their own age. However, they
are often unaware of danger and will take risks which other mentally handicapped
and normal children would not take. Many hyperactive children appear to have a
complete disregard for their own safety, and this can cause parents and teachers a
great deal of anxiety.

The teacher's task with a hyperactive child is to break through the child's de-
fences in such a way that he does not feel threatened or become more disturbed.
One way to do this is to provide him with the sort of bodily experiences he enjoys,
which are often vigorous play and free-flow movements such as swinging, sliding
and bouncing. The adult has to find ways of helping the child to accept physical
contact and support both from the adult and from the ground, while at the same
time providing the child with an enjoyable and satisfying experience.

One way of doing this is for the adult to hold the child under the arms, the
child facing away, and swing him round, his feet coming off the floor. At a later
stage the child can be swung facing the adult. Or the adult can hold the child by a
wrist and ankle and swing him in a circle, his back sweeping over the floor, so that
he is 'grounded' at the same time. Hyperactive children are often intrigued by being
pulled along the floor by their ankles. Two adults can swing a child between them,
each holding a wrist and an ankle, and this is much enjoyed. It should be noted that
during these activities the child trusts his weight to the adults. This commitment of
weight is significant as it indicates a beginning of trust and willingness to communicate.

It is possible that the free-flow movement may increase the child's excitement
and he may become noisier and more demanding. On the other hand, the child may
realise how close he was getting to the adult, and run off. The adult then has to
sense what the child is feeling and decide whether to sit down and leave him alone
for a while, and then, later, gather him up and give him another swing, or whether
to go and work with another child, upon which the hyperactive child may, or may
not, return to his adult partner and demand to be swung again.

The adult has to pursue this process of building a relationship with a hyperactive
child with great delicacy, and will observe that the child may try to manipulate the
adult in ingenious and skilful ways. If a hyperactive child can have regular movement

Fig. 5. Supporting a hyperactive boy.

sessions with the same understanding adult once a week, or more often if possible, the relationship play will gradually become less one-sided and change slowly to become more of a shared, reciprocal relationship. I have seen a beautiful hyperactive boy of nine who would do nothing but climb high and swing dangerously all the time shouting loudly. After weekly movement sessions with a student partner and good movement teaching at school, he gradually became less noisy and began to accept physical contact. After half a term he was able to sit on the floor and join the rest of his class in movement sessions. At this time the first indication of the boy becoming 'grounded' occurred, when he voluntarily slid down an inclined bench on his stomach.

In a hospital school in Norway I saw a physical education teacher working with a strong hyperactive boy of ten. She played with him until she was able to get him lying on the ground. She then lay across him, and, using her body as a rolling pin, she rolled the boy first one way and then back again. The boy enjoyed the sensation of being rolled and squashed, and became much calmer. He became much more able to relate to his partner and stopped his usual behaviour of running round the room shouting loudly.

The adult's task is to find some way of invading the hyperactive child's world to prevent him from becoming increasingly isolated. This may take the form of catching the child and hugging him tightly, perhaps rocking him. Gradually he should be released so that with effort he can wriggle free. I remember one hyperactive boy, played with in this way, who stayed quiet afterwards with his adult partner. The adult was on all fours, and the child remained curled up under the adult's body for some minutes as if he were in a 'house'. This boy used to flit from one piece of gymnastic apparatus to another, but on the last visit of the term he played on a crash mat, somersaulting over a student who was on all fours, and then explored all kinds of rollings and landings with the student for half an hour. The boy never spoke, but he had communicated through shared movement play. His mother said that the only nights he slept well were after his weekly movement session in the gymnasium.

An adult can help a hyperactive child become more aware of his energy and strength by getting him to experience these against the adult's body. Children enjoy tugging, and pulling against an adult helps the child to direct and channel his energy. Disturbed children are more likely to pull against the adult than push, because pushing demands and implies greater personal involvement.

Gymnastic apparatus can provide valuable activities for hyperactive children. Any experience of coming down is important, so jumping off a box on to a crash mat is helpful, as is sliding down a bench, and bouncing while either sitting or standing on a trampette (the child must of course be supported if he is standing). Hyperactive children often accept physical contact in connection with apparatus; they will allow someone to push them on a swing and will accept support on a trampette.

Children who reject human contact will also often accept it in a swimming pool. They enjoy being in water so much that they forget to protect themselves. Hyperactive children gain a great deal from swimming, and are usually calmer afterwards. One hyperactive boy was able to swim every day at school, and this resulted in him being more manageable in the classroom.

Hyperactive children can become more responsive to people and less threatened by being at ground level, but I have not yet seen such a child able to focus totally on himself and relate to his own body. These children seem to be aware of a general sensation of the whole body but are not interested in their hands, knees or feet. Although they are often agile in movement they have little awareness of their bodies. They cannot curl up as a rule because they always maintain an alert lookout. Unfortunately I have never worked long enough with a hyperactive child to discover if it is possible to help him to establish that parts of his body belong to him. The child appears to be running away from all experiences which might make him commit himself, and all the adult can do is to create situations in which the child feels it is safe to trust the adult and his environment.

Hyperactive children are most testing and exhausting children to teach. The adult who works with these children has to be able to respond to them through energetic physical play combined with stability and firmness. The adult must have a sense of humour and be able to create a non-threatening atmosphere of fun. Like all children the hyperactive child is able to assess intuitively qualities of emotional maturity and integrity in the adult and will only consent to involvement with someone he respects and trusts. The adult must not feel personally hurt by continual rejection; she has to persevere and have confidence that the child will eventually accept her. It is difficult for the adult not to want personal success, but any emotional pressure put on the child may drive him away.

It would appear, however, that these children can benefit enormously from a daily programme of physical activity, preferably shared by a team of adults, including parents, and starting when the children are very young.

Children with autistic tendencies

These children vary a great deal but they all have great difficulty in relating to people. Like other disturbed children, children with autistic tendencies tend to avoid eye and physical contact. They may not speak but often appear to understand what is said. They resist sitting or lying on the floor and maintain a guarded look-out. They are often good-looking children, pale and slim. They frequently make obsessional movements such as flicking one hand near their face, or they may be obsessively attached to certain objects and to certain sounds, such as an object being dropped. Rarely, but significantly, one of these children may look penetratingly into the teacher's eyes. After such a searching assessment I have often found that the child is more willing to participate in activities.

Children with autistic tendencies often enjoy music and will listen to records for a long time, but they seem to have no wish to move to the music and are often more intrigued by the mechanism of the record player.

When working with these children the teacher can make use of the same approaches which have been suggested for hyperactive children. The child with autistic tendencies may enjoy free-flow swinging but will probably only tolerate a very brief swing in the beginning. The child is more likely to respond to the adult if the adult is lower than the child and if there is an atmosphere of play. Young children with autistic tendencies need a great deal of physical play, a gentle kind of play rather than a vigorous one, and this play has to be on a one-to-one basis. As these children grow older it becomes increasingly difficult to break through their resistance to human involvement.

I worked with an adolescent boy with autistic tendencies from a hospital school who constantly flicked his hand in front of his eyes. After three consecutive days in which he had stimulating and enjoyable physical activity, which included swimming, it was noticed that his obsessional flicking had stopped. If children have satisfying and engrossing movement experiences their obsessional movements often begin to disappear.

Sometimes a teacher can make contact with a child with autistic tendencies through playing with him with a ball which they can roll between them or through adult and child holding the ends of a rope or a blanket and shaking this together so it moves like a snake. These children are fascinated by objects; it takes some skill to share the child's world and become part of it.

Like other disturbed children, children with autistic tendencies will sometimes accept help from an adult in order to be pushed on a swing, and may accept support and help in the swimming pool. They may find it almost impossible to relate to other children, but they benefit from being with them and are more likely to join in activities which they see others enjoying. Some of these children reject physical activity but it is possible to make contact with them through role play and the adult may be able to enter the child's world through drama. It is easy to neglect these children because, as a rule, they do not demand attention but tend to withdraw into a private world. If these children can have a one-to-one movement session once a week, with a skilled adult partner, they may begin to lose some of their resistance to new experiences, and relax enough to enjoy play, and to make human contact.

Multiply handicapped children

These children are both severely physically handicapped and severely mentally handicapped, and are sometimes described as 'profoundly handicapped' or 'special care' children. As in all categories of children in special education, the range of ability is extremely wide, but some generalisations can be made. The children are often doubly incontinent and unable to feed themselves. They may suffer from severe spasticity, from impaired vision or hearing; they may not be able to sit, crawl or stand. But they normally respond well to physical contact and gentle movement play, and are often responsive to eye contact and to the human voice. One has to remember that many of these children may be functioning at about the level of a baby of six months.

These children have to be treated individually, and a suitable programme of physical activities has to be worked out for each child based on a careful assessment of the child's needs. The teacher and her assistant should seek the advice and help of a physiotherapist in devising the programme and carrying it out. The assessment of the child's basic skills should include all aspects of development of the young child — his capacity for gross and fine motor control, muscle tone and strength, range of movement, seeing and hearing, perceptual motor skills, play and language (voice sounds), and response to stimuli of different kinds. A record of each child's progress should be kept.The teacher, assistant, physiotherapist and parents will all need to work together to help the multiply handicapped child if maximum progress is to be made.

Multiply handicapped children enjoy the free-flow experiences of being rocked gently to humming accompaniment, and of being slid along the floor on a blanket. I have seen a severely spastic boy lose some of his spasticity and become more relaxed as a result of being slid, and through being rolled gently from one side to the other as he lay on a mat.

Multiply handicapped children should be encouraged to find whatever means they can of moving along the floor, whether it is rolling, pulling themselves along on their stomachs, or crawling. Besides strengthening muscles this effort gives the children some sense of their independence and encourages them to explore. Teacher and child can feel immensely rewarded when a child who has not been able to move succeeds in pulling himself along for several inches. Children will need encouragement and help to strengthen their muscles so that the weight of the body can be supported against the pull of gravity. The long bones of the leg will not be stimulated to grow unless they have borne the child's weight.

All multiply handicapped children should have at least one session a week in a warm hydrotherapy pool because handicapped children can considerably increase their range of movement in water. For this there should be a ratio of one helper to each child, and it may be possible again to arrange for children from a secondary school to come and work with the children, or to ask for the help of mothers who live near the special school.

In all work with multiply handicapped children the teacher must handle the children firmly but gently, remembering that a great deal is communicated by the way in which the adult moves the children. The most important thing to give the children is a feeling of security. Working with each child provides an opportunity for developing a relationship as well as for giving the child essential physical experiences. If the handicapped child is given physical exercises without the element of shared play he will be more likely to resist and resent treatment.

There are Developmental Centres in Canada and America designed for the treatment and education of multiply handicapped children, and I have seen my own methods of developmental movement being put into practice in one of these centres. Students from a local community college were working with one child each, and the children were benefiting both physically and socially. The students played out of doors with the children, on grass, and in the sunshine. The children were rolling down a small hillock and were somersaulting over the students' shoulders. The children used the students' bodies as safe 'houses' and as a frame to climb under, over and around. All this was done with all the students sitting or on all fours; it is important to keep the child close to the ground.

The teacher who works physically with multiply handicapped children will probably be rewarded by seeing the children become more responsive and more able to relate to her and to other children. Many of the children may only become a little more independent but they will generally develop their resources as far as they are able.

Not all multiply handicapped children attend special schools. There are many multiply handicapped children in sub-normality hospitals who are considered to be too handicapped to attend the hospital school. Unfortunately, there are not enough physiotherapists to work with these children, nor enough nurses to give individual children stimulating play.

Most people who care for profoundly handicapped children become very fond of

them and feel rewarded with the faintest flicker of recognition and by the slightest
effort to develop a new skill such as trying to touch a dangling toy which makes a
jingling sound. The big problem for parents is when their profoundly handicapped
child grows older and becomes increasingly heavy to lift.

THE POST-SCHOOL-AGE MENTALLY HANDICAPPED

Most mentally handicapped children in a day school will go on to an Adult Training
Centre, which is run by the Social Services. Trainees spend most of their day doing
simple unskilled work for a local industry, for which they receive a small payment.
On the whole trainees have fewer opportunities for physical activity than they had
in the special school. However, I have seen very successful movement teaching in an
Adult Training Centre for sixty adults, everyone having a weekly movement class in
groups of ten or twenty. The effect on the adults is remarkable; a young woman with
autistic tendencies started to work with partners, and adults of forty and fifty enjoy
physical activity for the first time for many years. Some of the adults who have been
having movement classes for over a year are asking to take the class themselves, and
they can manage this over a short sequence of activities. They have gained a great
deal in confidence and are particularly helpful in working with other adult beginners.
The more experienced adults can develop new ideas which enliven their movement
sessions.

The alternative to the Adult Training Centre is the sub-normality hospital. The
adult 'patients' are not usually physically ill but are in need of care. On the whole
there are not many opportunities for creative and physical activities in most hospitals as nurses are often responsible for large numbers of hospital residents. However,
there is a move towards giving nurses some training in practical activities such as
swimming, art, possibly some outdoor games, and social dancing, so that they can
improve the quality of life for the residents.

All the methods and objectives described in these three chapters have been devoted to the needs of handicapped children from infancy to the age of sixteen. The
fact that at the moment schooling stops at sixteen for mentally handicapped children
is determined by an educational system designed for normal children whose needs
are different from those of handicapped children. Further thought is being given to
the development of handicapped adolescents after the age of sixteen, and it is being
increasingly recognised that it is the obligation of society to adopt a more creative
approach to these children when they leave school. This will take time, money and
expertise, but there is some hope that there may be something better in store for
handicapped adults in the future.

CONCLUSION

In these chapters I have described activities which I have found enjoyable and beneficial for mentally handicapped children. I have drawn attention to movement experiences which I believe to be essential to the development of these children, no matter how limited their range of abilities is. In my experience good movement teaching can have a profound effect on personality development as well as physical and cognitive development. It seems to be of particular value in terms of helping a child build relationships and develop self-confidence.

I have said little about how the teacher teaches, but this is of course as important as what she teaches. The teacher must interact with the child. She must respond to him and adapt to him. Both the child and teacher can learn from this two-way experience. The adult has to be willing to take part in movement play. She should enjoy it as the children do, but at the same time must also be able to assert her authority, should this be necessary.

Above all, the fundamental demand made on the teacher is to observe the children carefully and purposefully. Through observation the teacher can determine the children's needs and discover strengths and weaknesses. To do this the teacher must understand something of the nature and meaning of movement. As powers of observation develop, the teacher will become aware of basic elements of human movement and behaviour which may have been missed previously. There is a constant sense of excitement and discovery in work with the mentally handicapped.

My thoughts and suggestions about teaching movement to mentally handicapped children have been learned the hard way. For this reason I have deliberately tried to avoid precepts; do this or do that. In 1959 when I began work in this field, there was no pool of knowledge on which to draw and as a result I was dependent on my earlier training in physical education and physiotherapy, and my later knowledge of the teaching of Rudolph Laban. With this, together with the pleasure and insight derived from bringing up my own children, I ventured into a new world. Almost every week I learn something new, not least from my students whom I help to feel their way into an educational world very different from what it was twenty years ago. Today there is much more information available but there is still much to learn if we are to ensure the best for the mentally handicapped. The patience, insight and disciplined sympathy involved do not come easily, but they can be learned.

Further reading

Holt, K. (ed.)(1975). *Movement and Child Development*. Spastics International Medical Publications, London.
Jordan, D. (1966). *Childhood and Movement*. Basil Blackwell, Oxford.
Russell, J. (1965). *Creative Dance in the Primary School*. Macdonald & Evans, London.
Sherborne, V. (1975). Movement for retarded and disturbed children. In *Creative Therapy*, ed. S. Jennings, pp.68—90. Pitman, London.
Wethered, A.G. (1973). *Drama and Movement in Therapy*. Macdonald & Evans, London.
Bulletin of Physical Education, 12(1), 1976. Whole issue is devoted to physical education and the mentally handicapped.

Films by Veronica Sherborne

In Touch   Movement for the mentally handicapped. Student teachers explore movement relationships, and then work with one mentally handicapped child each.

Explorations   A group of drama students learning the art of movement. They explore awareness of their own bodies, gravity, weight, and interaction with others in movement.

A Sense of Movement   Shows six- and fifteen-year-old mentally handicapped children taking movement lessons. Progress in physical and mental development is shown and also how the children can develop a greater awareness and control of their bodies, and increase their capacity to make relationships through activities which are enjoyable as well as beneficial.

These films are available in Britain from Concord Films Council, 201 Felixstowe Road, Ipswich, Suffolk.

Section II : Music

4 THE IMPORTANCE AND VALUE OF MUSIC

At an early age all children experience musical activity. They are rocked and bounced, they are crooned to, they bang spoons on tables and soon discover and manipulate sound and rhythm. These early experiences of sound are important to the child when he later comes to make and appreciate music as we conventionally know it. A child's early paintings depend on tactile, emotional and visual experience and on experimentation with colours and objects. In the same way, music depends on the richness of early enjoyment of sound and rhythm.

Many mentally handicapped children are capable of singing in tune, playing a variety of rhythms on a variety of instruments during band time, and enjoying listening to and responding to a wide range of music. But music making for many mentally handicapped children is most appropriate, and therefore most valuable, if we include stimulation and awareness of sounds and rhythms in teaching programmes and arrange opportunities for the children to practise noise making for themselves.

Musical activity is particularly valuable to any child 'in difficulty', whether the difficulty is intellectual, emotional, physical or, as is so often the case with mentally handicapped children, a mixture of any two or three of these factors. Apart from being an enjoyable activity in its own right music making can influence the development of a child in many ways. Amongst other things it can:
(1) foster communication;
(2) express emotion;
(3) be a 'success' activity for even the most severely and multiply handicapped;
(4) help in language acquisition and development;
(5) provide pleasurable group experiences affording enjoyment and encouraging co-operation;
(6) be a part of our aesthetic heritage which children can appreciate and enjoy.

COMMUNICATION

A sound made by someone and heard by someone else can be said to have been communicated. Normally, however, communication occurs when the initiator and the recipient share some understanding of the meanings of a complex set of verbal and physical symbols. Some mentally handicapped children are unable or unwilling to communicate with others. Some seem unable to hear; some don't like to feel or to be touched; and some may even close their eyes so as not to see other people. For such children it is occasionally possible to make communication bearable by the use of sounds which have none of the emotional connotations of the human voice.

Sometimes a child's barrier against the spoken voice can be overcome by singing. For example, John, who was fifteen and not usually very co-operative, especially over matters like clearing up the classroom after cutting and pasting sessions, one day expressed his obstructiveness by kicking pieces of paper around the floor. He had had a lot of experience of being asked, coaxed, told, and made to help with the clearing up, and he had perfected a good range of negative responses. When his rather desperate student teacher burst into 'John, John, sweep up the floor, John, John, sweep up the floor, It's nearly time for dinner' to the tune of 'Skip to my Lou', he grinned and, as the song was taken up by the other children, grabbed the broom and very self-importantly swept the floor.

It is sometimes easier for a child to relate to an instrument the teacher may use rather than to the teacher. The instrument may be the source of pleasurable sounds, or its shape and novelty of its appearance may excite curiosity, but the provider of that experience can gradually become important to the child. This may become apparent when the teacher plays the instrument or it may be that the child will make the first positive contact by asking to use the record player or tape recorder.

A person can be seen to be affected by music in three main ways. He can be said to listen to music intellectually, physically and emotionally.

Intellectual attention

Intellectual attention to music is a voluntary activity. For example at the level of the skilled musician this happens when a phrase or group of notes or chords is placed in the context of what has been heard before and will be heard after, giving the listener a concept of the form of the whole piece of music. It happens when we draw on past experiences of waves, rocks and moving water to build a mind's-eye picture of Fingal's Cave when we hear Mendelssohn's overture. In the same way a child makes an intellectual response to a sound when the noise of the spoon scraping the food out of the tin of baby food excites him into recalling the activity of eating. Experience reinforced by pleasure encourages an older child to hope for an ice-cream when the van comes round playing its carillon.

Some school music work calls for greater intellectual effort than we habitually expect mentally handicapped children to make. For example, the usual band session is directed by the teacher from the piano. Much emphasis is placed on keeping to the beat, on stopping and starting to a visual signal, and on conformity. This can be excellent training as long as it is realised that communication is at a low level and that the intellectual activity can degenerate into automatism. Given the same instruments the children can, with some practice in the skills needed to control them, make highly musical improvisations. The elements of communication, listening, thinking and responding, can be high if the activity is organised in this way. It can also provide the occasion for individual and group discipline. If children are used to a lot of background noise, it is vital that the teacher plans so that what they hear is appreciated intellectually.

Physical attention

Physical reaction to music usually happens involuntarily. It is not by accident that martial music is played at Waterloo Station during the rush hour; it is hard to dawdle and drag one's feet to a quick march. This link between body movement and music has of course long been used to teach body awareness with mentally handicapped children. It is less often used directly to stimulate movement of the limbs or head of immobile special-care children. Children who are hyperactive can sometimes be persuaded to enjoy the sensation of slowness encouraged by appropriate slow, flowing music. A few children seem to be extra-sensitive to the physical effects of sound waves and react strongly against some music. Chime bars seem particularly liable to have this effect because of the persistence of their sound. On the other hand this physical property of sound, of being able to feel the waves, can be of great use when children have impaired hearing.

Emotional attention

The ability of music to create and communicate mood, atmosphere and emotion is widely recognised. Most of us have experienced 'goose-pimple' music which has a stirring effect, difficult to analyse. Soothing, happy music is played in supermarkets to help allay anxiety as we reach for the impulse buy we cannot really afford. The power of music to soothe has long been recognised. In Thailand, for example, teachers sing to each child at rest time. In China special songs are used to soothe and comfort those sick in mind and spirit; in the Highlands of Scotland grandmothers make mouth music to beguile bairns. These last examples which communicate a 'feeling' have a musical characteristic in common: they use a pentatonic scale (p.89), a scale without conflict that cannot produce a discord.

The emotional stimulation from music can also help children who otherwise never experience emotional involvement. It is impossible to build a relationship with these children without communication or response. Music can be experienced by a child in isolation, but there are also many ways of making music which call forth co-operation and lead to constructive and creative communication.

EMOTIONAL EXPRESSION

A child who is unable to verbalise his feelings must be helped to develop alternative modes of expression if his frustration is not to be expressed in negative ways. Some children can express their feelings by painting, while others play with clay, do wood-work, or fight with toy soldiers or guns. For many non-verbal children, music can afford emotional expression.

It is important that the teacher provides a suitable environment if a child is to use music to express aggressive attitudes. For example, a compulsive, loud drummer can be provided with a suitably strong drum which is not too taut and therefore not un-bearably loud for the rest of the class. He may need to be encouraged to play his drum to the teacher from outside the classroom like a Red Indian sending tom-tom signals. On the other hand the child who is withdrawn and introverted may often choose the quietest instrument to 'speak' with during an improvisation session.

'Conversation' in pairs using instruments instead of speaking is difficult for many adults, but it seems that young children, and children with speech difficulties, find this to be a satisfactory and sensitive means of communicating.

Children may choose a record to express themselves. Margaret was unable to tell us what was wrong, although there clearly was something troubling her, and as the week progressed she joined in fewer and fewer of the activities which she normally enjoyed. The only thing she persisted in doing, in between bouts of crying, was to choose a record and to pull me to the record player. It was always Mussorgsky's 'Night on the Bare Mountain'. This dark choice continued during her grandmother's protracted stay in hospital, but she discarded it completely some time after her grandmother returned home.

CHALLENGE AND SUCCESS

'Nothing succeeds like success' is a truism which is important nevertheless. In the short term, success strengthens and maintains motivation, and positively reinforces experiences. In the long term it adds to the child's picture of himself and helps to build his self-esteem. Such a positive self-image and the idea that one is of value to a group of which one is a part is an essential precursor to co-operation.

Success in any field has a spreading effect. Music seldom has associations of failure or difficulty for children. Surprisingly this may be because our expectation for men-tally handicapped children's music making has been depressingly low in the past. Too often our own imagined lack of musical skills tends to allow us to settle for very much less than the best the children can offer. Handicapped children are often held back through lack of real challenge.

The enjoyment of meeting a real challenge and winning is one which can happen in a music session. Judy was fourteen, cheerful and co-operative. She was fortunately placid, otherwise her athetoid spasticity would have been agonisingly frustrating. She set herself a challenge, to my mind an unrealistic one, and I was fearful that the re-sult of failure would be discouragement. With a chime bar held between her knees and a beater in her better hand she was determined to play her part in the accompani-ment the group was arranging for the song 'I've been to Harlem'. I would have been

content if she had managed to hit it at all, but she decided that it would sound better if she played on the first and the last words. We were recording the final version
on tape. All went well and it includes a joyful shout from the most animated Judy
I ever saw: 'I h–h–hit it, miss'. No praise was needed.

The very wide range of activities which can be included in 'Music' offers teachers
tremendous scope for planning individual work appropriate to the child's need at any
stage of his development. In some instances the slightest eye-blink reaction to a loud
sound may be the occasion for much rejoicing and praise. In others, praise may not
be given until much effort and work has gone into the playing or singing of a piece
at an acceptable musical standard.

Once a climate of good expectation is established, and a child begins to feel self-
respect as a result of real achievement, it is easier to get him to spend time building
his musical skills.

LANGUAGE DEVELOPMENT

We must look carefully into the connection between language development and
music. It is not enough to assume that because singing is fun, no-speech Johnny will
sing the words with the others and thereby magically learn to speak clearly. Insist-
ence on clear words without other allied work on speech will more often result in
silence than clarity. Group singing has much to offer socially and musically and a
timid child with speech may occasionally be encouraged to join in 'under cover':
but it can have the opposite effect. Careful observation of the children in the group
is essential and it may well be that individual help is what is called for. However,
many situations lend themselves well to music/language work. For example,
when holding a child's hand and going downstairs, sing:

start	up – f
down – f	up – e
down – e	up – d
down – d	up – c
down – c, etc.	start
or conversely going upstairs	

With a child who is linguistically at the babbling stage it is important for the
teacher and parents to continue to provide encouragement even when the babbling
period is long and drawn out. It is hard to continue with 'babyish' activities that
may seem to be socially inappropriate but nursery rhymes, rocking, crooning, nonsense sounds and conversations can be part of a child's music programme and contribute to his language development.

One way of fostering language development is by helping the child to listen. As
well as rich auditory experiences the teacher can provide simple, clearly perceived
sounds for a child to listen to. Later he can practise picking out his special sound

(for example the clear tick-tock of the Chinese wood blocks) against a variety of background sounds of increasing volume. It may be necessary to take a child who is highly distractable, highly active or who suffers from difficulties of aural perception, to a quiet unstimulating environment for this sort of work, but there are many games using sounds and silences which can be played with the class or group and which can help children to listen with discrimination.

Occasionally a child who is an elective mute may be stimulated to make sounds by participating in music making. Robert was not only mute but also so unco-operative that he could not be tested to ascertain if he had any significant degree of deafness. He was downright awkward, always at odds with the group, and if frustrated would continually fall off his chair. During a music session in which she was making up a song for each child, his teacher sang to the tune of 'Frère Jacques': 'Robert, Robert, Robert, Robert, fell off his chair, fell off his chair'. To everybody's utter amazement he sang: 'No he bloody didn't, no he bloody didn't, so there'.

Most of the music work which aids language development is much less spectacular. However protracted the child's pre-verbal stage of language development may be his needs must be met and it is important to continue to try to meet them in the context of the music lesson.

SOCIAL DEVELOPMENT

Groups of people who sing together often achieve a feeling of goodwill and well-being. A sing-song can reduce individual tensions and build a sense of group belonging. This is particularly useful when working with mentally handicapped adolescents.

When children are mature enough to profit from group rather than individual work there are many varied and useful musical activities. Most work is best done in small groups, for example when instruments are being used and the teacher wants to keep a high level of awareness and communication in the group. Some singing is delightful with a small group of children, but it can be an equally happy and useful experience in a large group. The children at a special school I know sing extremely sweetly and in tune at an exceptionally early age. The three factors which have brought this about are in my opinion, (1) that the children have a good background of classroom music work (instruments are available in most rooms and the teachers 'have a go'), (2) the children sing almost every day after lunch in the hall with obvious enthusiasm and enjoyment, and (3) their singing is not inevitably accompanied by a piano. They sing a wider range of songs than is usually thought to be suitable, and they do not confine themselves to 'children's' songs. The quality of the singing is outstanding and the smaller children can sustain unaccompanied rounds, on their own, and in tune.

It can be beneficial for older adolescents to include some form of singing and/or dancing in coffee and biscuit breaks. A sing-song during a coach ride, or at a picnic round a camp fire can also help adolescents to form good group affiliations. The songs and dances used during such sessions should be socially appropriate to the chronological age and size of the children. We are not helping them to integrate into society if we teach them dances that were fashionable at the time we ourselves stopped going to dances or which are suitable for young children. It is important for the teacher to watch Top of the Pops and to learn more than the words of the first line of songs. It is socially useful to mentally handicapped children if they can recognise the difference between 'soul', 'reggae' and 'rock'. If we dislike pop music or find it hard to understand, we should not lose sight of its importance to the children.

Social skills are dependent on early experience, but good social interaction only takes place after a child has learnt about himself and has become aware that he exists in relation to others. This takes a long time for some mentally handicapped children, but music can contribute to a child's learning in both these areas. Movement, nursery rhymes, and jingles like 'Round and Round the Garden goes the Teddy Bear', 'This little Piggy goes to Market' and 'Two little Dicky Birds' can teach the child about himself in a relationship with a secure, comforting adult. Waiting or perhaps fighting for the instrument he wishes to use in the music corner can similarly teach him a lot about how other people are likely to react to his personal needs. Sometimes, opportunities to learn co-operation occur in the music corner when one child is invited, or ordered, by another to play a name-answering game with the chime bars (p.91). Small groups using instruments must learn that there is a need for self-control if their music making is to be successful. Whole school gatherings can help make a child aware that he is 'part of a whole'. This experience is an important part of learning that others have needs which must be respected. Short formal occasions can be good practice for the self-control a child needs in public and in less 'understanding' places like shops, cinemas and churches. Some schools have a short 'service' with a clearly defined code of acceptable behaviour to which those children capable of benefiting from, and contributing to, the atmosphere can come. Other schools have a 'sharing' time when work done by one group or class can be shown or played or sung to the rest of the school. Quiet 'gathering' or 'listening' music and the experience of singing meaningfully together are important parts of formal occasions.

At the end of a day at school many children are tired and have a low tolerance to frustration. On the buses which take them home it can be a great help to the escorts if the children are encouraged to pass the time in singing. If old favourites are chosen, songs learnt in one class can be passed on to the other children. One mother of a severely mentally handicapped child was asked by another woman who was waiting at the same bus stop, 'How do you get kids into that school yours goes to? That place with the singing bus.'

AESTHETIC HERITAGE

Music and movement in dance form are part of our cultural heritage. As teachers it is part of our job to make as much of it as possible available to the children we teach. Many mentally handicapped children do not have a background of the experience we might take for granted. In any case most handicapped children, because of the slowness of their development, need longer than usual to assimilate this information. This means that teachers of severely mentally handicapped children need a particularly wide range of material at their command if they are to sustain their own, and the children's interest.

It is useful to build up a collection of nursery rhymes, songs, records, tapes and instruments. Also, as was noted in the previous section, it must be borne in mind that we are all limited by our own experiences and that we need to extend our own listening if we are not to impose narrow limitations on the children. Many children do have a musical diet of only pop, or television background music. While the validity of these forms of music should be recognised, the children also need the opportunity to hear other forms of music.

MUSICAL MATURATION

The principle that development depends in part upon the stages of a child's maturation has long been accepted. In art we realise that a two-year-old's whole-arm scribble, or a three-year-old's 'mummy' with arms coming out of her head are honest and valuable statements. We know that such a drawing by a three-year-old, even if his chronological age is fourteen or fifteen, tells us something of his experiences, his concept of himself and of the world, the extent of his neurological and motor development, and his emotional state at the time he made the picture. It also tells us something of the ability he has to express himself in the medium. It may afford the viewer a moment of aesthetic pleasure if the colours and shapes are pleasing, or a moment of emotional satisfaction if the picture is of him. These constitute a 'bonus' for the viewer. But these were probably not amongst the child's aims when he started the picture. What he produces is dependent upon his skills and training in the techniques of painting but is probably not the result of conscious aesthetic judgements on his part.

It seems to be less easy for people to accept that musical development also occurs as the result of musical experience and maturation. Too often music is regarded as a field in which *training* and some innate gift are the only important factors.

When we plan a programme of musical education for severely mentally handicapped children we must keep in mind the growth and development of the normal child. But we should not assume that deviations of musical ability from the normal are necessarily downward in the severely mentally handicapped child. He may have perfect pitch or, rather, very accurate relative pitch with his own voice. He may be able to keep a beat with super-accuracy. He may have a true strong rhythmic sense and be able to appreciate and copy complicated rhythmic patterns or to invent them in his own music making.

Michael, aged fourteen with a mental age of six, who has been living in a subnormality hospital since the age of three, can tell me, even if he is unable to see the guitar, when I should change the chord during the course of the song. He finds it disturbing almost to the point of distress when the wrong chord is used. He already has greater discrimination in this respect than many adult students. What hinders his development is not his lack of musicality but his lack of ability to tolerate frustration of any kind and his very short attention span.

In the early stages a child's musical efforts may be discordant to adult ears. He may spend much time exploring the sounds made by whatever materials are at hand. When he starts to use sound expressively, to sing songs that to us have no recognisable tune, we must be careful to accept what he offers. It is the quality of the effort which is important. Our enjoyment of this effort can be sincere. If we show our pleasure expressively and warmly it can also motivate further effort.

Many children with severe learning handicaps need more stimulation than normal children. Poor motivation and limited success can so easily negate the efforts of any teacher. Disappointment with the lack of results in turn may cause the teacher to discontinue music lessons, or to rationalise her failure to plan a suitable programme and adequately motivate the child by saying, 'he is not musical' or 'he is not ready for music yet'. It is important, therefore, to plan a programme of extreme simplicity which the child can enjoy and about which the teacher is confident of the child's ability to master the skills involved.

What is chosen to be taught must of course depend on what the teacher knows to be appropriate for the child. Once this has been decided, the following general guidelines might apply. To be of value to a child, whatever is chosen, be it a single simple sound stimulus or a complex rhythmic pattern, must be:

(a)   meaningful and pleasurable;
(b)   clear and easily perceived by the child;
(c)   presented in a stimulating way;
(d)   immediately reinforced by a reward, to motivate a child who has made a positive response;
(e)   repeated by the teacher several times;
(f)   followed by a situation structured to enable the child to repeat and use the stimulus for himself successfully;
(g)   presented in parallel form many times in many ways.

All children seem to develop musically through the same stages. However, with mentally handicapped children perceptual impairment may mean that we have to work in spite of, or to compensate for, a specific handicap. We must accept that there will be great differences in the pace and extent of musical development in any group of mentally handicapped children. However, in most cases development will come, given good teacher preparation and pupil encouragement.

5 PLANNING THE PROGRAMME

Once the value and scope of educational music making is realised, the possibilities can be very exciting. At first people often ask, 'What can we sing? What can we do? I don't play the piano.' When they realise the potential contribution of musical activities to a child's development, the question usually changes to something like, 'How can I fit all the things I now regard as useful and important into the day?'

The person best able to plan individual music programmes is the class teacher. A music specialist is of course invaluable in a consultant capacity, especially over matters of musical technique. In some schools a teacher with special responsibility for music is appointed. If the music specialist is merely used to play for assembly and to take children for music while their class teacher has a free period, little will be added to the musical life of the school. However, if there is a good co-operative spirit amongst the teaching staff and if a team teaching approach is used, the music specialist can spread skills and knowledge and give support to teachers who are unsure of their musical ability. For example, if a teacher cannot read music the music specialist can pick out the tune and teach it to her by rote. This will be enough for her to use it with the children. The music specialist can similarly give simple but useful directions such as 'Take a chime bar and start the song on this note' or 'Play these two chime bars alternately throughout to provide an accompaniment, starting with this one.' With the confidence gained from working with a sympathetic colleague all teachers can provide a range of musical activities which will be of benefit to their class. At the level of music which is appropriate to mentally handicapped children, every teacher has the musical skills required and is in the best position to assess the children's needs and interests.

If music making for a class is limited to time-tabled sessions, and particularly if it only occurs, say, once a week when the 'lady who plays the piano' comes into school, music will of necessity be no more than a formal activity. This may be better than nothing, but it is only part of what a child could be experiencing. While some music is best carried out fairly formally there is much that occurs incidentally, and there is much that is best pursued informally. Music making with the mentally handicapped can happen in a variety of ways and take a variety of forms. A convenient way of classifying these is as follows:

(1) environmental and incidental sounds and music;
(2) teacher-made sounds and music;

(3) sounds made by the teacher and children in one-to-one relationships;
(4) music and noises made by individual children on their own;
(5) music and sounds made by two children playing together;
(6) work in groups, large or small and with or without a teacher.
Each of these ways of exposing a child to music lends itself to different types of musical activities. Some of these are explored in the following section.

ENVIRONMENTAL SOUNDS AND MUSIC

It is from the background of everyday noises that we gain our earliest aural experiences. Gradually the child becomes aware that certain sounds hold particular significance for him. This is the beginning of aural discrimination. The development of the awareness of general and particular sound can be provided for in the classroom. Some of the sounds heard in the classroom are not within the control of the teacher. These are noises from outside, such as construction machinery, traffic or other children playing or working outside on a fine day. In some schools, thin partitioned walls or folding doors allow a high volume of sound to penetrate from other classes. In the classroom itself, if there is a good level of purposeful activity, there will be a characteristic buzz and murmur of sound. There will be voices, water pouring or splashing, hammering on the woodwork table, and music or sounds from the music corner. All these sounds provide good teaching material. Games can be made up which make the children aware of the quality and components of the sound in their environment. For example:

(a)   Make a silence, then name the things making any sounds the group can still hear.
(b)   Make a big picture of the objects which make the sounds one can hear in the classroom. Better still have a collection of the things themselves such as a bicycle bell or a milk bottle, or models like a toy dog or a Dinky bulldozer when the real thing cannot be used. Children can 'match' the sound with the object.
(c)   Common sounds can be 'taped' and 'What is it?' games played.
(d)   The teacher can change the general noise level of the classroom and draw the children's attention to the differences. For example children enjoy having a 'Whispering Time' when everyone tries to talk only in whispers and to open doors in the quietest possible way.
(e)   A pattern of sound on one or two chime bars can be used to signal that the teacher has an important announcement to make to the whole class. After this pattern, silence is expected.
(f)   The common classroom sounds can be isolated and when the children are familiar with them a story about the children and their teacher in the classroom can be made up. This story can be told live, or on tape, and then played to another class, or to the rest of the school.

A large number of severely mentally handicapped children have difficulties in selecting, and discriminating between, sounds. The ability to attend to one sound amongst others is fundamental to a child's ability to comprehend speech. Also much care should be taken over the giving of instructions. They should be short and clearly spoken, and a check should routinely be made that the child has comprehended the exact nature of the request or commission.

Perhaps the most important source of musical stimulation is the teacher's voice. Children are much influenced by voice tone. It is useful as a signal for young and multiply handicapped children, because the combination of pitch and tone may tell them much more than the actual words used. If one says 'foul and horrible hound' to a dog in a warm and affectionate way, he will wag his tail. Just as it is easier for children to perceive objects and pictures that are large, clearly defined and bright, we must remember that it may be necessary to overstate with our voices the signals which we want a child to pick up. The meaning of what we say also relies for clarity on the way we look and it is important to match our faces and bodies to the real meaning of our communication. The teacher should use her voice to indicate calmness, warmth, acceptance, joy, pleasure, pride and affection, as these are all signals which may well have to be taught as part of the child's emotional developmental programme. The more negative tones which are cold, harsh, hard or shrill are part of life's experience also, but should be used as objectively as possible, with great discretion, and not just as an outlet for the teacher's tension.

TEACHER-MADE MUSIC

A teacher must sing – no matter how limited she considers her own vocal ability to be. After all, if one has mastered the art of talking with understandable inflections, one cannot be totally incapable of hearing and copying pitch and rhythmic differences. The best way to build confidence is by humming and singing one's favourite songs, even if they are out of tune. If you can only sing two notes, then sing them often. Sing the nursery rhymes you know so well that you don't have to think about them. Very quickly a class repertoire of songs, snatches of tunes, and tunes to use with impromptu words for spur of the moment song making will build up. If you plan to introduce a new song into the group's music making it is a good idea to make it familiar to the children by getting it 'on the brain' and humming or singing it to yourself for a week or two beforehand. It may then need very little actual teaching.

When the transport escorts are converted to the cause of singing, their help can be enlisted in a more positive way. Class teachers can give them the titles and words of the songs as these are introduced in class. It is obviously more fun to be able to sing all the song and not just the opening phrase. Much valuable reinforcement and skill building can be done in this way. Each bus or taxi can have its own Song Book which can be put together by the teacher or older children.

Many of the following activities can be included weekly in the programme, always bearing in mind the importance of repetition.

(*a*)   Have a 'tune of the week' on a loop in a play-back tape recorder. Introduce this week's tune with a little ceremony at, say, Monday milk time.

(*b*)   Make sure the 'tune of the week' is played in the hall at service time two or three times that week.

(*c*)   Play at least the opening phrase of the 'tune of the week' on as many different instruments as you can get hold of. This is easy on a xylophone or chime bars and with very little practice the right notes can be found on a tin whistle, recorder or melodica.

(*d*)   Introduce the children to any real professional instruments that can be borrowed. These do not have to be 'properly' played. It is important that the children see, feel and handle the things which make the sounds on their records. It is interesting for children to see a grown-up experimenting with an unfamiliar instrument to see what sounds she can produce.

(*e*)   Organise visitors who will bring their instruments and play for the children. They may be drawn from the nearby secondary school orchestra. Perhaps the music advisor will come, or a sales representative from the educational music department of your nearest music shop. Professional musicians are often very willing to help handicapped children in this way. Visiting orchestras, pop groups and chamber groups are often happy to visit schools with a selection of instruments if they know of the need. Very often such people only need to be asked and will give their time free. If necessary, many authorities have funds for the payment of professional performers so that they may visit schools.

(*f*)   It is often possible to take the children down to a local concert hall where, during or after rehearsals, musicians will play and talk to the children. Neighbouring primary and secondary schools will often welcome a group or class from a special school at a performance or rehearsal of the school orchestra. Many schools have a reciprocal arrangement to see each other's school pantomimes or concerts. This is a good arrangement as a neighbouring school will be aware of some of the difficulties of self-control experienced by some special-school children. However, it may be advisable to arrange a fairly short programme on such visits.

(*g*)   If the class has a music corner it can be stocked over the course of a week with a selection of objects and instruments which make a particular class of sounds. For example, one week can be devoted to a collection of things which 'ring', the next to 'knockers', or 'shakers', or 'twangers', and so on. These can be introduced fairly formally before taking their place on the table or trolley, and their sounds contrasted and compared with those already there. The children will soon start making their own contributions and the sounds these make can be discussed and decisions made about whether the sound fits into this week's sound category.

Sadly, what limits many children's education is the limitations of their educators. It is vital that teachers are open to new musical and sound experiences. The cliché 'Ah, but I like what I like' can be a very dangerous one because the children will then be limited to knowing only that which the teacher likes. Enjoyment is of course an essential factor but bland pleasure is only a small part of the experience offered by music and sound. Music is often a challenge to our set aural ideas and it takes much hard work to ensure that we offer a full range of music from classical to pop, from trad jazz to experimental comtemporary, including Eastern as well as Western and African based sound. Only the class teacher can plan systematically to introduce such a wide range of experiences over a long enough time.

TEACHER AND CHILD

Many kinds of music work are best done with a one-to-one relationship of teacher and child. I have found that the best way to establish the first tenuous relationship with a withdrawn or autistic child is not by talking or touching but by gentle singing. For example Paul, with his dislike of eye contact, avoidance of physical contact, constant obsessive hand movements and near-constant hooting noises, succeeded in blocking most attempts at contact. Swinging was a favourite pastime; holding the ropes took care of the hand movements and he enjoyed the motion enough to keep quiet whilst on the swing. Eye contact, physical contact and even a laugh were won from him when I placed myself, singing, crouched in order to be at the right level for eye contact, in front of the swing. A helpful gentle push from behind sent Paul forward to knock me over backwards on to the grass. The first couple of goes produced an expression of astonishment on his usually impassive face; then the game was understood. No helpful push was needed; he was a delighted participator in the activity. In less extreme cases I have found it very useful to allow the motion of the swing to bring the child's eyes momentarily to the right level for eye contact whilst softly singing his name or 'Hello, hello, hello'. Similarly a child can be encouraged to crawl through a play tunnel if one sits at the other end and encourages him with a special song made up about him.

Just as each child in a group will probably have an individual work programme in areas like reading, number, social education and motor training, each child should have a planned programme of aural and musical development. It is possible to make great progress with individual children once an aim is defined and the work planned in small steps. Individual programmes, though, should be planned to take into account not only the child's musical and aural needs. For example, if the child has a short attention span the work planned must be of short duration. If a child has behaviour problems one-to-one teaching may allow the work to be carried on but a consistent approach to motivation and reward is important. It is also important that regular daily work on the programme is maintained. The average time spent with individuals may be as little as three minutes a day, but this must be regular. Once a programme has been planned a classroom assistant can facilitate the implementation of the programme.

The content of an individual work programme may vary from the simplest sound stimulation to the building of skills needed for creative composition, and the setting down of symbols which will enable others to re-create the work at another time. The following are examples of three such individual programmes.

An early experience and sound discrimination programme

This is the sort of programme I use when working with 'special care' or profoundly multiply handicapped children. The aim of this programme is to provide basic, simple and direct stimulation. It is intended to be partly diagnostic.

Ringing noise from bell

(*a*)   Prepare the environment. Make sure that the general noise level is low enough or take the child to a quiet, unstimulating individual work room. The child should be comfortable and secure and not positioned so that he can be visually distracted by movement or light.

(*b*)   The teacher positions herself where she can clearly see the child's face and eyes.

(*c*)   Shake the bell to one side of the child's head.

(*d*)   Note carefully any reaction such as:
    (i) a blink,
    (ii) an eye movement,
    (iii) a movement of the head, or
    (iv) any movement of the body.

(*e*)   Reward any reaction with whatever motivates the child.

The basic situation can be repeated and developed in many ways, such as those listed below:

(1)   Ring the bell within the child's field of vision.

(2)   Use bells with differing tonal qualities.

(3)   Put the bell in a soft ball or inside an Indian wooden lattice ball and hang it within hitting distance of any part of the body which the child might move either voluntarily or involuntarily.

(4)   Sew bells on to a wristlet or anklet of soft elastic.

The teacher should discipline herself not to say 'ding-a-ling-a-ling'. Such vocalisation is confusing at this stage; it might reassure the teacher but can obscure the child's true reaction to the sound, for if a reaction is noticed, the child may be reacting to the voice of the teacher and be unable to appreciate the bell sound.

Consciousness of rhythm

At the end of the session of individual work establish the following ritual:

(*a*)   Croon, hum and rock the child gently in time to the tune being made up, or the lullaby being used. The child must feel comfortable and secure.

(*b*)   Incorporate the child's name into the tune and rock to the rhythm of the child's name.

(*c*)   Extend this situation, using the rhythms of the words. Use 'Mummy', 'milk', 'dinner-time', the teacher's own name and any names of other useful or practical things in the child's everyday experiences.

(*d*)   Play traditional 'knee games' like 'This is the way the Lady Rides', 'Ride a Cock Horse' and 'My little Pony'.

It has been suggested that many severely mentally handicapped children can learn language best through close body contact. Certainly apart from the musical content of such work the child will benefit from the added confidence he gains and the close relationship with the teacher.

Such a simple two-part programme may have to be carried out daily for many months before any significant progress is recorded, and this can be discouraging. However, disappointment can be minimised if assessments of the child and the programme are made at regular intervals and modifications made where appropriate.

This very basic, simple example of a programme can be extended in the following ways:

Shaker and rattle noises

Singing of nursery rhymes, songs, jingles

Click, bang and drum noises

Playing of finger games and body awareness games like 'Round and round the garden' and 'This little piggy'

Blowing noises

While singing with the child use any one clear sound to which the child has shown some response to accompany the song

A programme to develop awareness of pitch and rhythm

I used this programme with Michael, aged eleven, who was one of life's enthusiasts. His hyperactivity had led to his exclusion from most group work and his noisy and inaccurate singing meant that he was not popular at service time in the school hall or at music time in class.

The aims were (*a*) to establish attention and strengthen the ability to focus on the task and ignore distracting stimuli, and (*b*) to practise limit-setting by encouraging Michael to exercise control over the degree of response he made to the stimulus.

Single note recognition and reproduction

(*a*)   Prepare a suitable environment.

(*b*)   Strike note F on chime bar *gently* by the side of the child's head.

(*c*)   Strike the note again and sing with it.

(*d*)   Encourage the child to sing with the note as it is struck again.

(*e*)   Reward as appropriate to the child. For example a musically advanced child
     may be rewarded for singing the correct in-tune note, another may be rewarded
     for attempting to make any sort of sound or response.

When a child is familiar with the sound of 'his' note on the chime bar, week by week
the same note can be treated in the same way using a variety of instruments like a
glockenspiel, xylophone, piano, melodica or guitar. It is important, however, that
the same note be used and not its octave above or below, as at this stage the idea of
the octave being 'the same only different' is confusing to the child.

Recognition and reproduction of a simple rhythmic pattern

(*a*)   Use the child's name if possible. 'John', 'Robert' and 'Angela' are good examples
     of jump, walk and skip rhythms respectively. Say the child's name and clap as
     you say the name.
(*b*)   Repeat the child's name and encourage him to say and clap with you. (If the
     child is not aware of how to clap his hands at the midline of his body this can
     be 'patterned' by standing behind him and holding his hands.)
(*c*)   While saying or shouting the child's name, walk, jump or skip with him as is
     appropriate, around the classroom, hall or playground.
(*d*)   Continue to use the child's name and reproduce the rhythm on a variety of
     objects which do not produce differences in pitch: for example a drum, the
     table top, the window (gently!), a wood block, or note (preferably 'his' note)
     on the xylophone.

Some of the ways in which this work may develop are as follows:

1(*a*)   Sound the note F. The child sings after it.
 (*b*)   Play the rhythm. Get the child to echo it back.
2(*a*)   Introduce a second note, D, in the same way. When the child can sing it confi-
      dently relate it to the first note by playing them one after the other. This is
      best done by sounding the higher note (the F) first, then the D. This is a natu-
      ral and easy call for the human voice. It is the cuckoo call, the 'coo-ee', or the
      chant of the football supporters.
 (*b*)   Play the games devised around the rhythm of the child's name to these two
      notes.
3(*a*)   Using just these two notes make up a simple song about something the child
      does every day and sing this song with him and with the chime bars.
 (*b*)   Use the rhythm of his name to accompany '*his* song' using '*his* notes' and '*his*
      name rhythms' on any suitable noise-making objects, tuned or untuned.

A two-part programme to build technical skill in the playing of instruments and in maintaining ostinato accompaniments

The first part of this programme is easily accomplished by most adolescents, but it
is necessary to ensure that tuned percussion instruments give good ringing notes

rather than the dead sounds they make when heavily and incorrectly struck. The programme was very helpful for Andrew who enjoyed woodwork and who at first treated the xylophone beater as a hammer.

Correct handling of percussion beaters

(*a*)   Prepare a suitable environment and select an appropriate beater. A child with spastic hands, or a child whose fine hand movements are poorly co-ordinated, will need to have the standard beaters modified. If the handle is too thin a larger hole can be drilled in the beater head and a thick dowel rod inserted.

(*b*)   Make sure that the instrument to be played is level, secure and at the right height for the child to play comfortably. (This is usually at about the height of the child's waist.)

(*c*)   Make sure that the child knows his 'thumb', 'first or pointer finger', 'palm', and which is 'up' and which is 'down'. It may be necessary to touch all these before one can begin to work on the beater hold, in which case a suitable programme to enable the child to learn these things may be thought of as 'music' or be part of the more general development of the language programme.

(*d*)   Stand beside the child and show him how you put the beater into your own hand. This should be done with the palm of the hand up and the beater grasped between the thumb and the first joint of the first finger.

(*e*)   Play a 'please' and 'thank you' game, taking turns with the beater and making sure that it is always held correctly.

Maintaining an ostinato rhythmic accompaniment

An ostinato is simply a repeating series of notes, usually in the bass. It can be used in many ways and can be played on any tuned or untuned instrument. It is important to remember that simplicity is often very impressive and that the combination of two simple ostinato rhythms can sound most sophisticated. The simplest pitched ostinato is very useful when working with a group which can't keep in tune, or for a teacher who feels that she can't help going flat or off key. It is very effective to play the rhythm on a single chime bar using the 'home' or finishing note of the song. This note can often be D, but any note can be chosen by singing the song through at a pitch which is comfortable, and then matching a chime bar to the last note.

Children can be taught how to maintain an ostinato rhythmic accompaniment in the following way:

(*a*)   Find a suitable short phrase of words such as the child's Christian name and surnames together — for example 'Andrew Brown'. Say the name over, out loud with the child. Clap the rhythm, and walk and jump it, in this way:

Say   An — drew Brown, An — drew Brown
Do   step   step jump, step   step   jump

(*b*)   Teach and establish the 'magic spell':

'When you say, you play,
When you "hush", you don't play.'

(*c*)   Teach and make a game of the actions 'When you say, you play, when you say "hush", you touch your head.' A very simple, clear-sounding instrument is best used, such as a Chinese wood block, or a side drum.

Say   An – drew Brown hush, An – drew Brown hush
Do   play play play head, play play play head

(*d*)   Incorporate Andrew Brown's accompaniment into the group session when the song is sung by the whole group.
If the tune chosen is like 'Lavender's Blue, Dilly Dilly', Andrew Brown fits the rhythm of the tune and the 'hush' activity is not needed.

Song   La – ven–der's blue   dilly–dilly
Play   Play play play play   play play
Say   An – drew Brown An – drew Brown

If the tune is like Frère Jacques it can be played by Andrew Brown like this:

Song   Frè – re   Jac – ques
Play   Play play play head
Say   An – drew Brown hush

It is usually necessary for children and teachers to continue to *say* as well as *play* for the duration of the piece of music.

MUSIC MADE BY THE CHILD FOR HIMSELF

Mentally handicapped children need to go slowly through the stage during which they can practise and re-experience what is presented to them. The music corner, if it is well stocked and thoughtfully planned and arranged, can contribute to the satisfaction of this need. Certain practical measures may be helpful. For example:

(*a*)   Pull a cupboard or rail of dressing-up clothes out to form a right angle with the wall and make your music corner behind it, at the opposite end of the room to where the quiet, concentration activities usually take place.

(*b*)   Have a peg-board about 2 feet high and 4 feet long on which to hang instruments.

(*c*)   Place chime bars, xylophone and glockenspiel on a sturdy table of a height at which most of the children can comfortably stand to play.

(*d*)   If there is room, have a low bench, stools, chairs or cushions on which the children may sit.

(e)   Carpet the area with 'wall to wall' carpeting. (This can be made out of sample carpet squares glued together on to sackcloth backing, or the best part of an old thrown-out carpet, cut out to fit and with its edges bound with iron-on binding.)

(f)   Hang old heavy curtains on curtain wires, one below the peg-board and behind the instrument table, the other on the back of the cupboard or piano pulled out to make the corner, and let them come down to the carpeted floor. Try to find old curtains of interesting colour and pattern.

(g)   Have a 'Closed' sign and establish that before 'story' time or 'talk' time the sign is put at the entrance to the music corner and 'we don't go when the sign is up'. It is generally true that adults find noise more of a hindrance to concentration than do children. Nevertheless, if the music corner is not to become a nuisance and thereby fall into disrepute it must be carefully situated and its times of free use clearly defined.

What is put out for the children to use in the music corner will depend on what equipment you have at your disposal, on the content of the group work you are doing, and on the programmes you have planned for individual children. The suggestions in the table opposite show some of the ways in which equipment placed in the music corner for the children's free use can reinforce and complement their other musical activities.

In a similar way the children can be introduced to and can manipulate the materials which make wooden and knocking noises, twanging and scraping string sounds and the enormous variety of air movement and blowing sounds.

If the interest is to be maintained the teacher must plan to stimulate it at suitable intervals by changing the focus of interest in the music corner. For example:

(a)   *Saturation.* Put out as many things as you can which provide an enormous variety of sounds.

(b)   *Selection.* As suggested above, or by the concepts of loudness and softness, or selected for a marked contrast in pitch, high and low.

(c)   *Skill-building.* For example, make available those instruments which are played with beaters (especially if the correct holding of beaters and the correct striking of bars is the theme of individual work programmes).

(d)   *Surprise.* Take all the instruments away. Put out a cassette-player with a loop of tape on which are the names and sounds of individual orchestral and solo instruments. (This is most effective if it is linked with visits by players who bring and play the 'live' instrument.)

(e)   *Suggestion.* Go into the music corner and use the instruments yourself to work out an accompaniment or to try out a song. This is much more stimulating to children than doing it for them. It is teaching by example and shows that the instruments are serious tools and not just toys for messing about with.

It is not a good idea to accept second-hand toy instruments for the classroom music corner, unless they are of exceptionally good quality and condition. All too often tin drums, out-of-tune glockenspiels and poor cymbals are rescued from school

Equipment	Experience	Songs and Activities
(a) 'Kitchen band': saucepans, lids, spoons, paint-scrapers, frying pan, jam jars with water in, cups hung on string, small bell, bicycle bell, etc. A variety of beaters (e.g. wood, metal, felt, rubber and soft heads)	Ringing sounds made by a variety of materials	German Band Frère Jacques Ding-Dong-Bell Oranges and Lemons Play tape loops of peals of bells Visit a local church to see and hear bells rung Get local hand-bell ringers to visit school
(b) Chime bars, jingling-johnnies, budgie-bell sticks or bracelets, temple bells, cymbal, triangle, gong, glocken-spiel Variety of beaters	Ringing sounds which are made by a variety of simple instruments	Sing and play a bell song* Work on bell-type ostinato accompaniments for any bell song Act the story of Frère Jacques with bells Make a 'bell tree' from a branch mounted in a heavy block and hung with differ-ent types of bells

jumble sales, or are handed on by older brothers and sisters, or harassed parents. These are not good enough for children who already have many handicaps.

MUSIC MADE BY TWO CHILDREN WITHOUT A TEACHER

Children following individual programmes with the teacher often wish to play out the experiences with another child in the music corner. This is very valuable, because the child may find himself for the first time in the dominant role of 'teacher', or may feel for the first time the need to play out the teacher–pupil role which may lead him into tentative experiences of co-operation with his peers. Big Michael was an unpopular child in his group. He was hyperactive and bossy, and anxious to have everybody and everything in its right place, so that people and things were apt to be damaged by the speed and force of his attentions. Small Michael, usually frightened by the tempestuous activities of big Michael, was dragged unwillingly to the music corner, sat on a stool, and had a chime bar and beater thrust into his hand. Big Michael commanded him to play his name, and sighed dramatically when small Michael couldn't do so. Big Michael, instead of raging with frustration in the expected manner, sighed again, and proceeded to 'teach' him how to do it using an economically shortened version of the methods he had just experienced during a one-to-one session with his teacher. This was sustained for ten minutes with little success on the part of small Michael and much 'teaching' on the part of big Michael, most of it surprisingly patient. Next day, little Michael took the chime bar to big Michael and they went back to the music corner together. They were eventually joined by several other children and a group formed and played 'What's your Name?', a game in which the answer to the question is played on a chime bar.

Listening games often work well when played between two children. For example:

(a)   One child turns his back. The other makes a noise with an object or instrument and the first child guesses which thing has made the sound.

(b)   A child hides, taking an instrument which he plays very quietly. The other child searches and traces the sound.

(c)   Two children at the piano take it in turn to 'talk' to each other by playing the black notes.

TEACHER-DIRECTED GROUP MUSIC

When a class contains sufficient individuals mature enough to tolerate and profit from group work, it is best to hold a short session every day. It is usually possible to allow some children who do not wish to join in to continue with some other activity as long as it does not disrupt the concentration of the group.

It is better for a group period to be too short than too long. Every class teacher will know the limits of toleration of group work in her class. This can vary from day to day and depend on the mood of the group's individual members. I hesitate to suggest an ideal or general lesson length. In my experience, when music work is first introduced the period for which interest and concentration can be sustained is quite long. There is a slight reduction of interest towards the end of the first term which can usually be overcome by introducing a novel stimulus. Once the children become interested in skill-building and are confident of enjoying the music period they will happily go on for longer than the half hour or forty minutes the teacher has allotted in planning the day. For infants and juniors I allow only ten to fifteen minutes of the morning for group music and when first starting music with older children, twenty minutes to half an hour.

An ideal group size is between six and ten children. I have, however, taken very exciting group sessions, including instrumental work, with groups of twenty and on several occasions with a whole school of two hundred children. The content of the programme must of course be adapted to the size of the group. In a school where lots of music goes on in each classroom no problems arise in large group work when only a few children can have a turn with the instruments.

The following list suggests some activities, not all of which should be included in every session, but which should be used regularly especially at the beginning and at the end of each group music session:

(*a*) A listening game.

(*b*) A familiar song, perhaps with accompaniment.

(*c*) Pitched name-singing.

(*d*) A rhythm game, such as guessing whether a member of the group out of sight of the others is walking, skipping, running or hopping.

(*e*) A listening moment: a very short snatch of a piece of music (preferably not more than thirty seconds long).

(*f*) The ceremonial introduction of a new sound or a new instrument.

(*g*) The introduction of a new song or rhyme.

(*h*) A finger-play, action game, acting song, or dance game.

(*i*) A 'concert', when those who will, may sing or play on their own for the entertainment of others.

(*j*) Instrumental improvisations, which may be either free or structured by the teacher.

(*k*) Movement and body awareness (if the children do not have a separate daily movement lesson).

(*l*) 'Echo' games: the teacher taps a rhythmic pattern, a note or a tune and the children repeat it back.

(*m*) A good way to end the group lesson is with a well-loved, well-known song, so that the memory of the session is one of confidence, success and satisfaction.

The most important rule is to remember always to end the group music-making *before* the children have had enough. Then, they will always want more and will look forward to the next opportunity to make music.

EVALUATION OF PROGRAMMES

The progress made by severely handicapped children can be extremely slow and this can be very discouraging for the teacher. Often one is persuaded by the child's lack of response to abandon a programme prematurely. It is not good enough to think 'he can't do it' or 'she doesn't like music' and to stop trying. The range of music activities is so wide that there is always something to be done with sounds which will interest and benefit any child however handicapped or disturbed he may be.

I find that the two most important factors to check, if a programme seems not to be working, are the suitability of the content and the motivation of the child. Very often I find we expect children with perceptual or behavioural problems to work in an environment which contains stimuli competing with ourselves for the child's attention.

6 ACTIVITIES, SONGS, INSTRUMENTS AND BOOKLISTS

Many games and activities which can be carried out in the classroom do not require the teacher to play the piano or guitar, or to know anything about the theory of music. Indeed if a teacher can play the piano and relies on the instrument to support all music making the children will be deprived of a large and important range of sound and music-making experiences.

The following activities do not require the use of the piano or any instrument demanding a high degree of skill.

LISTENING GAMES AND WORK WITH SOUNDS

The mystery game

Remove the lid flaps and one long side from a large cardboard (or wooden) box. The front and the sides can be decorated. When this is stood on a table it makes a secure screen behind which the teacher can move freely enough to make sounds with objects hidden from the view of the children. Many ways of using the Mystery Box can be devised. It is useful to attract attention by counting aloud 'One, two, three' immediately before producing the sound.

Some examples of mystery games

(1) Everyday objects like saucers, matches, a click-top biro, a nailbrush, and pennies can be placed in the box and the children can try to identify them by the sounds that they make.
(2) Two, and eventually three or four, sounds can be made at the same time and the children have to identify the individual sounds.
(3) 'Kim's game' can be played with sounds in a variety of ways. For example, three sounds can be made one after the other. The sequence can then be repeated leaving one sound out, the children being asked to identify the missing sound. This can also be done with sounds produced simultaneously.
(4) Instruments instead of objects can be used as described in (1), (2) and (3) above.
(5) Two chime bars, two shakers, a wood block and some jingles, and two scrapers can be played successively and the children asked to identify those sounds which are 'the same' and those which are 'different'.

(6)   Mystery contents game. Collect plastic margarine containers and put into four
       or five of them different-sounding foods — for example a little rice, sugar,
       cornflakes, dried peas or macaroni. If these are being used behind the Mystery
       Box they could remain uncovered, but as the contents do tend to get eaten,
       the containers can be covered either with their own lids or with an opaque plas-
       tic bag secured tightly with a wire twist closure. As with the everyday objects
       and instruments a variety of games can be made up based on the identification
       of the sounds.

(7)   Put the same contents into a plastic container, a metal tobacco tin and a glass
       jar. The children have to identify the different containers.

(8)   Make a large chart with samples of the contents of each container stuck on to
       it, each in a separate square. The children have to match the covered container's
       sound to the contents by putting the container on the appropriate square. This
       can be extended by using a picture of the 'filling' rather than the real thing,
       which in turn can be replaced by its name written in the square.

(9)   Use a variety of materials for 'filling': for example, a metallic group of sounds
       such as dressmaking pins, drawing pins, paper clips, small nails and large nails.
       Alternatively, use sand, pea-gravel, coarse gravel and pebbles.

(10)   Place as many instruments in the box as there are children in the group. Give
       the children one each of a duplicate set of instruments. When an instrument
       is played behind the box the child with the matching instrument has to play
       his.

Sounds in space game

(1)   The children close their eyes or sit in a close circle looking at the floor. One
       child or the teacher moves as silently as possible about the room, then stands
       still and plays whichever instrument he is carrying, perhaps a bell or a chime
       bar. The rest of the group point to the source of the sound and then look to
       check their accuracy.

(2)   Conversely the person moving about can play as he goes and stop playing when
       he stands still. Pointing can be done as the player moves or at the moment when
       he stops.

(3)   Play 'hot and cold'. One of the group or the teacher is sent outside the door
       while the group hides a sweet. The 'finder' moves around the room looking
       for the sweet. As they move towards the hiding place the group, who each have
       an instrument, play louder; if the child moves away from the hiding place they
       play more softly.

(4)   Play 'hot and cold' in other ways. For example:
       (a) play faster for nearer and slower for further away;
       (b) play 'ringers' (e.g. chime bars, bells and jingles) for nearer and 'blowers'
           (e.g. whistles, kazoos and car horns) for further away;

(*c*) clap or play simple rhythms, such as

Say   Mi — chael
Do   clap   clap

for nearer, and a different one, such as,

Say   Mi — chael Waite
Do   clap   clap   clap

for further away.

Listening games such as these give children the opportunity to acquire and practise some basic techniques of instrument handling, as well as the dynamics of loudness and softness, and different speeds. Much individual and group discipline is inherent in the activities and the elements of concentration and communication are very important. These games make a good basis of experience from which one can move on to instrument improvisation work, creative instrumental composition, song composition and song accompaniment.

IMPROVISATIONS WITH INSTRUMENTS AND VOICES

Instrument games

Question and answer games, echoing, copying and follow-my-leader games all encourage children to listen and to use sounds expressively.

Some examples of instrument games

(1)   The teacher claps or plays a simple rhythm and looks at a chosen member of the group who then repeats the rhythm on his instrument.

(2)   A game on the piano can be played with three people, one at the middle of the keyboard, one on the high notes and the other on the low notes. The player in the centre (the leader) plays a 'tune' — perhaps a thumping march — on the black notes, and then points either to left or right or to both sides at once. The other players play the same sort of tune at the signal. Since the black notes are a pentatonic scale it does not matter which notes are struck or in what combination they are played; the effect will be that of 'music'.
This can be repeated in a variety of ways. For example, the tune can be a fairies' dance or a lullaby for a baby. Or no clear signal is given and the players have to respond to the tune in turns or together in a random manner. A loud angry question can be answered by a loud angry answer or by a quiet gentle one, or the tune can start with low growly notes and work its way up to high tinkling ones.

(3)   The music group sits in a circle, each with an instrument, and plays 'pass the ball'. One child starts by playing a short rhythmic pattern on a wood block or running the beater up and down a xylophone. He then looks directly at another child who plays the same sort of phrase or something different. After playing,

each child chooses another child to pass the tune on to, either around the circle or across the floor, direct eye contact being the signal to play.

(4) A pairs game can be played in much the same way. A player and his partner 'talk' to each other at the same time as other pairs 'talk' to each other. If the children are new to this sort of activity it helps if each pair has a different-sounding instrument (e.g. chime bars, scrapers, shakers) so that they can more easily make out the sound of their partner. Later this type of selective help is not necessary.

(5) Make a set of cards each with a picture of an instrument clearly shown on it. The teacher or a child then lays the cards out behind the Mystery Box or a screen and chooses a card to hold up for the group to see. When the card is held up the child with the instrument shown on the card plays for as long as the card is held up.

This activity can be extended as the children get used to the game by holding up more than one card at a time or by having two groups working with two card selectors simultaneously. The instruments can be divided into groups of 'ringing sounds', 'wooden sounds', 'twanging sounds', etc., and each group can be controlled by a 'conductor' with the matching cards.

One of the purposes of this activity is to make individuals aware not only of the sounds made by their own instrument but also of those made by other members of the group and of the sound of the group as a whole.

(6) The instruments can be discussed and if pitched instruments like chime bars, glockenspiel, xylophone or large and small bells are used the group has to decide whether each instrument plays a high sound or a low sound. Once the group has been divided in this way and appropriate hand signals decided upon and learnt, a 'conductor' can be chosen who has to signal with one hand who is to play and with the other hand give the sign devised for a long continuous sound or single short sounds.

It is very useful to stimulate discussion of the work by recording improvisations and playing them back to the children. This helps the children to be aware of their individual sound's contribution to the effect of the whole. Short improvisations can be recorded, discussed, improved upon and re-recorded. If the children are used to the idea of playing to picture cues, as in the card game described above, the improvisations can be drawn on to card to form a 'score' which is read from left to right. Two scores can, with practice, be played by two groups simultaneously and the resulting composition can be an impressively sophisticated sound tapestry or picture.

The same games devised for instrument improvisations can be adapted and used to promote improvisations using the voice and the wide range of sounds we can make with our bodies. The teacher must forget her own inhibitions and refrain from passing them on to the children. Children respond, in my experience, very readily to 'mouth music', which is a traditional method of accompanying dancing in many cultures. It will also help the children eventually to sing more accurately in tune if they can enjoy and use the wide range of sounds that they can make with their own voices.

STORY TELLING, DRAMA AND MOVEMENT

Each of these activities is covered in other parts of this book, so I will give just a few examples of how music and sound work can be integrated with them. The ability of mentally handicapped children to play imaginatively is often under-rated, and if they have difficulty it is often because their experiences are restricted by over-protective parents and teachers. The richness of the everyday experiences of shopping, visits to theatres and relatives, trips to the seaside or abroad may well all be denied to many, particularly those who are in hospital or institutional care. The quality of the dramatic play of children is dependent on their experiences and on the way teachers help and encourage them to recall and make use of these experiences. It is helpful when composing groups to make sure that at least one lively Down's syndrome child is included in each group as they can help to 'lift' the tone of the class with their enjoyment of mimicry and drama.

Story telling

(1)   Some stories lend themselves admirably with little adaptation to the use of sounds in their illustration. Two such are 'The Little Red Engine' stories and the fable of 'The Three Billy Goats Gruff'.

(2)   Take a selection of instruments and put them on the table in reach of the music group. (In this case it is best to work with a small group of not more than six or eight children.) The teacher tells a story which allows the children to make sound associations and choose a suitable instrument from the selection available. For example:

'It was a dark and windy night and the wind was howling (*voice howls and wolf noises from the children*). The front door was not properly fastened and was swinging to and fro, creaking as it swung (*scraper noises made on a resi-resi home-made rasp*). I heard far away the sound of horses' galloping hooves (*coconut shell gallops*). They came closer, getting louder and louder (*louder coconut shells*). The front door slammed (*loud drum beat*) and I went out to see who was there. The front door was shut; I opened it (*resi-resi*). There was nobody there. In the distance I could faintly hear the sound of galloping hooves (*coconut shell gallops*) through the howling of the wind (*voice howls*).'

(3)   Adolescents enjoy making up their own stories and illustrating them in this way with music. The stories can be taped and played to the rest of the school at assembly or broadcast over the school's public address system.

Drama

Improvised drama, where the teacher leads but does not direct, often enables mentally handicapped children to live out situations of which they have an awareness but in which they are not usually allowed to participate freely. Very few props are needed but there is often a musical component, ranging from lullabies in a home-making play to 'space music' for astronauts. Three examples of drama are given below, all of which I have used with juniors and adolescents. The first two develop from music work, and the third is a story which is turned into a musical play.

(1)   The sounds made by the children are used to suggest dramatic situations. The new drum brought by a student teacher into the classroom was much in demand. Because it was a tom-tom one of the children inevitably said, 'It sounds like Red Indians, Miss'. Within minutes a wigwam had been improvised and feathers were being made. A council was called and the peace pipe passed around. Squaws were to cook a buffalo and the camp was established. The classroom remained an Indian camp for several days. Some white men were captured and tied up. A war dance was worked up with a throbbing accompaniment and much whooping. The soldiers galloped to the rescue, but in the ensuing battle everybody was killed.

(2)   A song can lead to a whole range of dramatic and musical work. 'Oleanna' is a folk song about Norwegian settlers in the United States. The story of the song suggested a popular television serial about a waggon train to some of the children, and a long 'play' developed which included cowboy songs, Red Indian dances and lullabies. Aaron Copland's 'Appalachian Spring' was used as background music.

(3)   The story of 'The Iron Man' was told to the group of adolescents. Several boys started to go around chanting, 'I am the iron man, the iron man, the iron man'. They started to act out and play parts of the story of the gentle monster. A digging song was made up for when the townspeople were digging the pit to bury the monster and a triumphant processional song was made up by the children and the teacher to accompany the final scene as the iron man was led to his new home, the town scrapyard. Eventually the play was staged with the aid of a student director.

Music can thus be used to initiate and stimulate drama, or it can be incorporated into dramatic play and thus give it an added dimension.

Movement

Some music can lead to movement and teachers can use this to stimulate action. A class of institutionalised children seems to have been trained not to move, but I found that music which was very loud and exciting got them off their chairs. Chair- and bed-bound children can also be encouraged to move using appropriate music. Records like those of the Tijuana Brass and Los Indios Tabajaras are excellent for getting arms, heads and shoulders moving.

Records with movement

It is too vague and too difficult for most children simply to be asked to move when a record is played. It is usually necessary to be more specific. If music is being used, it is usually better to think of the qualities that might be expressed in movement. For example, if it is heaviness I want, the music I play might be 'Dance of the Elephants' from Saint-Saëns' 'Carnival of the Animals'. If I want caring, quiet movement, I would play part of the slow movement from Rodrigo's Concerto de Aranjuez (for Guitar and Orchestra). There are also good recordings available of electronically produced sounds which are very suggestive of growth, contraction, and spiralling. In the following list I have included some of the music which I have found useful to create specific moods.

Sea and water music
Mendelssohn — Fingal's Cave
Debussy — La Mer
Sibelius — The Oceanides
Britten — Sea Interludes (from *Peter Grimes*)
Smetana — Vltava (from Ma Vlast)
Sibelius — Swan of Tuonela
Respighi — Fountains of Rome

Mysterious and eerie music
Saint-Saëns — Danse Macabre
Mussorgsky — Pictures at an Exhibition (The Old Castle and The Catacombs)
                    Night on the Bare Mountain
Holst — The Planets (Saturn, Uranus and Neptune)
Berlioz — Symphonie Fantastique
Grofé — Grand Canyon Suite
The Strawbs — Dragonfly
Sound and Silence — a recording accompanying the book of the same name by John
                    Paynter and Peter Aston (Cambridge University Press)

Quiet and peaceful music
Beethoven — Symphony No. 6: Pastoral (2nd and 5th movements)
Delius — Summer Night on the River
            On Hearing the First Cuckoo in Spring
            Hassan
Ravel — Daphnis et Chloé: Suite No. 2 (Daybreak)
Debussy — Prélude à l'après-midi d'un faune
                Preludes, Book 1, No. 10: The Submerged Cathedral
Rodrigo —Concerto de Aranjuez for Guitar and Orchestra (2nd movement)

Storm, battle and wind music
Tchaikovsky — 1812 Overture
Berlioz — Symphonie Fantastique (March to the Scaffold and Witches' Sabbath)
Vaughan Williams — Sinfonia Antartica

Holst — The Planets (Mars)

Loud, exciting and barbaric music
Honegger — Pacific 231
Mussorgsky — Night on the Bare Mountain
Shostakovich — Symphony No. 10 (2nd movement)
Prokofiev — Symphony No. 5 (2nd movement)
Strauss, Richard — Till Eulenspiegel
Wagner — Ride of the Valkyries

Light, gay dancing music
Prokofiev — Love of Three Oranges (March)
Tchaikovsky — Nutcracker Suite (Dance of the Sugar Plum Fairy)

This list is not intended as a definitive one; the choice of music and what it suggests to each individual is bound to be subjective.

Instrumental work with movement

Some instruments, like anklets and bracelets of bells, can be worn by children to enhance the effect of some sorts of movement. Pipes, if they are very simple with not more than two holes, can be played by one or two children while the others dance. These can be combined with one or two drums, and if a sequence of drums, pipes and drums is followed, a dance with some beginnings of form will emerge.

With older children it can be interesting to take a group of sounds with a clearly defined character as a basis for a piece of movement work. For example, take all knocking, clicking, rasping and percussive sounds and do a series of improvisations with these noises. The agreed final version can be recorded. Discussion will bring suggestions from the children, such as 'It sounds like woodwork, Miss', or 'It sounds like my brother's factory, Miss'. The factory idea was agreed upon and then someone suggested that we needed a whistle to blow to tell us to start the machinery. The whistle was added to the recording. A group was formed to represent the machinery and a self-elected worker decided he would operate the machine. Drawing on the experience of a visit they had paid to the offices of the local evening paper to see the printing of the early edition, the 'machinery' began to move as the tape was played through. They eventually decided that they should superimpose voice noises ('whooshes', 'whirrs' and 'psssss' as they moved to the persuasive noises on the tape. This integrated music and movement work was carried out with twelve- to fourteen-year-olds and formed the main part of half a term's work.

FINGER PLAYS, ACTION SONGS AND ACTING GAMES

Finger plays and songs which name parts of the body are particularly valuable to severely mentally handicapped children. It will probably take longer for such a child to become fully aware of his body and its relationships with space and objects. A good many handicapped children come into the category of 'clumsy' children, which is so often one of the characteristics of children suffering 'minimal cerebral disfunction'. These children particularly need daily movement sessions and if these are supplemented with songs and games like the old-fashioned 'Heads and Shoulders, Knees and Toes, Knees and Toes' it is to their advantage. It is important to verbalise the experience of movement and much regular work has to be done on these lines if severely mentally handicapped children are to know and understand the 'space words' like 'through', 'behind', 'in front', 'close to', etc. Many of the movements which we take for granted have to be taught to handicapped children and these can form the basis for songs to accompany actions. This has the dual purpose of making the action a consciously verbalised one and of teaching a group of words which present a stumbling block to many children in their language development.

A useful source of finger games is the Pre-School Play Group's booklet *Forty Finger Plays and Action Songs*, but it is often more effective to improvise songs and actions for individual children as the needs and circumstances of the individual child suggest.

Ring games are particularly good and care should be taken over their selection for use with different ages. It is also important that everybody has a turn and that the game does not require a 'heroine' (who is usually chosen to perform the major part of the action on account of her prettiness and tractability). Such a game is 'The Princess Lived in a Big High Tower', which is an enactment of the story of the Sleeping Princess. A better sort of story would be the ring game of 'Oats and Beans and Barley' (John Wagstaff's record, 'Songs for Singing Children'). In this game the principal characters change all the time throughout the game and everybody has plenty to do all the time. Many traditional games like 'In and Out the Windows' can be simplified if they are too complicated.

Some action songs use instruments and these are very popular. For example:

> I love to play on my big bass drum,
> And this is the way I play it,
> Brumm, brumm, brumm, brumm-brumm, brumm, brumm, brumm,
> And this is the way I play it.

This can be mimed and the sounds of the instruments imitated. It is important that the children *know* what a big bass drum sounds like if they are imitating it. A better song which demands minimal technical ability but which should consequently only be a small part of the instrumental activity of any group of children is 'The German Band':

> We're a band of fine musicians, we practise every day,
> And people come from miles around to hear Johnny play . . .
> His chime bar, his chime bar, they love to hear his chime bar,

(Johnny plays)

> Johnny, Johnny, Johnny, Johnny, Johnny, Johnny, John.

When everybody in the group has had a turn it is then the turn of the whole orchestra:

And people come from miles around to hear our orchestra play . . .

If nobody you know knows the tune it is very easy to make one up. Take the five chim chime bars D E F$^{\#}$ A B and play them with a beater as you say the first line over and over again. When several variations have been tried, like:

We're a band of fine musicians, we practise every day . . .
D D D D A A F$^{\#}$ E   D D D A A   D

decide on the version you like best and learn it thoroughly. The advantage of any tune made up for yourself in this way over the 'proper' tune is that it is pentatonic. If you give the children in the band the chime bars D, E, F$^{\#}$, A, B to play, whatever they play will sound good with your tune. The glockenspiel and xylophone can also be used if all the bars except those five notes are removed.

This band song can be played and sung very simply or it can be made more interesting for more competent groups by the inclusion of ostinato rhythms in the accompaniment. An introduction can be played before the song and between the verses, and some older adolescents and adults may enjoy playing the chords on an autoharp or dulcimer.

SONGS AND SINGING

Children who sing a lot are more likely to sing in tune and unselfconsciously. As I have said earlier, children whose singing is always heavily accompanied by the piano seldom sing as sweetly in tune as those who have developed confidence and good pitch discrimination by singing unaccompanied. The 'home' or finishing note played occasionally during the song should adequately support children's singing without dominating it.

It is very easy for a busy teacher to get stuck with a small group of songs with which she is comfortable and familiar and to use these so often that the songs become stale through over-use. A good song which is catchy is worth the bother of learning. It is important to get the words down on to paper as the tune can be more easily recalled with the help of the words. Many 'pop' songs can be included but the onus is generally on the teacher to teach the words as the children seldom pick up more than the first phrase from the records played on Top of the Pops.

Many teachers are more at home with nursery rhymes and songs for nursery-age children, but it is important with adolescents to sing the songs that are popular with their peers. There are many traditional and contemporary folk songs which are simple in tune and word and which are acceptable to children and adults. (David Ward has a superb bibliography of song books and an analysis of songs and their suitability for different ages and stages of development. These can be obtained from him at Dartington College of Arts, Totnes, Devon.)

I have found that it is helpful to consider the characteristics of songs when fitting them into the teaching programme. For example the little song 'Who's that?' is useful for teaching self-image, language work on prepositions like 'under', 'behind' and 'on', and it is an action song. There are many counting songs like 'Ten fat sausages frying in a pan, one went pop and another went bang. Eight fat sausages . . . ', and so on, which children enjoy. Perhaps the best one to use with a whole class of young children is the old song 'There were ten in a bed and the little one said roll over, roll over. And they all rolled over, and one fell out, so there were nine in the bed, and the little one said . . . ', etc. I have found it better to start with no-one in the 'bed' and add on the whole class until the 'bed' is full and someone falls off the end.

The following few songs I have found suitable for younger children. The tunes are given in chime bar letter names under each word for teachers who cannot read musical notation.

Swimming pool song
Guitar: One chord, D
Chime bars: D, A and F$^\#$
Accompaniment: Chime bars D and A played alternately starting with D on the word 'he'
Rhythm: (*a*)   Say the words
　　　　(*b*)   Say the words and clap what you say
　　　　(*c*)   Say the words and play the chime bars as you say them!

Words: When he went in—to the swim—ming pool Pe—ter got his hair wet!
Tune:　　　D D D D D D   D　　D D D D D A F$^\#$ D
Accompani-
ment:　　　　D　　A　　　D　　　A D　　A　　　D
Words: Splish, splash, splish, splash, Pe—ter got his hair wet!
Tune:　　　D　　D　　D　　D　D D D A F$^\#$ D
Accompani-
ment:　　　D　　A　　D　　　D D　　A　　D D

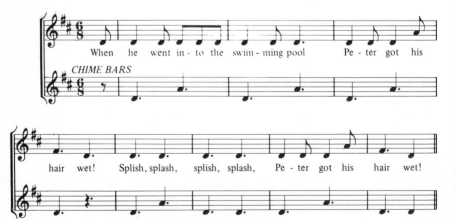

This song can be adapted to many situations. For example: 'When he went down from the top of the slide Mark shouted Whee' or 'When she banged the big drum Angela went boom boom'. It can be used to stimulate recall of experience, as an action song, for practice of speech sounds, and for improving self-image.

What's your name?

Guitar: One chord, D

Chime Bars: F$^\#$, G, A, E, D high, D low

Accompaniment: Chime bars D low, A. The D low is played throughout except when the child sings his name, when the A bar, which is the note he sings, is played

Rhythm: The notes for the words 'name', 'me' and the child's name notes are long. The rest of the song goes as you like to say it

Words: What's your name? What's your name? What's your name? Won't you tell me?
Tune: F$^\#$ G   A   F$^\#$ G   A   F$^\#$ G   A   A   D D A
                                                                       (high)(high)

Accompani-
ment: D   D   D   D   D   D   D   D   D   D   D D D

Words: It is Ed—ward, it is Ed—ward, Ed—ward is the name for me
Tune: F$^\#$G A   A F$^\#$G A   A A   A F$^\#$F$^\#$ D   E D
                                                    (low)   (low)

Accompani-
ment: D D A   A DD A   A A   A D D   D   D

This song can be useful to reinforce language work when prepositions are being taught. The child singing will sing 'me' and the other children will sing 'him'. The teacher and other children can point to the chosen child when they sing 'your name' and to themselves when they sing 'won't you tell me?' It is good practice for wait-ing, limit setting and control when the child has to sing his name only at the right time.

A school song to the tune of 'Frère Jacques'
Guitar: One chord, D
Chime Bars: D, E, F#, G, A, B
Accompaniment: Just play the D chime bar four times before you start and then on
                the beat all the way through
Rhythm: If you don't know the tune, the word 'best' is long each time and 'we're
              the best at' is sung quicker than the rest of the song

Words: Down—ham school, Down—ham school, We're the best, We're the best,
Tune: D   E F#D D   E F#D F# G A F#   G A
Accompani-
ment: D   D   D   D
Words: We're the best at Down—ham, We're the best at Down—ham,
Tune: A   B A G F#   D   A   B A G F#   D
Accompani-
ment: D   D
Words: We're the best, We're the BEST!
Tune: D   D D   D D D
Accompani-
ment: D   D

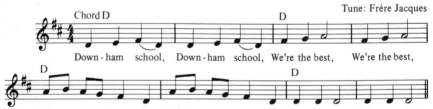

This is obviously a very simple song which is familiar to almost everyone. It is a tune which I have found to be very useful when I need a quick song for a special moment or want to record an event worth remembering, as it is so easy to fit whatever words one wants to it.

Play the bell
Guitar: One chord, D
Chime bars: D, F#, A
Accompaniment: Best without any, but it is a good idea to play D four or eight times
                before you start

Words: Play the bell . . . . *(child plays)* Ching,
Tune: D   D D   A

Words:	Play the bell	(*Child plays*)	ching,
Tune:	D D D		A
Words:	Tina's playing	ching, ching	(*as many times as*
Tune:	F#F#F#F#	D D	*you like*)

This little song can be used with a 'bell tree'. A strong twiggy branch is anchored into a heavy block of wood. Bells of various sizes, small cymbals, Indian bells, and any other objects which ring prettily are tied on to the 'tree'. The same tree can hold sweets at Christmas time, or as a beginning of term treat.

Who's that?
Guitar: Two chords, D and A
Chime bars: D, E, F#, A, B
Accompaniment: These notes D, E, F#, A and B make a pentatonic scale. You can
 play any of them together with any of the others and they will
 sound consonant (in tune). If you have plenty of chime bars you
 can give one to each of five children and allow them to play randomly, or you can put the bars in a line and get one child to play
 the rhythm of a short phrase like 'underneath the table' over and
 over again whilst the other four children play randomly. There
 are lots of good combinations to discover.
Rhythm: 'Who's that' and the child's name are long notes, 'underneath the' and
 'standing on the' are quick notes, and the length of note for 'table' and
 'chair' is somewhere in between the two. If you are in doubt just say
 the words over and over again to yourself out loud and a rhythm will
 appear; when it does you can play it like that. Your version is just as
 good as anybody else's.

Words:	Who's	that	un–der–neath		the	ta–ble?	Who's	that	un–der–neath		the	chair?
Tune:	D	A	E	E	E	F# E	D	D	A	E	E	F# E	D
Chords:	D		A				D	D		A			D
Words:	Jul–ian	is	un–der–neath		the	ta–ble,	Si–mon	is	stan–ding	on	the	chair
Tune:	DD	A	A E	E	E	F#E	D	D	A	A E	E	F# E	D
Chords:	D		A				D	D		A			D

(If the child has a long name add some extra notes. Any of the five will sound right but a D or an A will be easiest for the children to sing. Sometimes the children think up really good places to be and you may find that you have to fit in something like 'Arabella is standing in the sink with her socks off'. Don't worry about scansion, just add as many extra notes as you need.)

It is distressing to find older children being asked to sing nursery rhymes and infant songs. Some of the reluctance to sing, which is common in older boys and girls in special schools, comes from their realisation that often a lot of what they are asked to sing is socially inappropriate.

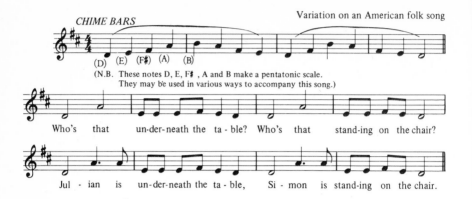

There are always one or two songs in the current Top Twenty which are quite suitable for use in school. Some modern songs, like 'I'd like to teach the world to sing' (the first part of which is pentatonic) and 'Everything is beautiful, in its own way' are songs which are very suitable for prayer or service time. A very useful tune is the Negro spiritual 'Go tell it on the mountain', as it is a pentatonic song the words of which can easily be adapted to make it a carol for Christmas or Easter.

There are many humorous songs which appeal to adolescents, such as 'You canna push your Granny off a bus' which is sung to the tune of 'Coming round the mountain'. A very firm favourite with older boys is a football song based on the tune of 'Frère Jacques'. A local version goes:

> We saw Argyle playing football at Home Park, at Home Park,
> We saw them losing, we saw them losing, UP ARGYLE, UP ARGYLE.

and a second verse went:

> We saw Argyle playing football at Home Park, at Home Park,
> We saw them winning, we saw them winning, UP ARGYLE, UP ARGYLE.

If the song has two chords, two children can accompany the group with guitars, each child playing when the group is singing the words which go with 'their' chord. They do not necessarily have to be able to hold the shape of the chord because if one guitar is tuned to an open D chord and the other to an open A chord by the teacher all they have to do is strum the strings with their right hand.

The following short list of songs can be played with very simple guitar chords:

One-chord songs

Frère Jacques	Mr Froggie Went a-Courting
The Animal Fair	Ten in a Bed
Lavender's Blue	The Barnyard Song

Two-chord songs

One Man went to Mow	Mrs Bond
Au Clair de la Lune	This Old Man
Bobby Shaftoe	Michael Finnegan
Skip to my Lou	Down in Demerara
Duke of York	Hush Little Baby
Let's all sing Together	Go tell Aunt Nancy
Nuts in May	Fairy Lullaby
London Bridge	Hot Cross Buns

Three-chord songs
Almost all other traditional and children's songs can be accompanied with three chords.

Children who sing sweetly and in tune do so because they have been given the opportunity to sing often. There are many moments during a school day when a song helps to pass time spent waiting. Each class can compile a song book and present a song each week to the rest of the school if there is a concert or 'sharing time' at the end of the week.

Older boys who are reluctant to sing can often be coaxed into song if they are given a kazoo to play so that they are using their voices to play the instrument. But on the whole, once a tradition of singing is established in any school there are few children who can resist joining in a good song.

INSTRUMENTS TO BUY AND MAKE

The only really essential instrument in a classroom is the teacher's voice. The cheapest way to build up a set of instruments is to start with individual chime bars and add good percussion as you can afford it. Much money is wasted if sets of triangles, cheap drums and poor cymbals are bought in bulk. I have found it useful to acquire the following in this order:

(1) *Chime bars.* D, A, F$^\#$, E and B, then G and C$^\#$, followed by low A and high D.
(2) *Snare drum.* A good one can often be found in second-hand or junk shops.
(3) *Tambour.* A good big tambour which can be tuned is invaluable for encouraging timid children to make large assertive movements, as they like to beat it hard with a soft-headed beater.
(4) *Cymbal.* A spun cymbal of not less than twelve inches diameter.
(5) *Guiro* and *two-tone wood blocks.*
(6) *Xylophone.* It pays to save up for the more expensive bass xylophone, because almost all the instruments used in classrooms have a highish pitch and your classroom music-making takes on a much more professional sound if you add some bass notes. Children are also nowadays very used to records which have a heavy bass, so they will prefer the deeper tone.

(7) *Glockenspiel.* Toy glockenspiels are often given to mentally handicapped children. They are of very limited value and usually have a short life. If you have the chance take the money instead and put it towards the cost of a small professional glock in a substantial wooden carrying box.

(8) *Piano.* Most schools have a piano which is too good an instrument to allow children the freedom to explore and 'mess about' on. A classroom piano on the other hand can be used by the children as a keyboard instrument or with modification it is very exciting to use a piano as a large harp. The front and the keyboard of an upright piano lift off and the exposed strings can be plucked or percussed with hands or beaters. If teacher and child have 'conversations' using only the black keys of a piano keyboard a very attractive improvisation can be recorded, as the black notes form a pentatonic scale (not D in this case, though, so you cannot play the other tuned instruments with it unless you acquire the chime bars which make up the same scale).

(9) *Kazoos.* These are very cheap and encourage non-singers and growlers to use their voices.

Most of these instruments are now stocked by music shops in big towns. It is worth going to The London Music Shop, Great Portland Street, London, if possible, or to The London Music Shop, Exmouth, where they have a marvellous selection of all types of instruments for school music making.

There are now several books on home-made instruments and I will only mention and illustrate a few of the simpler instruments. These will augment professionally made instruments or, if no money at all is available for the purchase of good commercially produced ones, this collection would start you off. You would soon, though, need to include a wider range of sounds which cannot be produced by home-made instruments.

1. Untuned xylophone

2. Cotton reel clicker

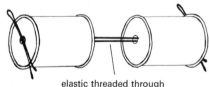

elastic threaded through reels and secured by hair grips

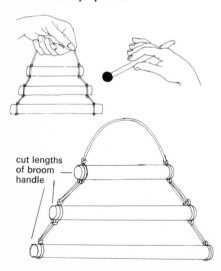

cut lengths of broom handle

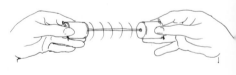

(1) *Untuned xylophone.* Broom handles are very useful and just the right thickness for making the blocks. If you experiment and cut the blocks to different lengths it is possible to tune them roughly. (Short pieces make high sounds and longer lengths make lower sounds.)

(2) *Cotton reel clicker.* This is fun for children who have good control of their fingers. It is fiddly to make and to play but not all severely subnormal children are clumsy with their hands. It doesn't make much noise so it is best 'featured' and given a small solo part.

3. Wood block

4. Resi-resi

ridges cut across
section of
bamboo

slit cut along length
to allow sound out

grooves cut to
give hollow sound

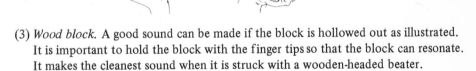

(3) *Wood block.* A good sound can be made if the block is hollowed out as illustrated. It is important to hold the block with the finger tips so that the block can resonate. It makes the cleanest sound when it is struck with a wooden-headed beater.

(4) *Resi-resi.* This is a variation on the guiro. First obtain some long, strong bamboo poles. The natural divisions of the pole show where to cut. The wood is hard so it is safest to put the section of bamboo which you are working on in a vice to cut it. The instrument can be tapped like a wood block and also makes a super creaking noise when a stick is scraped along the grooves.

(5) *Sandpaper blocks.* The blocks should be big enough for a child to hold easily. Different sounds are produced by different grades of sandpaper. The sandpaper does have to be replaced from time to time. The sound produced is similar to that of a shaker with fine material inside it, but sandpaper block is easier for a lot of children to control.

(6) *Rubber drum.* A circle of pliable rubber such as inner tube can be stretched over the top of the plant pot. It is difficult to get a drum like this sufficiently taut, but it is useful to have a 'soggy' drum around for the complusive hard drummer to enjoy.

5. Sandpaper blocks

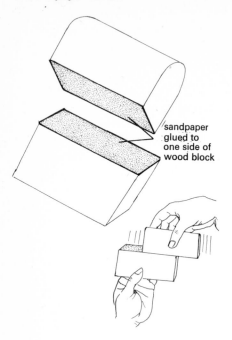

sandpaper
glued to
one side of
wood block

6. Rubber drum

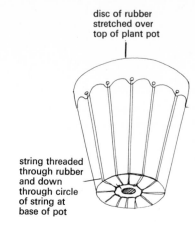

disc of rubber
stretched over
top of plant pot

string threaded
through rubber
and down
through circle
of string at
base of pot

7. Tom-tom

a laminate of
six layers
composed
alternately of
greaseproof paper
and muslin
glued together
by wallpaper
paste

plant pot

drum head
fixed by
either the
same method
as rubber
drum or by
sticking to
side of pot

8. Beaters

INSTANT BEATER

hammer from
dismantled piano

RUBBER BEATER

tap washers
glued together
and on to dowelling

FELT BEATER

wooden knob stuck
to dowelling and
covered with a layer
of cotton-wool and
a layer of felt

PLAIN BEATER

plain wooden
dowelling with wooden
knob

(7) *Tom-tom.* A much harder drum which produces a sharper sound is made with a head of different material. Layers of greaseproof paper and muslin glued into a laminate can be stuck on to a pottery flower pot. The head can be more easily broken than that of the rubber drum so a softer beater is needed if a child is still at the uncontrolled bashing stage.

(8) *Beaters.* It is a false economy to use dowelling which is too thin for beater handles. However, the materials for making many types of beaters are easily available from hardware and do-it-yourself shops and if one can save money by making beaters it is then easier to spare funds for tuned instruments which are harder to make satisfactorily.

9. Plant pot bell

10. Bell bracelet

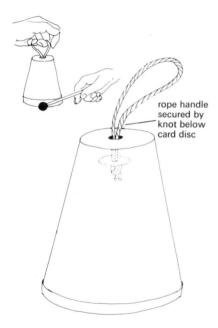

rope handle
secured by
knot below
card disc

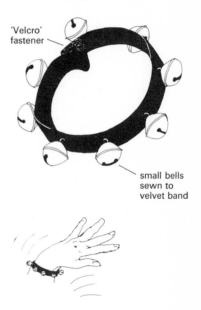

'Velcro'
fastener

small bells
sewn to
velvet band

(9) *Plant pot bell.* These are very easily cracked, but when sound a plant pot can make a lovely ringing noise. As with all ringing instruments it has to be suspended so that it can vibrate freely. Different sized plant pots produce notes of different pitch.

(10) *Bell bracelet.* Small bells sewn on to bands of soft material can make anklets and bracelets which can be worn by children who cannot hold objects. It is very difficult to control the duration of sounds made by bells so they should be used when a continuous sound is appropriate. Budgie bells make a pretty sound but not all bells are sweet, so it is important to try before you buy.

11. Cup-a-phone

12. Jingling johnny

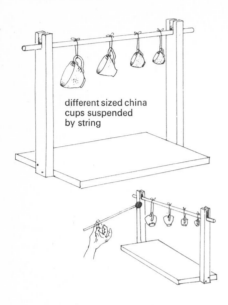

different sized china
cups suspended
by string

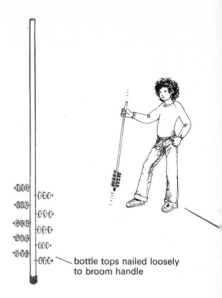

bottle tops nailed loosely
to broom handle

(11) *Cup-a-phone.* This is based on the same principle as the flower pot bell, and a gradation of large to smaller cups will produce low to high sounds.

(12) *Jingling johnny.* You can make a long jingle stick suitable for playing by banging it on the floor, or it can be short and either shaken, or gently tapped against the palm of the child's free hand to control the duration of the sound. A rubber ferrule such as you find on the bottom of walking sticks put on to the bottom of the long version helps to reduce unwanted noise.

(13) *Maracas.* Any suitable container can be used; the important thing is to make sure that the handle is firmly glued into it. Many different fillings can be tried, so that you make a set of maracas which produces a variety of sounds.

(14) *Plasticas.* These take very little time to make and children enjoy making their own. Bottles made of plastic come in many different shapes and sizes and some even have their own moulded handles. For classroom peace and to stop the contents being eaten I would advise gluing the tops on securely.

(15) *Shoebox ukelele.* This is too soft an instrument to be used in the classroom orchestra but it is a good one to make if there are no other stringed instruments available to the children.

(16) *Tea-chest bass.* It takes a fair amount of control to balance the broom handle and pluck it at the same time, but the popularity of the bass provides powerful motivation which encourages practice in the motor skills involved.

13. Maracas

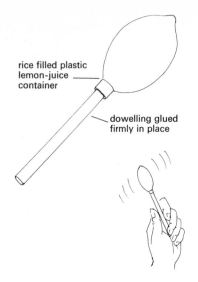

rice filled plastic
lemon-juice
container

dowelling glued
firmly in place

14. Plasticas

plastic bottle
filled with dried
peas or rice

15. Shoebox ukelele

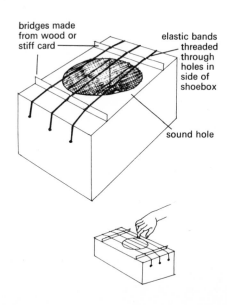

bridges made
from wood or
stiff card

elastic bands
threaded
through
holes in
side of
shoebox

sound hole

16. Tea-chest bass

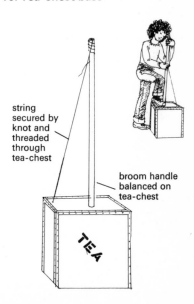

string
secured by
knot and
threaded
through
tea-chest

broom handle
balanced on
tea-chest

TEA

APPENDIXES

Materials suitable for use with young children

Books of songs

Songs from Playschool	B.B.C.	Feldman
Oxford Nursery Song Book	P. Buck	O.U.P.
Oxford School Music Book (Beginners)	Reynolds	O.U.P.
Nursery Songs	J. Gavall	O.U.P.
This Little Puffin	E. Matterson	Penguin
Sociable Songs	A. Mendoza	O.U.P.
Seven Simple Songs for Children	A. Mendoza & E. Rimmer	Curwen
Seventy Simple Songs with Ostinati	A. Chatterly	Novello
Songs to Sing and Play	A. Bently	Novello
American Folk Songs for Children	P. Seeger	Doubleday
Sixty Songs for Little Children, vol.1	W.G. Whittaker	O.U.P.
Echo and Refrain Songs	E. Barnard	Stainer & Bell
Sing with Chimes	O. Rees	O.U.P.
People Who Help Us	E. Hughes	Novello
Things That Help Us	E. Hughes	Novello
Eight Fun Songs	J. Pearse	Chappell
Faber Book of Nursery Songs	D. Mitchell & C. Blyton	Faber
Music for the Nursery School	L. Chesterman	Harrap
100 Children's Songs	W. Whyton	Essex Music
Appusskidu	B. Harrop	A. & C. Black

Records

Songs from Playschool (Decca)
Growing up with Wally Whyton (Hallmark)
100 All Time Favourites, Wally Whyton (Hallmark)
Best of Rolf Harris (EMI)
Singing Games and Action Rhymes: three, four, five (Kiddicraft)

Singing and acting games

New Nursery Jingles	E. Barnard	Curwen
Merrily Dance and Sing	G.E. Holt	Boosey & Hawkes
Children's Singing Games	A. Gomme	Curwen
Singing Games and Play Part Games	R. Chase	Dover
Nursery School Music Activities	E. Barnard	Curwen
Up and Down for Nursery and Infant Classes	D. Parr	Boosey & Hawkes
Go Ahead	D. Parr	Boosey & Hawkes
Clarendon Book of Singing Games	Wiseman & Northcote	O.U.P.
Games and Dances of the Maori	D. Willis	New Zealand Government Publications

Sound and instrumental work

Rhymes with Chimes	A. Mendoza & O. Rees	O.U.P.
Let's Sing and Play	A. Mendoza	O.U.P.
Tops and Tails	A. Mendoza	O.U.P.
Play and Sing	R. Addison	Holmes McDougall
Begin Making Music	R. Addison	Holmes McDougall
Playing with Sounds	E. Barnard & M. Davies	Curwen
Ring a Ding	Y. Adair	Novello
Music Makers	M. Berry	Longmans Green

Materials suitable for use with seniors

Books of songs

Oxford School Music Book	R. Fiske & J. Dobbs	O.U.P.
Scout Song Book		Boy Scout Association
Burl Ives Song Book	B. Ives	Ballentyne
Singing Together	H. Appleby & M. Fowler	O.U.P.
Faith, Folk and Clarity		Galliard
Sing a Merry Song	Swift & Clawson	O.U.P.
Something to Sing (Books 1 and 2)	G. Brace	C.U.P.
Sixty European Folk Tunes	R. Nobel	Novello
The Puffin Song Book	L. Woodgate	Penguin
Sing a Tune Series		Cooperative Recreation Services, Delaware, Ohio
124 Folk Songs	P. Seeger	Robbins
Listen, Let's Make Music	A. Hunt	Bedford Square Press
Sound Approaches for Slow Learners	D. Ward	Bedford Square Press
The Music Group	J. Horton	Schott
Fun with Drums	Nordoff & Robbins	Presser
Thirty Folk Settings for Children	A. Mendoza	Curwen
Appusskidu	B. Harrop	A. & C. Black
Making Music and Making More Music	A. Mendoza	Curwen

Records

Sounds and Silence (A record and book of interesting work with sounds in Junior
     Schools) (Cambridge University Press)
Songs for Swinging Children, J. Longstaffe
Instruments of the Orchestra, Yehudi Menuhin
Listen Now & The Town Musician, W. Clauson
100 All Time Favourites, Wally Whyton (Hallmark)

Materials suitable for all ages

Pentatonic songbooks

A Pentatonic Songbook	B. Brocklehurst	Schott
Just Five (Books 1 and 2)	R. Kersey	Belwin Mills

Books of rounds

Rounds from Many Countries	R. Anderson	Chappell
Round and Round Again	H. Newman	Hargail Press
Sing a Round	M. Wilson	O.U.P.
Graded Rounds	A. Mendoza	Novello

A music kit

Learning Through Music	G. & H. Lewis	New York Times Teaching Resources

(This is a complete programme of tapes, songs and instrumental work. It contains material suitable for a wide range of abilities and is well structured. The teacher who is 'unmusical' will find that she is free to concentrate on the children. The musical content is interesting, the instructions are clear and foolproof. The activities can be adapted to meet the needs of individual children and whatever instruments you have available can be used. It is expensive but since it contains material which would be suitable throughout a school it is a good investment.)

Useful addresses

Music publishers

Bedford Square Press (S.C.A.M.), National Council of Social Service, 26 Bedford Square, London WC1B 3HU

Belwin Mills Music Ltd, 250 Purley Way, Croydon CR9 4QD

Chappell & Co. Ltd, 50 New Bond Street, London W1A 2BR

Cooperative Recreation Services Inc., Delaware, Ohio, U.S.A.

Doubleday & Co. Inc., 100 Wigmore Street, London W1H 9DR

Holmes McDougall Ltd, Allander House, 137–41 Leith Walk, Edinburgh EH6 8NS

New York Times Teaching Resources Corporation, 100 Boylston Street, Boston, Mass., U.S.A.

Novello & Co. Ltd, Borough Green, Sevenoaks, Kent

Oxford University Press (O.U.P.), Music Dept., 44 Conduit Street, London W1R ODE

P.P.A. Publications, Pre-School Playgroups Association, Alford House, Aveline Street, London S11 5DH

Theodore Presser Co., Presser Place, Bryn Mawr, Pennsylvania PA 19010, U.S.A.

Schott & Co. Ltd, 48 Great Marlborough Street, London W1V 2BN

Organisations and associations

Advisory Centre for Education (A.C.E.), 18 Victoria Park Square, Bethnal Green, London E2

British Association for Early Childhood Education (incorporating the former
    Nursery Schools Association), Montgomery Hall, Kennington Oval, London
    SE11 5SW
British Society for Music Therapy, 48 Lanchester Road, London N6 4TA
Disabled Living Foundation, 346 Kensington High Street, London W14 8NS
MIND (formerly The National Association for Mental Health), 22 Harley Street,
    London W1N 2ED
Music for Slow Learners Project, c/o David Ward, Dartington College of Arts, Totnes,
    Devon TQ9 6JE
Orff-Schulwerk Society, 31 Roedean Crescent, London SW15 5JX
Standing Conference for Amateur Music, 26 Bedford Square, London WC1B 3HU

Further reading

*Books about music in education which are relevant to teaching the mentally
handicapped*

Music for the Handicapped Child	J. Alvin	O.U.P.
Music Therapy	J. Alvin	Hutchinson
They can Make Music	P. Bailey	O.U.P.
Slow Learners and Music	J.P.B. Dobbs	O.U.P.
Listen, Let's Make Music	A. Hunt	Bedford Square Press
Therapy in Music for the Handicapped Child	P. Nordoff & C. Robbins	Gollancz
Music in Special Education	P. Nordoff & C. Robbins	Presser
The Psychology of Musical Ability	R. Shutter	Methuen
Music Therapy	G. Thayer	Macmillan
Music for Slow Learners	D. Ward	College of Special Education
Singing in Special Schools	D. Ward	Bedford Square Press
My Kind of Playgroup Music	M. Shepherd	P.P.A. Publications
Heart, Hands and Voices	D. Ward	O.U.P.
Activities in Music with six year olds	M. Hope-Brown	Evans

Books on instrument making

Musical Instruments to be Made and Played	P. Roberts	Dryad Press
Make your own Musical Instruments	Mendell & Wood	Oak Tree Press
Designs for Simple Musical Instruments	R. Seifert	S.C.A.M., Dartington College of Arts
The Musical Instruments Recipe Book	E. Romney	Penguin
Making Musical Instruments	V. Blocksedge	Nursery Schools Association

Vibrations: Making Unorthodox Musical Instruments	D. Sawer	Cambridge University Press

Journals

Music in Education	Novello
Special Education; Forward Trends	Association for Special Education
MIND	National Association for Mental Health
Where	A.C.E.
Orff-Schulwerk Bulletin	Orff-Schulwerk Society
Guide Lines	College of Special Education, 85 Newman Street, London W1P 3LD
Journal of the British Society for Music Therapy	British Society for Music Therapy

Section III : Drama

7 DRAMA IN THE SCHOOL CURRICULUM: ITS AIMS, PURPOSES AND OBJECTIVES

'It's Mr Big! Are we going to do drama?'

Philip was greeted with exuberant cries as he walked into the small classroom. Surrounded by a group of rather undersized children, some in wheelchairs, he looked even bigger than usual. His first appearance had been a genuine dramatic confrontation. The class had come into the hall, a little tentatively, and suddenly a GIANT in big boots and wearing a sheepskin jacket strode in. He was carrying a pile of coats. There was also a group of people shivering with cold. 'He's taken our coats; please help us to get them back.' Some children ventured nearer to him. 'What's your name?', they asked. 'BIG!' was the stern reply. They retreated. The giant put down the coats and lay on them. The children crept back again and some touched his fur cloak, some managed to retrieve some of the coats. This game continued for some time. Two or three boys decided to help the giant and carried the coats back to him; others decided to help their adult friends. A giant pie was made but the giant refused to eat it. He got very angry. 'You must have a pill to calm you down', said one little girl. The giant made a great fuss but was persuaded to take the pill, a giant-sized one, and he went to sleep. Everyone ate some of the pie, got back the coats, and children and adults went to sleep, warm and comfortable. The giant was led away and the children very slowly woke up and went back to the classroom.

Many different activities developed from this incident during the following days. A castle was built from cardboard boxes. The boys dressed up in the giant's cloak and boots and repeated the story, remembering most of the details. Philip was measured. He lay down on a sheet of paper on the floor and an outline was drawn around him. Later this was painted and hung on the wall, another visual reminder of his size, particularly when the same thing was done with the smallest child in the room and the two figures put alongside one another. The story of Jack and the Beanstalk was listened to again with renewed interest and other paintings and creative work appeared. Movement took place to giant-like music and 'Fe! Fi! Fo! Fum!' was heard for a long time. Mr Big had become a hero and the children had felt the drive and stimulus of drama. The episode was not forgotten and it was several weeks later when Philip returned, dressed in his everyday clothes, to be immediately recognised as Mr Big. There was no doubting the warmth of his welcome, nor the children's readiness for more drama. (This episode took place during a session on drama in a hospital school. It was arranged by Mrs Dorothy Heathcote and the students taking the Diploma in Drama Education at the Institute of Education, University of Newcastle upon Tyne, and which the author was privileged to join.)

These children, all of whom were mentally handicapped, gained much from this activity. They had been involved in the development of the activity. They had been given responsibility to solve a problem and an opportunity to interpret and represent at their own level. Their ideas had been valued and acted upon. Possibly they had discovered unexpected personal resources and abilities. Subsequent classroom activities, although not all as obviously dramatic, reflected for some time to come the interaction that had occurred. Some, perhaps, were not as involved as others at the time, but they all wanted to participate when Philip returned.

The aim of educational drama is to create a situation in which a child becomes more aware of his whole self, physically, emotionally and intellectually. Through this self-discovery he may become more aware of his place in the world, his relationships with other people, and with the animals and objects he meets as he moves around. He may find out his limitations and his strengths. He will continually draw on his past experiences to reinforce new-found impressions. These aims apply to teaching drama to children at all levels, including those who are mentally handicapped. Indeed drama may be more valid as a medium for self-expression and learning for mentally handicapped children than for their more 'normal' peers. Their reaction to a dramatic stimulus is often on a simpler, more direct level and they are less cluttered by social inhibitions and attitudes. They will continue for many years to show their need to play out their experiences by imitation and spontaneous action. Teachers, however, must continually review their aims in planning programmes, remembering that their objectives may need to be different for almost every child. One child may have achieved much by a simple imitation of a hand movement, while another may have been able to assume a dramatic role and sustain it with some imagination.

DRAMATIC PLAY AND PLAY DEVELOPING FROM EXPERIENCE

A small child may follow its mother around the house, imitating her movements as she dusts, polishes and sweeps. The child may not comprehend the meaning of the work but enjoys imitating the physical actions. A few weeks later, all of these activities may be represented in play; stooping down to scrub an imaginary floor, or reaching up to polish a table. A little while later these actions may be seen in play with a dolls' or wendy house, or in the child running to get a cloth when something has been spilt.

Young children develop a deeper understanding of their world and their place in that world by imitation of adult activities and by play. This play tends to become more dramatic in character as their experiences widen. Before new impressions can be fully appreciated and before the child adapts his behaviour to meet these demands they must be linked with previous experiences. This happens symbolically in play. These newly discovered interests may be accompanied by verbal chatter and under-standing of the actions thus reinforced. Susanna Millar, in her book *The Psychology of Play* notes that 'symbolic or make believe play characterised the period of rep-resentational intelligence from two to seven years' (p.54). The delayed intellectual development of mentally handicapped children means that they may not play spon-taneously during those years, but at a later stage of their development. Lunzer and Hulme (1966) discovered that the play of mentally handicapped children resembles in many ways the play of younger normal children of similar mental age. Play also tends to become more dramatic as the child's experience widens. Most mentally handicapped children follow this pattern but again at a later stage of physical growth and at a slower rate. Each state appears to last much longer. Thus it is not surprising for a ten-year-old mentally handicapped child still to enjoy playing with sand and water. Dramatic work offers an opportunity to extend their activities in imaginary situations and in new roles. Strong physical actions and imitative games will be en-joyed at an age when other children enjoy more sophisticated and representational dramatic activities.

In dramatic work with mentally handicapped children it is therefore often necess-ary to teach them how to play, and to encourage the development of skills that appear to develop spontaneously in other children. It may be necessary for them to be taught how

(1) to move with enjoyment;
(2) to develop sensory and motor co-ordination;
(3) to play out their experiences; and
(4) to symbolise these experiences in dramatic play.

These skills are obviously not solely dramatic skills, and drama and the development of these skills must be seen in the context of the whole curriculum. Drama should not be isolated to an occasional session in the hall. There will of course be times of particular concentration on dramatic work when a dramatic activity is taken in iso-lation, but teachers should be aware of the links that can exist between experience and the various forms of self-expression that may result. A visit to a farm may result in many classroom activities, some of which may be primarily dramatic, but others may involve music, movement, or art and craft. Similarly movement activities, music, or a painting may become a stimulus for imaginative play. Alternatively an idea which originates in dramatic form may lead to other forms of creative activity.

It is important to remember, however, that many mentally handicapped children may not respond in an expressive way until they are adolescent or have had consider-able experience with basic and simple activities. It is important to remember to re-turn continually to the simplest objectives.

Dramatic play may also be used to foster general development. For example a teacher may want to encourage a child to know the names and movements of body parts. The child may have looked in the mirror and heard the names of the eyes, nose and mouth many times. Finger plays and touch can, however, reinforce this learning. 'Now what do we do when we go to sleep? We shut our eyes like this.' The child will probably imitate the teacher in a very unnatural way. He may screw up his eyes, peep out, cover his face with his fingers. The teacher may have to show the child time and time again, perhaps adding the traditional gesture of resting the head on the hands. Generally children will begin to imitate this action on their own and as the dramatic work continues, to a suggestion such as 'They got into their beds and fell fast asleep because they were so tired', the children will curl up on the floor and relax. Eyes will be closed and an imaginary blanket pulled up. The action is being represented in symbolic form. There is understanding and interaction between teacher and child. At a later stage mentally handicapped children will do this for themselves or with their toys and may begin to talk about it as they do it. 'Now then, go to sleep. Cover yourself up and don't kick off the bedclothes', said Mary as she put her teacher to bed at the end of a tiring journey. Make-believe, the first step towards the willing suspension of disbelief and a prerequisite for drama, is present in Mary's actions and language. But Mary is fifteen years old.

DRAMA THROUGH CONSTRUCTIVE AND CREATIVE PLAY

There comes a stage in children's development when their play takes a step forward. An observer can see that toys and other objects are used in a much more creative and constructive way. At the same time the child becomes aware of the strength of his movements and enjoys making an effort. He will push and pull, kick and splash about, drive a toy car with determination and build his bricks with some care and precision. None of these actions in themselves is essentially dramatic but every now and then one such activity is carried out with imagination.

Although the teacher will usually encourage constructive activity, materials must also be provided which can be destroyed. A piece of paper may be torn to shreds to make snowflakes, or a box battered to make a new shape to create a spaceship. Sand, water, clay, cardboard boxes and scrap material, old curtains, hats and shoes can all be stimuli for dramatic as well as creative activity.

Ben had responded to a finger play with interest.

> Here we see the deep blue sea,
> Here is a boat,
> Here is me,
> All the fishes down below
> Wiggle their tails
> And away they go

Without any direction he walked across to his toy box, emptied it and got in. He started pretending to row, then he leant out and said, 'Here's a fish.' He climbed out of the box and went around the room, bringing his fish back to the boat. He did this several times and then walked off. Later he was asked to put away his toys. 'Are you putting them in the boat?', he was asked. 'No,' he replied, 'it's the toy box'.

Drama, through creative play, often provides an opportunity for 'letting off steam', for some violence and aggression, but under controlled conditions. Children often find difficulty, though, in knowing when the climax of an activity has been reached. In the playground this may end in a fight or a quarrel; tears and recriminations may follow. Teachers must learn to anticipate this in class and help to bring the group back to reality in a gentle way.

John was building a motorway in the sand tray. It was an elaborate construction and his toy car sped up and down. His teacher could see that he was so involved in his play that he was getting exhausted. His movement became more and more violent and he ended by crashing the car into the banks of the sand that he had so carefully created. A look of relief came over his face when his teacher said quietly, 'Come and wash your hands, it's time for dinner.' He went off happily but obviously tired out.

It is necessary to develop the skill of knowing when to step in or out of the action, and when to help in the process of unwinding from the climax. This may sometimes be done by assuming an imaginary role of someone who has particular powers. The children may respond to a magic word like abracadabra or a Dr Who character who can control unruly monsters. The pattern of the lesson can be structured to end on a quiet note and the teacher can directly slow down the action. Most stories lead the listener from an exciting point to an easier situation. 'They lived happily ever after' may be more symbolic than real in ordinary life, but it represents a conclusion that children often need.

Such actions have a strong link with dramatic activity at a later stage and teachers will be ready to reinforce these by providing materials and opportunity for this natural development. Sometimes constructive play involves the child in a dramatic role within the action: 'I am a policeman, driving a police car.' And at other times the child will impersonate the thing he has created. For example, if he has made an aeroplane from two pieces of wood, he may run around the room making aeroplane noises with his arms spread out like the wings of the plane. These actions are the seeds from which role playing, dramatic situations and even dialogue will grow.

Children often appreciate, however, that the real world has security and love and may be a pleasanter place to live in than the world of fantasy. 'Let's go back to earth and back to our houses', said one boy as the spaceship seemed to be soaring ever further away. The tone of his voice indicated his anxiety. He found a way out of his dilemma within the drama: 'I'm going to pull this lever and reverse the engines.' This revealed unsuspected emotional control to his teacher and his decision was accepted by the rest of the group. Many mentally handicapped children continue their make-believe roles into their real lives, as do many young children. This should be accepted for what it is by the teacher and parent, and conversation and action accommodated to the fantasy situation so that unwinding can occur slowly.

All constructive and creative play is not dramatic but provides another form of expression. Painting and modelling, for example, also strengthen emotional discipline and concentration. Teachers who are responsible for a class throughout the day will be able to provide opportunities for many activities which will continually interact with the more specifically dramatic.

DRAMA AS A GAME WITH RULES AND AS A PART OF REAL-LIFE EXPERIENCE

Fantasy, make-believe and the willing suspension of disbelief all appear in children's dramatic play. Gradually this involves the acceptance of rules. Unwritten and unspoken, they can be recognised in the game which developed between the children and the giant which was described earlier. Such rules are very flexible and sometimes may not be discerned by the teacher. Ruth, a Down's syndrome child, frequently carried on with her role long after the play had finished. Imaginary friends frequently appear. Little gangs may form with their own codes of honour, private language and social behaviour. Often it is only when rules are shared in this way that the teacher will get any indication of the level of sophistication that has been reached. Sometimes the rules may be alien to the adult for in essence they represent a move away from dependence on adults towards the assumption of personal responsibility.

As children become more confident in themselves and about the world around them, and as socialisation progresses, the need to make symbolic representation of experience lessens. The real world gains in significance and offers endless opportunities for discovery and adventure. Opportunities for travel and the quality of some television programmes have opened up the real world to all children. This must be remembered when choosing subjects for drama and improvisation. The dividing line between fact and fiction may be strongly drawn by many mentally handicapped children as they begin to know from their experiences how machines work, how plants and animals grow and even about men walking on the moon — facts which were not so readily available twenty years ago. The rules of the game, however, usually still permit excursions into fantasy, as is obvious from adult enjoyment of James Bond and other romantic or escapist films and television programmes.

However, real-life experiences can be most useful for dramatic representation since they generally provide both a problem and a solution. The purpose of drama is not just to act out fantastic stories but also to help deepen the level of thinking about the questions stories raise. Drama may help children to ask 'why' and 'how' It is interesting to note that children do not often spontaneously act out stories they have heard, but usually choose topics they have seen on television or which come from their own lives.

Preparation for visits and representing events afterwards provides opportunity for dramatic work, for practising oral skills, and can also help to develop social competence. The part played by festivals in the school year, be it Harvest, Christmas or an open day, with their accompanying ritual are an endless source for developing a feeling for drama. The children are involved in a very simple way without elaborate rehearsal but can become powerfully impressed with the drama of the occasion. Similarly much can come from the seasonal changes with their rituals of behaviour, involving dress, food and activities. It is from these very obvious occurrences that language will be stimulated.

Teachers of mentally handicapped children are in a stronger position than many teachers in being able to see the purpose of interaction between the areas of creative expression. They may not always be aware that they are 'doing' drama. Alternatively some more obviously dramatic activities may be an indirect method of teaching. A treasure hunt can be an opportunity for sense training. Listening to a story may often stimulate the kinaesthetic sense although no movement has occurred. 'Start from where you are most confident' says Brian Way in *Development through Drama* (p.8), and this should be remembered by all who are hesitant to begin something which they feel they know little about.

DRAMA IN EDUCATION

It is perhaps unfortunate that the word 'play' is used for the sorts of activities which have already been described and also for the form of writing which involves dialogue and characters in the development of plot and atmosphere. Many people seem to associate drama only with the latter form and therefore only think that they are 'doing' drama when a play is being rehearsed. There may be a lot of time spent on learning words and movements and an audience may be thought to be necessary for the final performance. This may mean that dramatic activities are confined to a very small area such as the platform in the hall, originally intended for one or two people to use for the school assembly. To view dramatic education only in terms of theatre performances can sometimes result in neither an educational enterprise nor a theatrical event.

Some teachers do have skill, interest and creative ability in theatre arts. They may find that by working on a play for performance they can use their skills to draw a fully involved response from their children. They can often evaluate the progress made by individual children from such work and parents and visitors are often impressed with the achievement. Play production for an outside audience can stimulate a lot of fun and excitement, particularly if the play is colourful, topical and allows for spontaneity. It is not the author's intention to decry this approach, but sometimes the idea of producing a play is such a daunting undertaking for some teachers that they either never tackle it, or suffer by seeing the children move in a stilted, unnatural way, speak in exaggerated intonations and perform like robots. Rehearsals become a painful battle with bored children, and this applies equally to drama in all schools, not exclusively those for the mentally handicapped.

Drama in education should not be an opportunity to show off individual expertise on the part of the teacher or the children. Discipline, control, social awareness, confidence and some use of language may be acquired by putting on a play for public performance, but these must be weighed against the progress which has been made in understanding and thinking at a deeper level. Teachers who are convinced that play production is an essential part of the school curriculum will find many books on drama and theatre to help them. In these chapters the emphasis is on educational drama, drama which can be regarded as part of the total education of the child. This sort of drama does not seek an audience or elaborate staging. It may occur in a corner of the classroom or throughout the whole school. Sometimes a group of children may want to show what they have been doing to others, and a spontaneous performance may then occur. Sometimes the performance itself will become the game. Ticket sellers and usherettes with programmes, sweets and ices will be as important as the actors. Dressing-up clothes should always be available in the classroom. Sometimes extra costumes and head-dresses can be made in art and craft, sometimes parents can be enlisted, but as far as possible the adult concept of the theatre should be avoided. Similarly with properties and scenery, the imaginative use of an everyday object can be as real and effective for the child as the more realistic imitations. The provision of a wigwam is unlikely by itself to conjure up many ideas of North American Indians, but hiding under a table may be a very realistic cave for the bears if the children have thought of it for themselves. The important point is that with children whose imagination is limited we should introduce as many real things as possible for them to see, touch and use, but they are unlikely to see the difference between the real and make-shift until their all-round experience has been deepened.

Teachers of mentally handicapped children are faced with more difficulty than teachers in ordinary schools in providing realistic stimuli. Mentally handicapped children do need to be kept closer to reality and to have their impressions of the world constantly reinforced. Only the best is good enough because they cannot easily make comparisons and selections. This is not a contradiction of what has been said above but is meant as a reminder to teachers of their need to be constantly alert to the dichotomy of their position. A child or a group of children may become interested in cowboys and Indians following a programme on television. Some may begin to play with imaginary bows and arrows, guns and swords, horses and feathers. The teacher will want to reinforce this activity with good illustrations and with as many real objects as possible, but bows and arrows or guns and swords are not playthings and imitation ones should not be used in play because of the danger to eyes and limbs. A modern archery set may be available or a demonstration by an archer may be arranged and the actions can then be imitated. Wigwams, totem poles, Indian head-dresses and cowboy hats can all be made by the children. These outward signs become a follow-up of the children's interests. Alternatively, on some occasions the introduction of some unusual objects can be a stimulus for a proposed visit or project. For example, seaweed and shells can be a stimulus for a visit to the seaside. Dramatic movements may result in response to their shapes and peculiar feel, but the teacher must be ready to accept an improvisation of a visit to the seaside which is based on eating ice creams and using slot machines.

While mentally handicapped children, along with the rest of the population, have a large exposure to both real-life and fictional drama on television, they will also gain much from watching live theatrical performances, particularly those prepared for children. Teachers should try, where possible, to make links with local theatres and colleges, and encourage their visits to the school. Theatre in Education groups can be very helpful, not so much by performing to the children, but rather by involving the children in the performance and the follow-up activities.

As always it is the individual teacher who will contribute most. It is helpful to have experience of drama work and the theatre, and those who are trained in this area may approach it with more confidence and originality. But teachers with a sound knowledge of educational theory and practice, and of children, will not require great skill or expertise in drama.

The benefits which have been discussed as deriving from participation in dramatic activity cannot be evaluated as, or claimed to be, solely the result of work in drama. Drama is, and can only be, one part of the whole learning process. But dramatic activity supported by other classroom activities may account for an increase in confidence, in physical freedom, and in an extended language flow with a variety of vocal range. There may also be greater social awareness and competence. The imaginative response to stories may become deeper. Concentration and involvement in work may be lengthened, and perhaps the teacher may see awakening powers of comprehension and self-expression.

'Can we do drama *now*?'

8 SOME DRAMATIC ACTIVITIES

'A man walking across an empty space is drama' (Peter Brooks)

DRAMA ARISING FROM EXPERIENCE

It is a bright sunny day in summer. The children, aged between thirteen and fifteen, come into the classroom and move to a well-known pop record. Some can dance rhythmically, others move energetically but heavily. Some are not able to show much response beyond following the others with hands, feet or eyes, but when the music stops they break into chatter. They gather around the teacher. 'I'm hot, are you?' 'Let's have a rest for a while.' There is a short discussion on feeling hot and cold. The children feel the floor, the radiators and the walls, some of which are cold to the touch, some hot. They pretend to eat ice cream and sip a very hot drink. Some pretend to put on swimsuits and go into a pool, some lie in the sun and sunbathe.

There is a short period of rest, and when they sit up discussion follows about the journey which took place the previous day by bus to the park. All the everyday events which occurred are recalled and it is agreed that they will go on another trip today — in the classroom. Chairs are arranged to represent the bus. A driver is chosen, and his conductor, and the passengers. Having collected all the things they want to take with them, they get on the bus and start the journey. Someone points out things to look at, recalling other bus rides. The driver tells them that they have arrived. The action is halted while we all organise the next move: finding a picnic place. The teacher steps into the role of the park keeper or some official. 'No one can picnic here without a ticket.' This is an unexpected problem. Decisions must be made, ticket bought, and kept carefully. The picnic meal is prepared and eaten and a queue formed to buy ice creams. An ice cream stall is erected and a vendor selected. Games with imaginary balls, and hide and seek are progressing well until someone falls over. Spontaneously a first-aid kit is produced and the patient attended to. She is supported back to the coach, suffering bravely. The rest of the party collect their things and take their places again for the return journey. Everyone is very tired. On arriving home one has fallen fast asleep and doesn't get off. Numbers are counted and the missing one found but he is too tired and has to be carried. 'Perhaps he is ill?' 'Has he eaten too much ice cream?' 'Was it sunstroke?' The nurse must be sent for. The boy must go to hospital and be put to bed. Three or four children are engaged in this activity, which has arisen quite unexpectedly; the rest decide to visit him and take him presents. Fortunately he recovers and can come home with them. There may have to be a party tomorrow to celebrate his recovery, but for today he will be cheered up with a familiar song.

This very simple example of dramatic activity illustrates how everyday experiences can be fed back and the class led from known and familiar to more spontaneous and imaginative actions. The group may work together on common ground but individuals will supply ideas for their own exploits. 'Drama is concerned with the individuality of individuals', writes Brian Way in *Development through Drama* (p.3). (This is an excellent book which has given many teachers confidence in starting drama in education, and teachers of the mentally handicapped will find much in it that they can use with their classes.)

When working from experience into drama it is usually necessary for the teacher to begin a session by recalling a recent experience, but the subsequent development of a session can generally be left to the children. Generally one child will introduce some other event such as a small accident, another child will recall the outcome of that, and so on. In this way the drama will lead forward spontaneously, usually on a pattern of development quite different from that which may have been envisaged by the teacher. Gradually more imaginative ideas which have been met in stories, poems, songs or on television may be introduced. The park may become a desert island and the park keeper a monster, the bus may become a boat or an aeroplane, but the principles remain the same. A situation is met and a problem arises which requires a solution. In turn the solution involves decisions being made and actions taken. Generally the solution should be arrived at by the children, as this may lead to other problems and other solutions, but to begin with the problem-solving may have to be suggested by the teacher and it will then need to be of a very simple nature. For example:

(1) In order to get to the land everyone will have to take their shoes off and walk barefoot. People in wheelchairs are the lucky ones; they won't get wet.

(2) The Queen must be helped to find a name for her new baby.

(3) In order to get through the forest, everyone must hold hands and creep on tiptoe.

(4) The Princess must be made to laugh by a funny dance or song.

When they are asked to draw on their own resources children tend to become more involved in drama and begin to create dramatic situations around familiar objects and day-to-day events. Drinking and eating, getting undressed and going to bed, sleeping and waking up, and getting dressed constitute frequently repeated activities in children's lives and consequently occur frequently in their imaginative play. Teachers can draw on these as sources of dramatic situations. Amongst the most readily and easily acted out are:

(1) drinking and eating hot and cold food;

(2) eating food we like and food we don't like;

(3) feeling very hungry and having a big feast;

(4) observing birds and animals eating and drinking and imitating them;

(5) feeding different sorts of animals;

(6) making beds, nests, dens and magic castles;

(7) dressing-up in everyday clothes or clothes required for special events.

The subject of food is always useful, particularly as it can be extended in a number of ways. For example:

(1) discussions of how meals are prepared can be held and then acted out;

(2) parties can be held and linked to reality with shopping trips;

(3) banquets and picnics can be prepared and enjoyed.

These situations can also be repeated by varying the mood. The weather may change or there may be a need to hurry. Salt may have been used instead of sugar and everything has to be done again. The permutations are endless. In each case the real experience will support the representational.

Comedy is popular with children and can be introduced to reinforce involvement and participation, but generally the emotional attitude will be arrived at by suggestion and participation. Mentally handicapped children can often create a mood with simple and disarming sincerity. A class found a situation hilarious in which an old lady, played by a child, kept dropping her parcels from a loaded shopping basket while trying to cross a busy street. The drivers seemed to take little notice other than swerving to avoid her and tooting their horns. The mood changed dramatically when two of the children, recognising the old lady's plight, went to help her and saw her safely across the road.

Visits and visitors are sources of dramatic activity. The milkman, the postman and the dustman all provide extensions of experience for the child, and to see them at work, coming to the school and home, and then to talk with them and examine their uniforms is valuable. Later, visits can be made to the post office, the dairy or even the refuse dump, which will not only extend their understanding and social competence but will provide more topics for dramatisation. After a visit of a fireman in full uniform, one boy said, 'That's the best thing we've had in school'. Feelings like this can obviously lead to exploration and follow-up with a high degree of personal involvement. For example, the visit of a postman or a visit to the post office can be followed up in lots of ways:

(1) set up a post office and have people buying and selling stamps and postal orders;

(2) write letters to people and go on an imaginary walk to the post box;

(3) wrap some imaginary parcels and take them to the post office (include one extra-large one that won't fit through the door or on the scales);

(4) have a class letter box with its own collections.

Teachers never lack ingenuity in providing these enrichment opportunities but sometimes do not realise the opportunities that drama offers for extending the activities.

The ritual of the normal day is filled with situations that provide the basis of much scripted drama and which can be valuably explored with mentally handicapped children. Everyday situations such as meeting people, arriving at a new place, playing with friends, quarrelling with enemies, crying or laughing, waiting hopefully, leaving to return home or to travel, starting a job, coping with success or failure, and home with all its rituals and people, all require their own emotional response.

Teachers can draw on these activities for dramatic work with considerable emotional and cognitive benefit for the children, and at the same time help to bring home and school life closer together.

DRAMA ASSOCIATED WITH MOVEMENT

Dramatic activity is often the natural outcome of work in movement, and movement is essential to drama. The principles which underlie the teaching of movement have been elaborated in section I, and the similarity with those involved in the teaching of drama is obvious. Four factors of particular relevance to drama are: (1) the development of skill, control and co-ordination of the body as a whole as well as its various parts; (2) the development of spatial and body awareness; (3) the development of a sense of rhythm, climax and 'declimax'; and (4) the use of the body with motivation and purpose. But as with all aspects of drama, it is important not to bring adult concepts of formal movement to the work. Observation should be made of young children and young animals at play. It will be seen how skill and control are achieved by repetition, by trial and error, through contact with each other, and by a growing awareness and confidence in creating something new from a learned experience.

Skill, control and co-ordination

This is an area of almost total overlap with movement activities, although at the higher levels there is a gradual divergence of purpose and orientation. Initially the orientation is towards the development of simple functional activities like kicking, crawling and rolling, but gradually these are used with purpose and intent. At a later stage they can be used almost symbolically. Stamping and clenching the fist can be signs of frustration and anger without any practical use except the relief of feelings and tensions. In this way the initial physical activity may be used for some dramatic purpose. Teachers of mentally handicapped children will need to spend time on these movements which most children discover for themselves.

Development of spatial and body awareness

Awareness of the body, including the head, face and limbs may be induced by touch and gentle physical manipulation involving a play element. For example, the hands may be held together to clap, allowed to drop and then lifted to clap again. After some repetition the movement may be imitated by the child without help. Facial movements can be felt as well as seen. Children can be encouraged to imitate blinking, winking, pouting and smiling and to experiment with funny faces and expressions. Children should be allowed to feel the teacher's face and allowed some control over her face as well as their own. Many finger plays and nursery rhymes are centred on parts of the face and these can be used to accompany movements.

There is a strong need for children to feel physical support to deepen their sense of movement and induce a feeling of peace and relaxation. Swinging from an adult can be contrasted with the security of being cradled and rocked. Bodies, including the teacher's, can be crawled over and climbed up, pushed and pulled and compared with inanimate objects. To be able to pull or push an adult helps to increase personal responsibility. The support of the adult can gradually be transferred to the ground and children allowed to lie on their backs or stomachs and kick and thrash. They will gradually become aware of the strength and effort required to push themselves along, to roll and eventually to turn a somersault or stand on their head. Slowly they will become more aware and gain in responsibility and confidence. When these activities are practised in a play atmosphere they will be valuable long after the child has learnt to crawl and walk.

Other dramatic activities which help to develop body awareness include sitting on the ground in various shapes; spinning around like a top; moving forwards or backwards without using arms or legs; and imitating insects, fish and reptiles that they have seen or monsters that they have imagined. Gradually their bodies will respond to their imaginations. Teachers will sometimes have to demonstrate but it is vital to be willing at the same time to accept the children's ideas. The emphasis throughout must be on the personal enjoyment of the activity. When laughter or vocal sound can be heard it usually signifies a considerable release of tension. There are many variations of these types of exercises, all of which should have a playing, experimental nature. So many children have by-passed this natural form of development because they do not approach it spontaneously, and, for some, circumstances may prevent them being given the chance for noisy active play.

Control and co-ordination of movement in more conventional ways will develop as free movement progresses. Children may need to be taught to stand still, to sit down slowly, jump up, and walk on tiptoes. These will require concentration and effort but this can be encouraged by using imaginative themes. It is often important for teachers to observe the part played by the head and the eyes, and although critical comments should not be made, some suggestion to look at the light bulbs, at pictures on the walls, or to find treasure will encourage better posture. Sometimes more of the earlier play activities need to be repeated, and sometimes music can be used to accompany these movements. Through these movements the children will gradually become more aware of their bodies and the space around them.

Dramatic movements can encourage the use of a child's personal space, above his head, on the ground, and within touching distance of the next person. Young children tend to bunch together and often bump when they move in unison. They need help to appreciate pace, size and shape. Initially most children will be active at the same time and many will be doing individual activities. As social awareness develops they will begin to work together, help each other and learn from each other. The teacher may encourage children to explore their personal space by getting them to:

(a) crouch into a small shape and gradually grow upwards while staying on the spot;

(b) start as a statue or a doll and slowly come to life;

(c) eat some magic food which has the power to make a person into a giant or a
      dwarf; or

(d) melt from a block of ice into a pool of water.

When the children are ready to work together, some of these things can be done in
pairs or groups and actions contrasted one with another, sometimes touching hands,
sometimes intentionally not touching but quite close. This may lead to games such
as follow-the-leader in which the teacher can participate if she wants.

Adjustment to the hall or a new room may be encouraged by creeping all around
the walls in various ways, such as crouching, tiptoeing or walking backwards. Ob-
stacles, which must not be touched, may be placed around the room and a path must
be found around them. The sense of the use of space in large and small movements
and some feeling for variety in the timing of movement should also be encouraged.
Response to music in dance will then follow more easily.

Concepts of size, weight and texture can be strengthened through dramatic movement. One of the class might be asked to wrap a parcel, carry it around the room,
give it to someone else and help him unwrap it. Other objects can be chosen. They
might be closely related to things the children may have seen recently, and can be
as large and unwieldy as a lawn mower or a carpet, for example, or on the other
hand as small and as precious as a jewel or a silk scarf.

Experience gained in these very simple ways will link directly to later activities
which require a more imaginative response and will also help with group work. This
groundwork often shows when a new child joins a class of seniors. His embarrassment
is in contrast to the skill and freedom of the others who can quickly become involved
and react spontaneously and appropriately.

Development of a sense of rhythm, climax and declimax

It is usually easier to say that movement, speech or music lacks rhythm than it is to
define its presence. It is usually visible in dance, and audible in music and spoken
poetry, but our response to rhythm is felt deep within ourselves. Many mentally
handicapped children have the ability to respond to rhythm and can dance effectively
and with pleasure, but for many it is a long slow process to acquire some kind of rhythmic co-ordination in even the simplest of actions. Many children enjoy the sensation
of stamping their feet in time to a nursery rhyme or a song, but rhythm consists of
more than the mere regularity of beat. A rhythmic pattern is composed of a much
more subtle variation of time, stress or force, and spatial movement. It can be seen
clearly in the movement of the waves, ever changing yet constant in character. John
Keats' sonnet 'On the Sea' may convey this sensation to an adult in words, through
poetry:

>It keeps eternal whisperings around
>Desolate shores, and with its mighty swell
>Gluts twice ten thousand Caverns, till the spell
>Of Hecate leaves them their old shadowy sound.
>Often 'tis in such gentle temper found

That scarcely will the very smallest shell
Be mov'd for days from where it sometime fell,
When last the winds of heaven were unbound.
Oh ye! who have your eye-balls vex'd and tired,
Feast them upon the wideness of the sea;
Oh ye! whose ears are dinn'd with uproar rude,
Or fed too much with cloying melody —
Sit ye near some old Cavern's mouth, and brood
Until ye start, as if the sea-nymphs quir'd!

Debussy has captured the mood of the sea in 'Le cathédrale englouti', and others in dance or the plastic arts. All these are creations of adults with mature minds. How then can children discover this sophisticated entity, particularly when movement is clumsy and speech limited?

Teachers can do much by their own example. The way they move and speak is a constant reminder to their classes and impressions can be formed kinaesthetically. Children, by listening to poems or music, or in movement through rocking, swinging and other similar activities, can be helped to develop a greater awareness of rhythm. These can be accompanied by music, such as lullabies and nursery songs, which can reinforce the body feelings involved. Action songs and games with words can also be used to encourage variety and allow for repetition. Well-known examples are 'A farmer's in his den', 'Punchinello', and 'Here we go round the mulberry bush'. Obviously here we have the area of overlap between music, drama and movement.

Movement to narrative may also be used to good effect. At first, simple narratives can be made up by the teacher, based on familiar everyday actions. An effort should be made, however, to ensure that the narrative has some climax and that there is an opportunity for the children to unwind at the end. The spoken voice or music can be used to set an atmosphere of anticipation or quiet. Gradually more surprising suggestions can be made so that there is some stronger element of suspense involved. Some teachers may want to use music with movement in dramatic work and may follow some of the well-known schools broadcasts. Generally, though, these are not entirely suitable for use with the mentally handicapped and it is usually wise to tape them and use only those parts that are suitable. Sounds may be recorded by the teacher, and the children invited to interpret them. Sounds like a grandfather clock striking, a dinner gong, crackling paper or running water may all be used to stimulate improvised movement. Percussion instruments also encourage a variety of responses and may often be a useful way to signal to the class that they must stop and listen, or freeze in a position. The response to a drum will also be very different from that produced when a cymbal or bell is struck.

In dramatic work it is often necessary to show mentally handicapped children how to carry out an action, as they may not have developed images of their real experiences. Some of the things we ask children to do in drama can be very confusing. For example, a child may know all about washing his hands and know how to do it, but it may be confusing to be asked to do this in the middle of the school hall in the middle of the day without any soap or water. However, this transference of a skill from the real to the imaginary does represent a most significant development in learning.

Showing children how to represent activities and skills can be done too frequently and should be done with restraint. There are no absolutely right or wrong ways of doing things and the teacher must be willing to let the children work things out for themselves. Sometimes they know better than the teacher how to use some new toy, especially if it has been on television. If a child's reaction to being shown how to do something is negative then it would be unwise to continue.

It is at this stage that the early work in movement shows its significance. A class of children who can use their bodies imaginatively will participate in other, more demanding ways with greater confidence and skill. However, the skills involved in a particular activity can be broken down and taught directly to the children. For example, mock fights crop up frequently in dramatic work, be it in a cowboy episode or with monsters from Dr Who. The art of conducting a mock fight can be learnt in slow motion. Of course the children must learn to stay at arm's length and mustn't touch at all but at the same time can learn the moves that they would use in a real fight. These can be accompanied by realistic groans and shrieks. It is useful to follow sessions like this where there is high output of energy with contrasting light movements. From these some form of dance drama may be encouraged wherein the contrasts in mood and movement are highlighted.

Throughout sessions which concentrate on movement the children should be encouraged to present contrasts of strength, in large vigorous movements and in flowing delicate ones. Pace will also have to be varied according to the urgency of the situation. Jack may climb up the beanstalk in a very different way from that in which he comes down, and the giant will set off to catch him in a different mood from that in which he returns home to the castle at the end of the day and promptly falls asleep. It is likely though that this feeling for contrast will be achieved more readily in group work which involves some sort of processional ritual. A slow, solemn occasion or a hurried, busy one will evoke a more sensitive and naturally felt response than one which arises superficially. Contrasts may also be encouraged by the use of light and darkness, shadows and pools of light from stage lanterns; by noise and absolute silence; and by movement and stillness. All sessions should include times of rest and quiet. Many children need to be helped to achieve this for their work to gain in depth and understanding.

> Teach us to care and not to care
> Teach us to sit still.
> (from 'Ash Wednesday', T.S. Eliot)

It cannot be overemphasised that the acquisition of skills in movement is essential to the development of dramatic work. On the other hand some teachers may feel that the outcome of their movement work lies in the area of expressive dance. The close link between movement and drama makes it possible for some teachers to use the disciplines of drama more satisfactorily, while others who have had personal experience in dance can use their expertise in this way, and both can benefit the children. The latter group of teachers will probably want to be more ambitious and imaginative in their movement work and may need and want to go well beyond the suggestions of this chapter. There are also many students and teachers who have had little prior experience in movement studies or drama. It is hoped that this chapter will encourage them to have the confidence to introduce drama into the curriculum and also provide some ideas for their work in school.

Mentally handicapped children, like all children, offer much inspiration to the teacher, if the teacher provides the means and the opportunity as well as the example for drama and movement. There are many areas of personal development, such as range and depth of emotional expression, aesthetic standards, simple moral concepts and, perhaps most importantly of all, sharing and working with others, that cannot effectively be acquired in a closely monitored programme. The drama specialist and the movement specialist must each make a claim for the place of their subject in the curriculum. It is important for teachers to realise that these subjects are mutually supportive in school, and only in their fully artistic forms of ballet and the theatre do they make distinctly different demands on the performer.

DRAMA AS AN EXTENDED GAME WITH ITS OWN RULES

Extended dramatic activity offers an opportunity for the mentally handicapped child to deepen his experience of life by re-living experiences and representing them actively. The ability of some mentally handicapped children to understand and participate fully in this sort of activity may be limited but their interpretation of stories, myths and legends will involve them in problems in which they may see solutions to their own real-life problems. Fairy godmothers do sometimes appear at the right moment; diligence does have its reward; the wicked are not always punished but retribution may follow; the big bad wolf is finally overcome by the good little pig. Extended dramatic activity can also help to develop social competence and an awareness of others. The child can see that other people need help and that *he* can provide for their needs. The princess who arrives in the storm needs food, her bed has to be made, her clothes dried and she may even need to be told a story before she goes to sleep.

However, participation in extended dramatic activity does involve an acceptance of the rules of the game. In particular it requires participation in role playing and the willing acceptance of an imaginative situation as if it were real. Until children are ready to do this they cannot be expected to act out a story in dramatic terms, and may only be able to follow the directions of the teacher. Between about five and nine years there is, for most children, a growing awareness of the difference between fantasy and reality. There is a sense of sharing with an adult the knowledge that for the time being this or that does not exist, and behaviour and language will be geared to this awareness. Mentally handicapped children may develop this capacity later than normal children, but for most of them it will occur and become something that is accepted from then on. The rules may be acquired in many ways. Some arise spontaneously during play. 'You can't do that, you're the Daddy.' 'I'm the one who puts you to sleep!' Some are traditional. Games appear at certain seasons with their own rules which differ in different parts of the country. Some will be learnt in the classroom or playground with balls, cards and puzzles.

The acceptance of the rules of the game is reflected in the following incident with a group of young children. At the beginning of the lesson a length of coloured material was brought into the room and a story told about it. It had been brought in for them by an old lady who wanted them to think of something to do with it. Some children picked it up and held it up high in the air. Without any instructions or suggestions the rest of the class got up and stood underneath it. 'It's a tent.' No one dared to walk on it when it was put back on the floor. It had assumed a magical property. The children circled around it, trying to decide what else it might become. 'A racing car', said one boy. 'A magic carpet', said another. Finally it was folded with great care and the teacher was instructed to take it back to the old lady with their stories. The next day one of the children asked the teacher, 'Did you meet the old lady today?' 'No, not today', was the reply. 'I didn't think you would', he replied. His reply and look indicated that he knew that *that* game was over.

Before embarking on extended drama with a group of children the teacher must obviously decide whether the children have reached this stage of acceptance of the rules. Usually it will be evident in games in the playground and in class, but games like hide and seek, statues, or grandmother's footsteps are good indicators of a child's ability to suspend his disbelief and take on a role. All of these games also have their dramatic content. When involvement is strong, the teacher can adopt a role herself from which she can possibly bring the class to a fuller dramatic situation.

Any teacher with imagination who knows her class can easily plan and develop an extended dramatic episode. A pirate might appear in the class one day, and after a brief moment of suspense the teacher asks him what they can all do to help him. He wants help to find his treasure. The children are ready to co-operate. Some quickly gain enough confidence to show him possible hiding places. The treasure isn't there! He says he will come back again when they have had time to look at his map of the desert island where the treasure is hidden and make suitable preparations for the journey. He leaves some instructions with a boy who volunteers to be his lieutenant. Some work is suggested to the class and various activities ensue. A boat is made from boxes, food is prepared, and tents and fishing lines made or found. Maps are traced and paintings done of the island. Some dressing-up clothes are collected. A few days later the pirate returns and all is prepared to set sail in the *Jolly Roger* for the desert island. Some children suggest hazards that they might encounter on the journey. The teacher suggests some others. The sea may be rough, there may be sharks, the ship might sink, and the natives on the island may not be friendly. Generally the children's suggestions should be accepted, no matter how trivial or how gory. It may be difficult to find roles for some of the children, but beads can be held ready for the natives, a drum can be beaten, a dance of friendship practised. Eventually the treasure will be found, and all can return for a ceremonial meal of celebration.

Much of a story like this will develop from ideas put forward by the children and usually they will find roles for themselves. Some will want to be pirates, some natives, some will change roles in the middle — but this is not casting in a play. The episode must have initial structure and a basic plan but the development must remain flexible. No audience is required or expected. The acting does not require much acting skill, rather a willingness to suspend disbelief, to play out a role imaginatively and to allow unexpected events to develop to their own conclusions.

The teacher's satisfaction comes not from acting ability she may foster, but in the use that is made of skills associated with the children's learning and thinking. The themes that are suitable for exploration in this way are endless. The way in which they are developed will vary in detail and outline for the sources are vast. The rewards, too, are far-reaching.

DRAMA AND ORAL SKILLS

The term 'oral skills' is used here to cover all those areas in which speech is used. Most of us probably spend more of our waking time in this activity than in any other, and most normal children have acquired some considerable skill in this area by the time they are six. For mentally handicapped children the development of oral skills is frequently one of the most significant areas of difficulty. Some mentally handicapped children never develop any language skill and for most development is limited and patchy. The acquisition of language and the problems of speech delay are highly complex subjects and it is beyond the scope of this section to embark on a detailed treatment of this. However, drama is one way in which mentally handicapped children can be encouraged to develop and use language skills. Dramatic work gives children an opportunity to play with speech, to enjoy making sounds and repeating them and to discover for themselves a need to speak. Michael Croft in *Speech Delay: its Treatment by Speech Play* notes that 'speech cannot be taught, a child cannot be forced to talk, he can only be helped to enjoy and play with speech as far as he is able.' (p.1). Understanding what is said is acquired more quickly and is mainly dependent on the child's ability to hear and respond to the meaning of the speaker. Children in institutions may not understand that a nurse is trying to help them because she says the words in a different way from their own mothers. Teachers must remember this in their first contacts with children.

Listening and learning to listen with understanding are a vital aspect of early language learning and must be a priority for teachers. There are many ways in which the teacher can foster the development of listening skills, most of which will not be restricted to the drama lesson. Some aspects of drama work can, however, be used to good effect. Children can be encouraged or required to listen to sounds outside and inside the classroom and be asked to distinguish between them; the teacher can vary her voice from a whisper to a shout; percussion instruments can be used in a game-like situation to give signals; and simple listening to poems, stories, music and songs all help. It is rare to insist on silence in the classroom but in a drama lesson it is easy to create this sort of situation so that children can learn to listen without distractions.

In learning to talk, children pass through a babbling stage when they explore the possibilities for making sounds by using the different parts of their mouths. Children with speech delays can benefit from this sort of sound play. This can be ideal for dramatic activities when inhibitions are down. The teacher can make sounds to the child, the child can make them back, children can make them to one another. Whether a child responds or not, he may gradually become aware of the sounds he can make himself with lips and tongue.

Imitation of adult language is an important factor in language acquisition. The monologues of young children are well known to mothers and children and of obvious importance. In turn it would seem sensible to accompany actions with speech as much as possible. Thus: 'Now I shall put my coat on', 'I've lost a button! Where is it? Oh, here it is in my pocket.' Talk in dramatic play in the home corner, wendy house or shop reflects the extent of this sort of development and can be stimulated by the teacher introducing dialogue.

Mentally handicapped children tend to play silently and may need to be encouraged to 'make Teddy tell me'. Puppets can also help in this respect, making the things that the speaker dare not say easier to produce.

Movement work can also encourage the development of speech. Much of the work suggested for movement will help to release tension and many body movements can be accompanied by 'ooh's and 'aah's. Tiptoeing and creeping around with 'ssh' sounds adds to suspense and also represents basic communication. Laughter can be used to similar effect. Movement also encourages physical contact with adults and other children. Simulated meetings, greetings and farewells all represent language practice. The teacher can begin by greeting each child, shaking hands and asking each child to do the same. This can be followed by conversations about the weather, new clothes or holidays in the same way that would occur in any social situation.

Older children can be encouraged to develop a nonsense language which the other children have to try to understand. There needs to be a fairly secure use of language, though, if this is not to be confusing. It may help eliminate self-consciousness. Younger children may be able to join the teacher in a narrative illustrated by sounds.

> Teacher: I got in my car and it went prr prr
> (children repeat what teacher says)
> Teacher: I came to the corner and went TOOT TOOT
> (children repeat)
> Teacher: I went through a big puddle and it went SPLOSH!

This can continue, but a little at a time with many repetitions will be the most valuable way. Alternatively a story can be made from sounds. The teacher scratches on a drum: 'What was that like? A mouse? The wind?', etc. Another sound and there is an extension of the story. Listening and stillness can be contrasted with sound and movement.

Language development and socialisation often go hand in hand, and when children can work in groups there will be more opportunities for them to extend their talking: the shopkeeper chats to his customer, the bus driver to a passenger. Telephone conversations can be very popular. The teacher can join in, taking a role to introduce variety and stretch the level of thought. There will be continuous feedback between the dramatised scene and the level of talking, each enriching the other. Some of the formalities of language may be acquired in this way. It is wise to expect or require a response in sentence form and not accept single words, except from the very young or where they are appropriate responses. Accuracy of utterance, however, is far less important than developing interest and communicating meaning. Unless you have the guidance of a speech therapist pressure on the child to make a 'correct' sound may be harmful and could result in stammering or silence.

As with 'normal' children, much that mentally handicapped children hear, say and even learn, may not be fully understood initially. Gradually, however, ideas can be assimilated and understood. Finger plays, nursery rhymes and action songs all have incongruities. How many times has the reader been around a mulberry bush, let alone on a cold and frosty morning? But a 'confroty morning' is more meaningful than just a 'morning'. The action and rhythm have a stimulation that is carried over into everyday language. It often seems that words can be sung with more variety than they can be spoken and the incorporation of song into drama has many benefits of this kind.

Some children will need to be taught certain words very carefully, but repeating from memory puts the mentally handicapped child at a great disadvantage. Many will speak in a stilted, unnatural fashion when reading or repeating from memory. For this reason scripted plays seem to have little relevance, except perhaps for the older children. Practice in more creative drama encourages the use of language and provides the children with opportunities to speak fluently and with variety even if colloquially.

It must always be remembered that children find their own ways of communicating and that speech is but one of these. Although it is important to foster oral language all these other means of communication should be accepted with understanding, particularly in dramatic work.

A DRAMA PROGRAMME

Drama so often arises from an unexpected source that it is difficult, if not impossible, to draw up a detailed programme of activities in advance. It is possible, however, to approach drama work in a systematic way and the following suggestions may be helpful.

Time

The length of time over which a class is capable of participating in purely dramatic work varies enormously, but since it does require a good deal of concentration twenty minutes to half an hour tends to be the optimal period for most mentally handicapped children.

Place

If there are a lot of children in the group, or the classroom is small or cluttered, it may be easier to use the hall, but generally the familiar surroundings of the classroom are less daunting and more conducive to creative work. If possible the room should be arranged so that there is space to move in the middle of the room rather than in the small area at the front of the class. The children are not performing to an audience and will generally all be involved at the same time.

Noise

A drama lesson should never become over-noisy but there may well be percussion instruments, a record player, or an explosion involved in some activity and some noise is inevitable. It is important that if a noisy activity is planned or does develop some attempt is made to control the noise level so that it does not disturb other classes. Teachers vary in their acceptance of noise and it would be unfortunate if drama were damned in a school simply because of uncontrolled noise.

Discipline

A pre-arranged signal such as a beat on a drum, a tambourine or a cymbal can be a particularly effective technique for gaining attention and controlling activity in a drama lesson. If it is introduced early enough it can become an accepted part of drama routine. If some children find co-operation difficult or have extreme difficulty joining in dramatic activity, it is sometimes helpful to work with them closely or individually, but at times they may have to become an audience and be left to watch. It is always helpful to have extra adults in the room during dramatic activity to give physical support where necessary, particularly when working with multiply handicapped children. Through their participation they may also encourage the more self-conscious children to participate.

Movement

This may at first be quite free but the teacher will choose to draw attention usually to one part of the body and seek to get variety of shape, weight, strength and pace centred on that area.

Relaxation

Relaxation and quiet should intersperse activities. This may be an opportunity to play a record, read a poem or make quiet sounds.

Topics for dramatisation

These should be discussed by the class so that their ideas can be used as much as possible. An object, a length of material, a crown, an illustration of an episode from a story, or an event in real life can be used as an initial stimulus. Questions can then help lead towards a dramatic confrontation and the adoption of suitable roles by the class.

Usually the children will work together, but sometimes individual children may want to try out ideas on their own. As far as possible the children must feel that they can make suggestions and that these will be put into action. The teacher must alternate between active involvement and standing aside. Action may have to be interrupted for discussion: 'There are big rocks on the moon. Can you climb up them? Let's practise carrying a heavy pack on our backs.' After a brief practice the action may have to be repeated. A climax may then need to be arranged. A new figure may be introduced who must be questioned. The class should be left to discuss what they should ask and how they should approach the character. 'She's asleep, so we must whisper.' Or, 'Is she deaf? Shall we shout?' Mentally handicapped children may often have to be shown what to do when the action is new, but their interpretation should remain their own. If the children can convey the mood within their own terms they are more likely to want to continue to experiment for themselves.

Structure

The drama lesson involves a combination of freedom and structure. On the one hand it permits a less objective approach where individuals may be given the freedom to discover their own ways of solving problems. 'Shall we cross the river by the slippery plank or over the stepping stones?' On the other hand it needs structure and discipline. The teacher must have specific aims for any lesson even if the children respond in a creative and subjective fashion. For example the teacher may want the children to:

(a) make an imaginative leap and imagine a stream running through the centre of the classroom;
(b) come to understand the difference between firm ground and running water;
(c) adapt their behaviour to meet the conditions they encounter in the running water of the stream and then on firm ground; or
(d) understand words like slippery, slimy, rotten, deep and shallow and then use them in their dramatic activity.

Most of these aims will have been encountered and perhaps achieved even before they discuss the actual crossing of the river.

A lesson plan

A drama session should include movement, talk and imaginative dramatic work. As has been suggested in the previous chapter the more closely these are related to each other and to the work of the day the more successful the outcome is likely to be. The drama session can contribute to the generalisation and transfer of skills acquired in other work. For example a group of children may have been working on a closely structured programme to develop the concepts of quantity with its associated words, such as 'large', 'small', 'heavy' and 'light'. A drama lesson might thus be created on the theme of shopping, or packing a suitcase, or posting letters and parcels.

If the theme is shopping, the lesson might develop as follows. The basket gets heavier and heavier as more and more goods are taken from the supermarket shelves. 'I've got four tins of fruit and four tins of soup.' If the basket is dropped on the way to the bus or the goods are eaten, the light basket can be swung all the way home.

In developing a lesson along these lines the teacher may plan it as follows:

(1) A real basket and real tins may be used and the increase in weight actually felt as each tin is put into the basket.

(2) The basket may be carried, walking slowly.

(3) The real basket and tins may then be put aside and the action mimed, the class imitating the teacher.

(4) The teacher might lead the class through an imaginary supermarket, selecting imaginary tins for imaginary baskets.

(5) The real basket might be looked at again and tried for weight.

(6) With only one or two tins in it the children run and drop the real basket, losing the tins and picking up an empty basket.

(7) With imaginary baskets the children can re-play the scene, collecting imaginary tins and then dropping the basket and losing the tins while the teacher narrates the episode.

(8) The teacher may tell a short story about a boy and a girl doing the shopping and hurrying home. On the way home they drop their basket, break some things and lose others. They go home very slowly.

(9) Or the story may be developed into a more dramatic scene with a cast of shoppers, children, and mothers at home.

(10) The lesson may end naturally with a quiet period or some kind of united celebration, but there should be a chance to unwind before returning to the routine of the day.

Follow-up

Sometimes an idea may continue to appeal for a long time, gradually developing into a play with some shape and a climax, so that the children may want to show their work to visitors. Sometimes after a short while the ideas have ceased to draw fresh inspiration and a change must be made. In many cases, though, drama will provide a stimulus for further creative work in the classroom, be it painting, model-making or building with blocks. For example, after work such as that described above, problems could be set in another lesson which the children have to try to solve. How can they best help someone who has had an accident with a basketful of groceries? What will they say to explain what has happened? How would they look if they had broken a dozen eggs? Such opportunities for extension work should not be missed.

When a piece of work is to be performed before an audience there may be a few more details to attend to such as dressing-up clothes or properties, but these rarely add to the children's original ideas, just facilitate their expression. Their involvement is in the action in which they have found a new role; perhaps a new way of moving and talking, perhaps a world where they can do all that they want — the land of make-believe.

Further reading

Barnfield, G. (1968). *Creative Drama in Schools.* Macmillan, London.
A book which is designed for teachers of drama in secondary schools, but which should give basic ideas to teachers in special schools about the theory and practice of creative drama, dance and play production. It also shows how dramatic work can be encouraged by teachers without special training in movement and drama.
Bruce, V. (1965). *Dance and Dance Drama in Education.* Pergamon Press, Oxford.
A comprehensive survey of the study and practice of movement and creative dance, based essentially on the theories of Rudolf Laban.
Craft, M. (1969). *Speech Delay: its Treatment by Speech Play.* John Wright & Sons Ltd, Bristol.
A book which should be helpful to parents and teachers. It is intended to support the specialised work of the speech therapist.
Goodridge, J. (1970). *Drama in the Primary School.* Heinemann Educational, London.
A book which is rich in suggestion and source material. Although much may be beyond the scope of many mentally handicapped children, teachers will find much that is stimulating and helpful.
Gray, V. and Percival, R. (1962). *Music, Movement and Mime for Children.* Oxford University Press, Oxford.
A good introduction in these areas which is linked with the radio programmes.
Jeffree, D.M. and McConkey, R. (1976). *Let Me Speak.* Souvenir Press, London.
A book of learning games designed to stimulate language development. Designed primarily for parents but a good source of ideas for the teacher with lots of ideas that can be incorporated into many classroom activities.
Jennings, S. (1973). *Remedial Drama.* Pitman Publishing, London.
A useful handbook for teachers and therapists written by a person who has considerable experience with the handicapped.
Jennings, S. (1975). *Creative Therapy.* Pitman Publishing, London.
A collection of readings related to the use of creative activities in therapeutic situations, and with disadvantaged and handicapped children.
Jones, A. and Buttrey, J. (1970). *Children and Stories.* Basil Blackwell, Oxford.
All who tell stories to children should read this book. The authors write with insight

and experience and attempt 'to look at [the] story as a phenomenon of the human mind that we all have a share in creating'. There are very helpful book lists as well.

Lunzer, E. and Hulme, I. (1966). Play, language and reasoning in the severely subnormal child. *Journal of Child Psychology and Psychiatry*, 7, 107–23.

McCaslin, N. (1974). *Creative Dramatics in the Classroom*. David McKay Co. Inc., New York.
A broad survey of the subject which sets out to answer basic questions for beginners. There is a chapter on creative drama in special education.

McCaslin, N. (1975). *Children and Drama*. David McKay Co. Inc., New York.
A collection of essays by leading practitioners in Britain and the United States of America.

Male, D. (1970). *Approaches to Drama*. Unwin Educational Books, London. An analysis of the aims and scope of a variety of methods of teaching drama, stressing the links with other areas of the curriculum. Contains a very complete bibliography.

Matterson, E.M. (1970). *Play with a Purpose for the Under-Sevens*. Penguin Books, Harmondsworth, Middx.
There are many practical suggestions in this book which should prove invaluable in helping teachers and students initiate or follow up dramatic play.

Millar, S. (1969). *The Psychology of Play*. Penguin Books, Harmondsworth, Middx.
Some of the psychological theories of play are presented in a way which is easy to read and to relate to the practical situations which teachers meet in the classroom.

Scher, A. and Venall, C. (1975). *100+ Ideas for Drama*. Heinemann Educational, London.
Many useful ideas to start a teacher thinking. Not ideal to be used exclusively.

Skard, A., Pickard, P.M. and Flekkoy, M. (1969). *Your Child is Growing*. The World Organisation for Early Childhood Education, Copenhagen.
The book is aimed at parents, personnel in institutions, teachers and students who want to know more about children and how to strengthen their relationship with them.

Slade, P. (1954). *Child Drama*. University of London Press, London.
A well-known standard work. This book and a shorter version, *An Introduction to Child Drama,* present a personal philosophy and a way of working which have influenced teachers of drama for many years.

Way, B. (1967). *Development through Drama*. Longman, Harlow, Middx.
Many practical examples are given to support the author's philosophy that drama is concerned with the individuality of individuals. A clear distinction is made between drama in education and in theatre.

Section IV : Art and Craft

9 PREREQUISITES FOR SUCCESSFUL ART AND CRAFT

When he was fifteen, I taught him to knit. For weeks I sat by his side explaining the symbols of a knitting pattern and watching his first stumbling attempts.

But this was the turning point in Paul's life. He is now twenty-three. He produces the most beautiful garments in Fair Isle, Shetland and Aran. He designs pewter jewellery, spins and weaves, stitches fine and intricate tapestries and is skilled in many other crafts.

All Paul's work is exhibited and sold from our home. We have visitors from all over the world who come to see Paul and buy his beautiful work. I feel sure that he must get some sense of pleasure from hearing his work praised and admired, although he can never express his feelings even to us his parents.

But Paul has become something of a legend in our small village and I feel very proud to be known as just 'Paul's mother'.

(Rena Griffiths writing in *Parents' Voice*, December 1976)

While few children may ever reach such a sophisticated level in art and craft as Paul, art and craft can become a true leisure-time activity for mentally handicapped children, a time when they can gain emotional satisfaction from working with their hands. A sense of inner satisfaction which it can bring is of particular importance to the mentally handicapped since they may never know the joys which reading and writing can bring. Like music and drama, it is a means of communication through which we can express our innermost thoughts to others. For the mentally handicapped child with limited ability to express such feelings verbally, art and craft has particular importance.

First and foremost, art and craft activities are enjoyable activities at which even the most severely handicapped child can achieve some degree of success. Art and craft can be a 'fun' time for mentally handicapped children; a time when everything they do is right, and whatever they produce is a work of art; a time when there are no right or wrong ways of doing things. These facts are very important when we consider how many other times in the day the mentally handicapped child can achieve as much success as his teacher. Even children with severe multiple handicaps can participate in some way in most art and craft activities. An immobile child, for example, can be held or propped up and, as long as he is covered with protective clothing, he can use fingers, hands or feet to make patterns in paint. Special materials may be necessary; for example a half-inch-wide paint brush, built up at the sides for easier grasp, and G-cramps to hold paper and board steady. But a work of art it will be, nothing less.

At the same time art and craft activities contribute on a broad plane towards the mentally handicapped child's whole social and intellectual development. At a basic level, art and craft work fosters the development of manipulative and motor skills. All art and craft involves motor activity of some kind, ranging from the fine motor control involved in the use of scissors or needle and thread to the gross control involved in finger painting. For many children with associated physical handicaps and impairments, the simple control of a paint brush is an important achievement. In view of the emphasis that has recently been placed on motor training the importance of this 'natural' training should not be overlooked.

At a higher level the exploration and organisation of thoughts for expression in creative work is important. Painting a picture of something from his environment involves the child in explaining the environment and developing ideas about it and its functioning. It requires the child to develop powers of observation, to be able to select important features and characteristics, and to be able to make sufficient sense of these to communicate his findings to others. All these are extremely important skills for any child to develop.

On the emotional plane art and craft activities have further benefits. The way in which art and craft is a vehicle for the expression of the emotions has already been mentioned. Children with limited speech may find painting easier than talking and through paint be able to express ideas, emotions, and reactions to situations and experiences. Similarly emotional satisfaction can be gained from working with the hands, whether it be thumping clay or, with greater dexterity and co-ordination, manipulating tweezers to stick seeds on a collage. The therapeutic value of art and craft should not be overlooked either. Thumping clay or manipulating tweezers can provide a much-needed outlet for many children. For others the expression of inner conflicts and stress which creative work allows, represents a potentially important benefit.

Art and craft work can also help the child to gain confidence in his own ability and to develop a more positive self-concept. Mentally handicapped children are generally deprived of normal school achievement but art and craft is one area in which the mentally handicapped child can function within the normal range of performance. This is particularly important with regard to the community's assessment of the child. Home–school relations, and more importantly the family's expectations for the child, can benefit from the production of art and craft work which can be taken home and displayed alongside other art work in the home.

THE TEACHER'S TASK

Teaching art and craft to mentally handicapped children is not without its problems. In addition to the physical difficulty which the children may experience handling tools, the organisation of the thoughts they wish to express often constitutes an in-surmountable barrier to anything approaching sophisticated art. Some mentally handicapped children also seem to resist pressure to produce free expressive work, tending to persist with pattern-making rather than attempting new activities such as work with clay. Teaching art and craft, therefore, must involve more than provi-ding materials and encouraging free expression. It must involve considerable direct teaching and structuring of activities. It is perhaps this structure and direction that distinguishes art and craft with the mentally handicapped from art and craft at any other level with any other group of children. The suggestion of highly structured art and craft work may be an anathema to some specialist teachers but without it the subject would not be realistically geared to the needs of the mentally handi-capped. The task of the teacher is to strike a balance between the freedom of creativity and the need for structure. The teacher's success in striking this balance determines to a large degree the success of the art and craft programme.

If art and craft is going to be maximally beneficial to the child, the teacher must think in terms of stimulation and the enrichment of the environment to provide ad-equate experiences for children who have difficulty recalling experiences; of develop-ing observation skills and helping the child to become aware of the environment; and of developing basic skills and seeing the relationship of these basic skills to other areas of the curriculum. To this end it is important that the teacher develops a simi-larly critical awareness of materials which are appropriate at various stages of develop-ment and of materials which will help stimulate the child. Most importantly the sig-nificance of discovery learning must be recognised: discovery of limited but signifi-cant information; discovery of things such as the feel of paints, clay, papier-mâché and other materials; discovery of the varied uses to which objects can be put, and the ways in which objects are created.

Teaching art and craft to the mentally handicapped comes closest initially in nature and content to teaching art and craft to nursery children, particularly be-cause of the importance given at both levels to art and craft as an activity in its own right, where the activity is seen as being as important as the end product. The final product of any lesson, be it a painting, a model, a decorated fabric or an amorphous lump of clay, obviously has importance and its quality is relevant to the enjoyment the child receives, and the skills that he develops and demonstrates in making it. But of equal significance is the process itself and the enjoyment that goes with simply doing. Recognising the importance of simply doing not only helps to increase the child's enjoyment but also can result in the teacher gaining greater satisfaction.

While it is not possible to enumerate specific teaching skills to apply in every situ-ation the following suggestions may help to make the activity beneficial and enjoy-able for the child:

Experimentation

Exploration and discovery should be principal components of any art and craft lesson. The child should be provided with opportunities to explore materials and their qualities. He should be encouraged to mix paints, experiment with consistencies and colours, explore texture and shape, and make mistakes however disastrous and messy they may be.

Observation

Communicating ideas through any medium requires observation and identification of features of the environment. Most children need help to develop observation skills and to become aware of the environment's more subtle aspects. Some of this help can be provided incidentally through discussion when the children are engaged in a task. Some will require more direct teaching through directing their attention to details in their everyday surroundings, to proportions of the body, to relationships between parts of an object, and to features of their own work.

Imitation

While copying or reproducing work produced by the teacher or by others may not be truly creative, it can be a valuable activity and opportunity should be provided for this. Such activity can help provide a model on which the child can organise his own thoughts and a vehicle within which to develop component skills.

Trial and error

The freedom to make mistakes and learn from mistakes should be provided in all activities. With mentally handicapped children this frequently means considerable mess, but it is better to prepare for this by taking appropriate precautions than to restrict the child's freedom.

Reinforcement

There is much joy to be gained simply by creating something and for most children art and craft work has great intrinsic motivation. However, reinforcement of success and effort should not be forgotten and every opportunity taken to reinforce children for their involvement in the task and for the quality of the end product. Displaying work is one way of reinforcing children but verbal reinforcement and attention are extremely potent motivational forces and should not be overlooked.

Discussion

While there should always be time available in any lesson when children can work quietly without interruption, there is also a need for discussion and interaction. This can be either on an individual, small group, or whole class basis. It should aim at intellectual and aesthetic appreciation and development, for it can never be taken for granted that mentally handicapped children know something. Their attention frequently has to be drawn to important factors, their understanding needs constant exploration, and their interest needs constant stimulation. Verbalising about work is one way of encouraging this.

RECOGNITION OF MENTAL HANDICAP AND WORK PREPARATION

In any class of mentally handicapped children the teacher may be faced with a considerable range of abilities and problems. At a gross level the primary causes of handicap in a group of children may be different, and further complicated by the presence of any number of secondary disabilities. More importantly, the specific strengths and weaknesses, which even those children who share the same diagnosis display, can vary significantly. Some children may have good fine motor control while others may be totally immobile. Some may have good powers of intellectual organisation and expression, others total confusion and disorganisation. The obvious implication is that planning and work preparation must be based on an awareness of these individual differences. Objectives for any lesson must be geared to meet the needs and abilities of each child. For example in one lesson the teacher's aims for some children may be their simple involvement, for others it may be the use of tools, or the development of a specific motor skill, while for some the end product may be the aim. But in any lesson these objectives must be clarified. The teacher must 'know' each child and what can be expected of him. This usually poses no real problem as most art and craft work with mentally handicapped children is carried out by the class teacher, who knows the children's educational and emotional needs and abilities. If there is a specialist art and craft teacher, liaison is necessary between the specialist and the class teacher.

Associated with this is the need to ensure that any specific activity is within the ability range of the children. As has already been noted, many mentally handicapped children do have associated perceptual and motor problems. With these children it should not be assumed that they are capable of using scissors or other tools, or that they know how to use tools without instruction. On the other hand, well-intentioned but misguided efforts sometimes result in children being denied the use of tools such as scissors and putty knives — but these are not dangerous if the children are taught how to use them.

With mentally handicapped children motivation is an important consideration. The nature of their disability renders some mentally handicapped children generally lethargic and uninterested. With others, past failure has stifled natural curiosity, and for some school in general may hold little interest. But above all this, creative expression rarely occurs at any level without some motivating force. No artist produced a masterpiece simply because someone provided him with the materials at two o'clock in the afternoon and told him to paint a picture. The artist needs inspiration and so do children. With mentally handicapped children the teacher usually has to be the source of this inspiration. There are endless ways of getting initial interest and it is up to the teacher to be imaginative and creative herself in thinking of different ways to stimulate the children. Some children will respond readily, others will require an extremely imaginative and gifted teacher to constantly and consistently motivate them.

At the same time there is much in art and craft work that is intrinsically motivating. Particularly in the early stages of art and craft the exploration of materials can be extremely exciting and stimulating. Squeezing and squashing clay, messing about with paints, and experiencing the texture of different materials represent new experiences for many children and can serve to generate enthusiasm for work. At this stage the teacher's task is to provide materials and ensure variety of tasks. If this initial enthusiasm is to be maintained, however, more systematic efforts usually have to be made.

At this stage it is perhaps worth saying that children easily pick up attitudes from the teacher. Thus the teacher who is enthusiastically exploring new ideas and activities with the children will tend to foster the same enthusiasm and curiosity in the children. To this end it is important that the teacher is familiar with the materials and techniques that are introduced. It is advisable to try out techniques and experiment with materials before embarking on a lesson. But remember that art and craft should be fun. It is permissible to make mistakes. In fact extremely interesting art frequently results from mistakes. Don't have expectations that are too high, but aim for enjoyment and many problems of motivation will disappear.

Mentally handicapped children also need time and space to work at their own pace and in their own way. There is need for time for them to become familiar with materials before they are asked to work with them to some specific end. For example, when clay is introduced time should be allowed for the children to experiment and play with it on their own before being asked to make anything. Similarly in introducing batik work, time must be allowed for the children to become familiar with melted wax, before being asked to use it with fabric.

The teacher must be willing to devote plenty of time to art and craft work, particularly when a new activity is introduced. Initial results may often be disappointing, but given time to experiment, time to repeat, and time to enjoy the work good results will often come. Actual work space is also important, if the children are to feel free from fears about damaging or dirtying the work area.

While it is desirable for children to be given the opportunity to explore and discover, it is often advisable to limit the range of materials for mentally handicapped children. For example the choice of colours can be limited to minimise the possibility of disappointing results. If the children are working with red card, it often makes sense to remove the orange crayons from the crayon box as the children will produce little of interest with this combination of colours. While the importance of experimentation has been emphasised in previous sections this has to be balanced against the need to maintain the child's interest and motivation. Nothing stifles a growing interest more quickly than disappointing results.

On a practical level it is worth stressing the need for thorough preparation. A good lesson with any children is one which runs smoothly with all required materials to hand. Interruptions to creative work are usually extremely disruptive and difficult to rectify. The teacher disappearing for long periods into the storeroom or off to the office for forgotten materials frequently results in behaviour disturbances which then taint the remainder of the lesson and usually result in at least one child being unable to give complete attention to his creative expression. At the same time it is important that the teacher does not do everything for the children. Art and craft lessons provide an excellent opportunity for the encouragement of independence and self-discipline. Children should be encouraged to participate in lesson planning and preparation as well as clearing up. They should be able to plan work for themselves, fetch materials they want, and generally create what they want to create. As with most work with mentally handicapped children there is a delicate balance to be maintained: a balance between teacher planning and pupil independence.

RELATIONSHIP OF ART AND CRAFT TO OTHER ASPECTS OF THE CURRICULUM

There is a danger that art and craft activities can be presented in isolation from the rest of the curriculum and treated as an independent activity. While art and craft merits a place of its own in the curriculum it is important to recognise the value of relating it to other school activities. Art and craft can be satisfying and fulfilling on its own, but it can also extend and vitalise work undertaken in other parts of the day. Art and craft can be used to illustrate other work or it can become an integral part of the learning process, in a project. This is not to suggest that it should always be related to other work, but its value in this area is considerable and should not be overlooked.

Art and craft offers many opportunities for enriching and extending other classroom work. For example, with mentally handicapped children the teacher will frequently be concerned with the development of the senses, and specific lessons may be taken where texture and colour are explored. This can obviously flow into art and craft lessons where considerable 'natural' exposure to textures and colours occurs. Similarly art and craft work can be used to illustrate themes that have been explored in class. For example, nature study can be extended into art and craft work with pictures or collages devised to illustrate animals and plants that have been seen or discussed.

A natural home for art and craft activities is in project work. It is here that creative work can be most directly linked to other learning. There are, however, occasions when art and craft can be a starting point of a learning experience and help to make that experience more meaningful. An obvious example is work involving the teaching of the four seasons. All four seasons have their own beauty which can readily be represented in two- and three-dimensional form by children. Building a frieze based on autumn colours, and using leaves and grasses as well as paints and other materials, can provide considerable insight into the feeling and significance of the seasons. Much more significant learning is likely to result than from talk and discussion. Many similar themes lend themselves to this sort of treatment and help to provide a rich source for exploration of the environment.

DISPLAY

The display of items produced in art and craft lessons is important both in terms of reinforcement for effort expended and of stimulus for further effort. Putting children's work on display is an effective way of encouraging them to participate in subsequent work. For mentally handicapped children this can represent an all too infrequent boost to their confidence and self-esteem. The ability to mount an attractive display is therefore an important teaching technique. The skill to do this comes more easily to some people than to others, but there is a good deal which can be learnt about it.

Many teachers, for very admirable reasons, tend to saturate their classrooms with displayed materials, with the result that no single object is obvious above the general level of background colour. It is important that only a limited amount of material is displayed at any one time, otherwise children soon come to notice nothing. Too much colour and too many objects on display limits the display's significance and is almost as bad as a bare, sterile room. Similarly it is important that the display is selective. It is not necessary or desirable for every piece of work of every child to be displayed. If it is, the importance of having a piece of work displayed will be reduced. This should not be taken as a suggestion that only 'good' art is displayed. It has already been noted that the quality of the finished product is not the primary object of art and craft work. Display, however, should not be a formality, and the selection of a piece of work for display should be seen as an achievement by the child. This selection can obviously be based on multiple criteria which include the quality of finished product, but which also include factors such as effort and originality. Implicit, however, in this concept of selection is the notion that all children should have some expectation of having their work displayed regularly. Display of work should not be viewed as a contest, rather as a reward for effort.

It is important that display is not limited to the classroom. Display areas should be available outside the classroom and occasionally outside the school. School buildings vary in the provision of areas for display purposes but there are usually corridors, halls and entrances which can serve admirably. An important point to bear in mind, though, is that the display is for the children's sake and not a means of decorating the school. Remember, too, your 'glory' holes. Most schools have them, and often the accumulation of junk in them can be written off, used or stored elsewhere and the space used more purposefully for display. If you are fortunate enough to have large areas available for display, do things on a large scale. It is important to remember that everything does not have to be done in modules of a standard size piece of card. The use of large spaces encourages variety in the end product. Make use of this.

Display does not simply mean pinning up children's work. The manner in which work is displayed is vital. There is an enormous difference between something which has been thrown on to the notice board and pinned with a couple of drawing pins, and something which the teacher has taken care to display to its best advantage. Preparation needs considerable attention. All two-dimensional work should be mounted before being displayed, giving due consideration to suitable backing. Cheap white cartridge paper and sugar papers in black and dark tones make good backgrounds. The colour of the mount should have a relationship to the colours of the work that is being mounted and should complement the picture and not compete with it. Double mounting using a dark sugar paper with a light cartridge paper can be even more effective.

Even spacing on three sides, larger space at the bottom

A double mount using dark sugar paper and white cartridge. This often makes a very ordinary piece of work look twice as good

When pieces of work are put together on a background, consideration should be given to spacing. The whole mounted piece should be an attractive design. In fact some thought can be given to treating display as an art and craft activity, with the children working on the display, producing decorative trims and features. It is also worthwhile spending some time mastering the art of printing. Labelling displays, putting children's names on work, and using key words on displays add to the value of the display. Good, legible printing makes it more likely that the children will be able to make sense of the display and thus obtain greater benefit from it. If you have difficulty with printing there are aids that you can use, the most effective and easiest to use of which are probably plastic templates and Letraset. When displaying work, do avoid drawing pins. They are unsightly objects when they are dotted all over a picture. Far better to use staples or Blu-tack; they damage the picture less too.

Displaying work obviously requires appropriate display surfaces. With materials such as Blu-tack it is possible to use wall space without damaging most paints or plaster. However, if possible have all wall space at eye level covered with soft board, remembering when you do that a child's eye is lower than yours. In most cases this will not be possible because of cost or building design. Large, framed pinboards may be an alternative solution. These should ideally be covered with a neutral, self-coloured backing. Brightly coloured material will interfere with the work on display. Hessian backing is useful as this doesn't show pin marks. Plastic-faced display panels are also available and these have the advantage of being able to be written on directly with wax marking pencils, but do not take pins so well. Another idea is to have small portable pinboards, about two feet by three feet. With a picture cord attached these can be hung in any free spot or rested against a wall. Portable boards can also be used for temporary displays in halls or other public areas. If it is not possible to have pinboards there are plenty of other means of display, and even if you have pinboards other means should not be forgotten. Old clothes horses and folding screens make excellent display areas. These can be covered with cheap, unbleached calico which can be dyed if necessary. Work can then be attached using dressmaker's pins, string, hooks or tape. The backs of cupboards and bookshelves, and the leading edges of shelves can be used if other areas are limited. You may also try using corrugated cardboard, which can be bought in rolls five feet high. This makes an excellent temporary display surface as well as providing an interesting background which can itself be decorated. Suspended cardboard cylinders and sheets can also be used to display work.

While wall boards are the best means of displaying two-dimensional work, tables and other horizontal surfaces are necessary for the display of three-dimensional objects, although these can be suspended from ceilings or placed on window ledges or shelves. For more interesting display of three-dimensional work use rostra or collect two or three tables of different heights, perhaps a few giant building blocks from the nursery, a stool, a chair, whatever is to hand, and arrange them in the display area. Bear in mind that children need to be able to see the objects on display comfortably. When the setting is satisfactory cover the lot with a large piece of calico or neutral hessian. Lengths of material chosen to complement the items on display can be draped around to enhance the setting. You then have an excellent base for a display, particularly a display which involves a variety of art and craft forms.

Finally it is important that displays are changed before they become tatty and as soon as the children lose interest in them. A good classroom should present an ever-changing panorama and reflect the prevailing interests of the group and the work in which they are engaged. It is impossible to give a maximum time for material to be displayed but it is important that this is not too long lest the display loses its impact and becomes an unnoticed part of the general background. Equally it is important that the children have time to see and appreciate it before it is taken away.

ENVIRONMENTAL CONSIDERATIONS

Ideally a room should be set aside and equipped specifically for art and craft activities. This makes life much easier for the teacher and facilitates the achievement of the sort of aims that have been advanced for art and craft in this chapter. The provision of such a room is by no means essential, however, and excellent art and craft work can be carried out within the confines of the normal classroom. If art and craft is to be taught in the ordinary classroom and space and equipment are at a premium, a mobile trolley or cupboard can be of considerable benefit. The cupboard can be fitted out with a range of art and craft materials and moved to whichever room it is needed in. Precise design of a mobile cupboard is obviously a matter for the teacher and the school, but fig. 6 shows one which the author has found convenient. A cupboard of this size seems ideal for a basic stock of tools and materials. In the drawers you can keep tools such as scissors, paint brushes, pencils, crayons, pins, jugs, rubber gloves and small quantities of powder paints, glue, plaster of Paris, and other usable materials. On the shelves to the left of the cupboard items most frequently used can be stored – things such as small boxes, bottles, fabric and paper scraps, waste materials for decoration, or anything else that is currently required. At the back a hessian pocket will hold newspapers, large sheets of polythene, sugar, crêpe and tissue paper, and card. The Formica surface provides a useful working area for the teacher or the children.

Whether or not you have a specialist room it is important that there is adequate lighting and if possible vision and access to the outside world. For mentally handicapped children it is essential that the floor is easy to clean and able to stand up to spillage. Large sheets of polythene or newspaper can be spread on the floor but some mess is inevitable and it is important that the children are not subject to restrictions that may inhibit their creative spirit and their willingness to explore. Equipment should similarly be chosen to minimise the difficulties that may be encountered. Non-spill pots should be available for mixing paints; paste should be mixed in squat, heavy containers that are not easily knocked over, and paint brushes should have

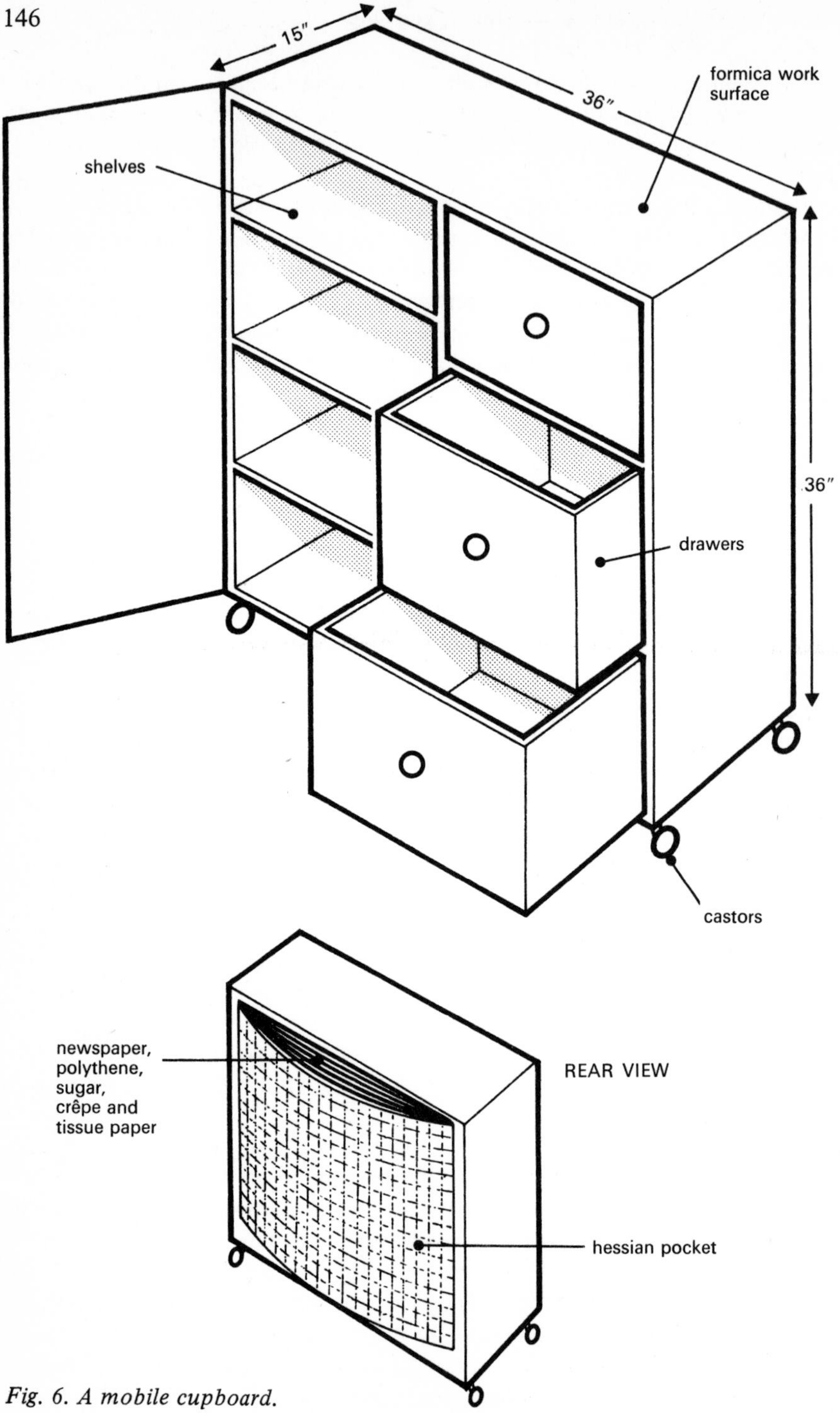

shelves

formica work surface

36″

15″

36″

drawers

castors

newspaper, polythene, sugar, crêpe and tissue paper

REAR VIEW

hessian pocket

Fig. 6. A mobile cupboard.

their handles shortened to increase ease of use and minimise the likelihood of knocking other equipment over with them. Care should also be taken to provide space that allows for efficient storage of paper and other equipment and yet which allows easy access for the children when they are collecting and returning items. Cupboards should thus be low and easy to reach so that materials can be obtained by the children when they are required without having to wait for the teacher to lift down a box of crayons from a high shelf. A storeroom is ideal for bulk storage. If a paper storage cabinet is not available, shelving or vertical slots can be used so that different types of paper do not have to be stored on top of one another. If the children are to be encouraged to be self-sufficient and independent, items such as this must be easily accessible, for there is nothing more stifling to slowly emerging independence than a disaster in the storeroom as a result of an attempt to obtain a sheet of paper.

In a specialist room furniture must be chosen with care and thought. Tables and other working surfaces should cater for the wide range of heights that may be found in any school, and be sufficiently flexible to cope with the problems of wheelchairs and children with additional handicaps. Formica and other non-absorbent surfaces have obvious advantages over wooden surfaces. A strong woodwork bench with vices attached is essential if wood or metal work is to be attempted and also provides a firm base for other heavy activities. Easels of varying heights and types can be useful but can create problems of their own. Some easels are not particularly stable and tend to move around even when rubber ferrules are attached to the legs. Also, paper has to be secured to them with clips and can slip under heavy hands with rather messy results. They also require the use of thick paint as thin paint tends to run without very careful application. Moreover they are easily upset, as are the paint and water containers resting on them.

Perhaps the most important requirement for furniture in the art and craft room is that it should be adaptable. For some work it is necessary to have a large floor area cleared, for other activities a solid block of desks or tables. Tables and chairs that stack are valuable from this point of view, as are hinged, drop-down tables attached to the wall which can be brought into use when needed and used as display space at other times. Alternatively old trestle tables are collapsible and can also be used as mobile display surfaces.

It is essential to have water available for art and craft. Running hot and cold water is the ideal but if this is not available portable fibreglass units can be as efficient. Smaller barrels, caravanning containers, or ordinary buckets will also serve but these are generally not easily manipulated by mentally handicapped children.

A sink is similarly essential, and there should preferably be more than one at different heights. Once again improvisation is possible although usually not without disadvantages in terms of the restrictions it imposes on the child with poor coordination and motor control.

A small but important point is the value of having a few extra electric sockets in the room. It can be an advantage to be able to play music while children are working, or to show slides as motivation or background. An overhead projector to enlarge templates for picture and frieze work can also be a valuable piece of equipment. All of these require electricity and it is frustrating to be unable to explore different avenues such as these because there simply aren't enough power points in the right places.

Considerable thought must be given to the room's efficiency, for while non-handicapped children can cope with problems such as the lack of running water this can present an insurmountable distraction to the mentally handicapped child. Mentally handicapped children have to learn to live in an imperfect world but there are many other occasions for confronting them with its complexities when the resulting confusion will not have such a limiting influence on their learning.

An apron or an old shirt for protective covering is essential for all children. Fear of making a mess or dirtying clothes can be most inhibiting.

Finally it should perhaps be stressed that art and craft does not have to be, and indeed should not be, restricted to the classroom. While the classroom provides a base for most work it can be limiting. Sometimes the room is just not big enough or is unsuitable for the materials you wish to use. Activities such as mixing cement, stuffing animals with straw, painting scenery, or making a full size mural of an elephant are all more appropriately carried out in the playground or *in situ*, outside the classroom or school.

MATERIALS

The materials required for art and craft with the mentally handicapped differ little from those that are required for any children, although the greater wastage of material underlines the importance of 'acquired' or junk materials. There is a large number of educational suppliers and their catalogues will suggest materials that can be purchased. However, before ordering any materials or equipment make sure that they are suitable for the children. If possible visit the supplier's showroom before ordering. It is also important to obtain tools that will stand up to hard use, but remember that price is frequently no real guide to quality.

Because of the varied interests and needs of teachers and children it is difficult to compile a list of 'essential materials'. However, the following should provide a useful basis for any art and craft stock list, and allow for a considerable range of activities to be undertaken.

Basic materials

Only specifically art and craft items are listed. Many others can be 'borrowed' from general school stock or scrounged from families or friends.

Crayons: of various sizes and adequate colour range.

Brushes: including traditional fine artists' brushes, glue brushes, stencil brushes, and general household brushes up to two and three inches wide.

Paper and card: of all sizes and weights. Sugar paper is the standard old faithful, but obviously the more different types of paper that are provided, the better. When ordering try not to let personal colour preferences dictate choice too much. Children's choices are often very different from those of adults.

Paints and inks: standard stocks will be powder and poster paints, but don't forget house paint and more exotic lines such as fluorescent paints. Inks are less useful but can come in handy. Include ordinary writing ink as well as Indian and waterproof inks.

Modelling materials: include plasticine and other similar modelling compounds, potter's clay, plaster of Paris, and items such as balsa wood and art straws.

Woodwork tools: a hammer, saw, screwdriver, pincers, pliers, and a good stock of nails, screws and panel pins, and wire. G-cramps have many uses too.

General equipment

The items listed here, equally indispensable, will form part of a general school stock which can be borrowed for art and craft activities:

General stationery: rulers, pencils, pens, pencil sharpeners, erasers, drawing pins, straight pins, rubber bands, glue, paper clips, bulldog clips, long- and short-arm stapling machines and staples, adhesive tape, scissors.

Cleaning and mixing materials: rubber gloves, paper towel and dispenser, spoons for mixing paint and paste etc., polythene jugs, dishcloths, a washing-up brush, a broom, a dustpan and hand brush, plastic bowls and buckets, towels.

General equipment (which can perhaps be based in the art and craft area): a safe guillotine, paper punches and duplicating facilities all have obvious appeal for art and craft work.

Kits

There are currently many kits on the market which facilitate experimentation with different activities. Many of these may prove to be too difficult for some mentally handicapped children, but this should not be assumed before they have been tried. Suitable kits include ones for balsa modelling, brass rubbing, bead craft, candle making, enamelling, jewellery, fabric dyeing, marbling, mosaic, origami, plaster modelling, plastic embedding, polystyrene modelling, printing, stone barrelling, and weaving. Many teachers prefer not to use kits, but for the inexperienced they provide a good introduction to the activity as well as to the materials that are required. Usually these kits contain a clear and simple set of instructions. If a kit is found to be suitable, materials can be ordered to suit your particular requirements.

Acquired materials

The bulk of the art and craft teacher's materials will be 'acquired'. Acquired materials cost nothing and more importantly they provide great variety in texture and appearance, and opportunities for experimentation with different surfaces. Amost anything can become part of this stock of acquired materials, but a basic stock should include the following:

Paper: of all kinds, including magazines and newspapers, gift wrapping paper, wallpaper, corrugated paper, brown paper, metallic paper, cellophane, tissue paper and greaseproof paper.

Paper items: such as bags, paper straws, bus tickets, stamps, greetings cards, paper plates, pastry cases, doilies, sweet papers, chocolate-box straw.

Containers: cardboard boxes of all kinds, plastic bottles and boxes, metal boxes, tins and trays, and all types of cartons.

Jewellery: sequins, beads, chains, old brooches and decorative pins.

Sewing items: all types of materials, buttons, braid, cotton, wool, zips, items of clothing, cotton reels.

Natural objects: bones, shells, feathers, pebbles, stones, straw, nuts, pine cones, driftwood, loofah, eggshells, 'raw' wool, leather and sawdust.

Household items: coat hangers, plates, beakers, bottles, tiles.

Hardware: metal chain, wire mesh, clocks, machine bits, old film spools, wire.

Food: cloves, sago, lentils, rice, fruit stones, peas, beans, peppercorns, and pasta of all shapes and sizes.

Availability and care of materials

The condition and availability of materials is crucial to the children's involvement and concentration. The lack of a vital colour, appropriate brush or suitable pencil can be extremely frustrating and destroy an entire creative effort. It is therefore not petty to suggest that materials such as brushes should be washed out after use, pencils resharpened, yarns and threads untangled, paints made workable, and claywork tools cleaned before they are needed again. The same applies to stock, which should be kept at appropriate levels; wherever possible avoid allowing materials to run out in the middle of a project. A good supply of materials requires good stock control. Keeping a record of day-to-day requirements over an extended period is perhaps the best way of forecasting future requirements.

Some of these points may seem obvious to the experienced teacher. They are, however, vital to the success of art and craft work. They make lessons run smoothly and help maximise the children's involvement and creative effort.

10 SOME SPECIFIC ACTIVITIES

While it is possible in some subject areas to plan a sequential programme of activities it is generally not possible to do this in art and craft. Nor is this necessary, for most of the materials used in art and craft have no characteristic which makes them more suitable only for one particular age or ability level. The quality of the finished product may vary with age and ability, but the artistic merit does not. The finger painting of a five-year-old multiply handicapped child can, and frequently does compare, with that of his 'normal' peers. Most materials such as clay, paint, and fabric can be used by virtually all children including the most severely and multiply handicapped. Wood and metal may have a more limited use but should not be denied to young and less able children. Obviously the young multiply handicapped child is not going to be able to make a bookshelf or a bracelet, but wooden blocks glued on to thick cardboard can result in a most effective collage.

In this chapter suggestions are given for activities which the author has found useful, and possible, with mentally handicapped children of a wide range of age and ability. The activities vary from the very simple to the more complicated and demanding, and some will not be suitable for particular children. In deciding what activities to provide for a group of children, the teacher must consider the age, ability and interest level of the children, and adjust her aims accordingly. If a teacher is working with a group of children whose co-ordination and manual dexterity is limited, any attempt to make clay coffee mugs is likely to produce little apart from frustration for all.

The suggestions that are given in this chapter are not meant to be exhaustive for it is possible to include an enormous range of activities under the heading of art and craft. Rather they should be regarded as a basic range of activities which allows for variety within any school year and over the period of a child's school attendance. In each instance only brief introductory comments have been made. In many cases, if the teacher is going to pursue an activity, further background reading and experiment may be necessary. Fortunately there is no shortage of useful and practical books on the market and a list of some of these has been included at the end of this chapter. Most of these are cheap and readily obtainable. But most do not deal with teaching mentally handicapped children and the teacher will have to adapt the techniques and methods suggested. Generally the adaptations necessary are simple, and it is hoped that these chapters will provide some helpful guidelines. Pauline Tilley's book, *Art in the Education of Subnormal Children,* is the only book which deals directly with the problems of teaching art and craft to the mentally handicapped. It is to be recommended.

TEACHING COMPONENT SKILLS

In the previous chapter the importance of teaching component skills was noted. The fine and gross motor handicaps found in mentally handicapped children make it important for component skills to be taught directly and be seen as an integral part of the art and craft programme. It is of little use taking it for granted that children will know how, or be able, to handle tools such as pencils, crayons, brushes, scissors, bodkins or pens. Much training in the use of tools and the development of skills can occur naturally within the context of other activities, but it is important for the teacher to pay attention to this aspect and ensure that opportunities do arise for skills to be practised. The following activities can be useful in the direct teaching of motor skills:

Paper tearing

This is simple activity required for many tasks and of considerable value to children with co-ordination problems. It can involve tearing: newspaper for papier-mâché; coloured magazines for mosaic patterns and pictures; or tissue and crêpe paper for collage work and picture making.

Paper cutting

This is also an activity which benefits co-ordination. A graded approach to teaching this skill is important. Initially very large, easy cutting should be undertaken, with finer and more demanding work being introduced gradually. In a class project the more capable can do the finer cutting, the less capable the grosser work. A sort of assembly line can develop with each child working at his own level.

Using scissors is often difficult for mentally handicapped children. Initially it may be necessary to draw lines for the children to cut along, straight to begin with but progressing to wavy lines or specific shapes later on. Subsequently shapes can be provided for children to draw around and then cut out. Eventually children can be asked to cut out illustrations from magazines for scrap books, friezes, models, collages and the like. This skill can be practised with materials other than paper, although it is best to allow the children to develop some degree of skill with paper – which is less expensive and easily replaceable – first. The scissors themselves are important. They need to be of a reasonable quality, move easily, and actually cut. For safety it is important to buy round-ended rather than pointed scissors. Remember to make sure that left-handers are catered for.

Paper folding

This skill is important for many activities requiring good perceptual-motor co-ordination. It too should be approached through grades of difficulty, with the folding of large sheets of paper preceding the finer tasks. Card is easier to begin with than paper as it is less flexible and thus more easily manipulated by unco-ordinated hands. Folding can be directly linked to cutting skills if paper or card is folded and then cut along the folds.

Pasting

This skill is frequently used in art and craft work but is often taken for granted; little care is taken to make its teaching a graded process. Pasting is most easily tackled initially on a Formica work surface; then if too much paste is applied the object can still be lifted clear without damage. If newspaper is used instead, as it often is, the result is more likely to be a torn piece of paper or picture when the object to be pasted adheres to the newspaper. Scrap book work gives good practice and picture making can also involve this skill. Initially cold-water paste should be used, but as skill and needs develop it is necessary to introduce more appropriate commercial glues and adhesives.

Tracing

Tracing is a very useful skill but not an easy one to acquire. Greaseproof paper is one of the strongest and cheapest papers available. Thick lead pencils are generally suitable although felt-tip pens and crayons are sometimes easier to use. Initially simple, bold, uncomplicated pictures should be provided, with paper clips or bulldog clips to keep everything in place. If necessary, acetate overlays rather than greaseproof paper can be used for early practice. Acetate doesn't tear, no matter how clumsy the child, and can easily be erased and re-used if water-based felt-tipped pens are used. Its transparency is also helpful.

Threading

For most activities with fabric, and some with card, it is an advantage for a child to be able to thread a needle, but this is a skill which requires a high degree of visual motor co-ordination. As such it can be seen as the climax of a long developmental process. The beginning of this process can be seen in the common play activity of putting large blocks on to dowelling sticks. This is not usually an art and craft task but it may be necessary in some cases to introduce this sort of activity into the art and craft lesson or at least suggest its use in the ordinary classroom if children are eventually going to be able to thread a needle. If the children can manage threading on large apparatus, provide smaller items. Coloured threading laces with a metal tag at one end and a bag of small coloured beads provide valuable practice which is in itself a craft activity. Coloured plastic straws can also be threaded through the holes in a sheet of pegboard. A piece of pegboard, twelve inches by twelve inches, slotted into a groove on a block of wood so that it stands vertically, is useful for this. Once threaded, the straws can be bent or knotted to make a picture or pattern. As skill increases, a large, blunt-ended bodkin with a huge eye can be threaded with rug wool and basic needlework can begin on a piece of rug canvas. Coloured string or nylon waste is also useful for this work as it does not fray or break easily. Some children may not progress beyond threading a large bodkin and weaving this in and out of large-holed canvases, but they will then be able to make things like peg-bags, string bags, and cushions. Other children will progress further and manage work on embroidery canvases and other materials requiring finer yarns.

Rolling

This is a skill which underlies success in a large number of three-dimensional activities with materials such as clay, plasticine, dough and papier-mâché. Again this is a skill which can be developed gradually as children learn the importance of the amount and consistency of pressure applied. Early work is probably best done with plasticine, progressing to clay and finally to papier-mâché. Initially it is easiest to concentrate on using the hands for rolling but eventually the rolling pin can be introduced. Practice in this skill need not be artificial as many objects made by rolling can easily be decorated. Snakes, snails and slugs always seem to appeal to children and, if made from clay or papier-mâché, can be brightly painted or coloured. Clay plaques and wall tiles are also popular and useful end products.

CORE ACTIVITIES

The following core activities are teachable at virtually all ages and ability levels and are tasks that children can undertake at their own standard with a good chance of success. Furthermore they are activities which can be varied sufficiently to ensure variety in the art and craft programme over a number of years. Indications are given where tasks are more suitable for one age or ability level than another.

Picture making

There are many ways of making a conventional picture and it is important not to become set on using paint and a paint brush. Similarly there are many materials on which a picture can be made. Card or sugar paper are the most frequently used and perhaps most convenient, but newspaper, cardboard, wallboard and three-dimensional objects are equally suitable for picture making and can add new dimensions to art work. Sometimes children find a large sheet of fresh white paper inhibiting. Coloured or printed paper can help here. Alternatively the teacher can put a squiggle or bold dash of paint on the paper to provide a starting point.

The following specific activities illustrate some of the many ways in which variety can be introduced into picture making.

Finger and toe painting

Finger and toe painting provide interesting ways of picture making and can also aid the general development of body awareness. With finger and toe painting don't be afraid to use lots of paint, but do make sure the children wear protective clothing and that their own clothes are rolled up out of the way or removed. Be prepared even to give a bath afterwards. Finger and toe painting has obvious appeal to the young and less able child but is also enjoyed by older and more capable children. Do not use quick-drying paint though.

Brush work

This is the most obvious method of picture making and, as a result, easily overlooked. Brush work is of course important, but has its limitations for mentally handicapped children. Few are likely to attain any degree of fine skill with a brush and many other techniques offer more interesting possibilities. When brush work is undertaken, try to introduce as much variety into the activity as possible. Different sorts of paints can be used, ranging from powder and poster paint, through oils, to ordinary house paint. Different sorts of brushes can be used, ranging from standard artists' brushes to house-painting brushes and brooms. Base materials can also be varied enormously, from the traditional card of sugar paper through to wall board or actual walls. When planning brush work, think in terms of variety — variety of size, shape and texture; this adds to the children's interest in the work as well as to the value of the finished product. If you are going to do much brush work you must also think of specially modified brushes and materials. A half-inch paint brush with a specially built-up handle and G-cramps to hold the paper steady will make work much easier for the handicapped child.

Marbling

The main value of marbling is perhaps that it's easy to do. There are kits available but the basic requirements are only a tray or a tin such as a roasting tin, some paper and some oil-based colours. Put the water in the tin and float the colours on the top; then all the child has to do is place the sheets of paper on top of the liquids to produce a pattern. By moving the colours on the water using a small stick, any number of very different patterns and designs can be produced from the same batch of paint. While this may have obvious limitations from a creative point of view it can be extremely useful with very young or multiply handicapped children, as it allows them to produce sophisticated patterns which they may have no chance of creating by any other method.

Stencils

Perhaps not acceptable to the purist, stencils do have their value. They can produce pictures with recognisable objects and animals in them, and are good for effective border and edge work. They can be most useful with the very young and the multiply handicapped. With most groups the teacher may have to provide the stencil, although older and more able children can make their own with guidance and instruction. Two important tips are to keep the paint fairly dry, as this will prevent running, and, if you can afford them, to use stencil brushes. They make the work much easier and the finished product more satisfying.

Wax resist

This is another easy way to achieve variety in picture making. It involves simply drawing on the paper first with a wax crayon or a candle and then covering the whole picture with a fairly thin colour wash of powder paint. The wax resists the paint and shows through the picture as a pattern. Most children can manage the waxing as well as the painting, but with the very young or the multiply handicapped the teacher may have to do it or guide the child's hand, without limiting the child's feeling of success. Even though the child's contribution may only involve painting on the colour wash and holding the crayon while the teacher guides his hand around the page, the end product is interesting and a true creative effort.

Wax patterns

This is a way of using up old wax crayon stubs and at the same time producing interesting patterns. All the child has to do is to break or grate up the crayons and spread them over half a sheet of paper. He then folds the other half over to cover the chippings, covers the whole thing with a few layers of newspaper and irons it with a warm iron. As the wax melts it spreads to form a pattern. This can be attempted by virtually all children. Care is needed with the warm iron, but the teacher can help overcome any difficulty and prevent danger. Unless you have a large stock of old crayons or use crayons at a rapid rate, this is something only to be done occasionally. But it can provide an exciting treat for the severely handicapped, particularly those with extreme motor difficulty, for it is an activity that requires a minimum of motor control yet results in exciting pictures.

Printing

Printing is an interesting way of producing varied designs, with the added advantage of fostering awareness of the texture and structure of objects. There is an endless range of objects which are suitable for printing, but the following offer variety at minimum cost:

Fruit and vegetables, such as apples, pears, carrots, potatoes, cabbage, swede or onions, can be cut into any shape, coated with paint and pressed on to the paper. The use of fruit and vegetables in this way is particularly popular as most children can bring and prepare their own vegetable and then use it to make their pattern. The motor skill required is minimal.

String can be glued in coils or in varying thicknesses on to a block of wood to make a printing tool which is used in the same way as the vegetables. This is not quite as easy for the children to prepare as a vegetable block, but appeals to the older and more able, or to any age group if the teacher prepares the block.

Blocks of wood or sticks can be cut or carved into particular shapes and then used as printing sticks. This too is suitable for all if the stick is provided, but perhaps only the more capable can manage to produce their own stick or block.

Sponges or loofahs give most interesting effects, particularly over large surfaces. They can be messy to use but are suitable for all ages and abilities.

Lino cut patterns are perhaps the most effective for pattern making, but not all that useful for severely mentally handicapped children because of the high degree of co-ordination and skill involved in the cutting. A lino cut can be prepared by the teacher but this does limit the value of the work.

There are also many variations on roller techniques which can be most effective. Painting on glass and then running a paint roller over it on to paper can produce interesting patterns. More exciting patterns can be produced by introducing leaves, seaweed or feathers into the process, although this does need a greater care and skill. Also, rolling off the top of an ordinary picture can produce an interesting variation by producing a mirror image.

Pattern making

Pattern making is always interesting to children but can become too rigid and should be used in moderation. If it is always done with some specific purpose in mind this should limit its frequency and also help maintain a high level of motivation and interest. For example it can be used effectively in making book covers, general background material upon which to display other work, wallpaper for a wendy house, or decoration for the classroom. There are many different ways in which patterns can be made:

(1) Make a growing pattern by drawing a shape on a piece of paper and drawing other shapes around it until the paper is full. It can then be painted or coloured.
(2) Use vegetable or other prints to produce a varied or repeating pattern.
(3) Use extra-thick paint made up from powder colour and detergent and put a pattern into it using a comb or a pastry wheel.
(4) Use acquired materials to provide a large number of different shapes and combine them into a pattern.
(5) Use a number of brushes tied together to make a pattern through powder paint thickened with cold-water paste.

(6) Use very thin powder paint on sugar paper and allow it to run freely to produce the patterns.

(7) Sprinkle dry powder paint over a thin powder wash to produce new colours and patterns.

A very simple method of pattern making is illustrated in fig. 7. The pattern is made with string and sugar paper using two colours. The sugar paper is folded in half, then opened out and laid flat on newspaper. Two lengths of string are immersed in different colours of very thick powder paint for several minutes until saturated. One at a time the two pieces of string are lowered on to one half of the sugar paper to form an abstract pattern. One end of each piece of string is left protruding from the edge of the paper as illustrated below.

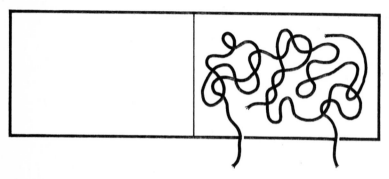

The other half of the sugar paper is folded over the string. This is covered with newspaper, taking care to leave the ends of string showing. A magazine is placed on top of the newspaper and pressed down to keep the sugar paper in place while the strings are pulled out one at a time. Finally the magazine and newspaper are removed very carefully and the paper unfolded to reveal the pattern. Fig. 7 shows an example of a pattern made in this way.

Pattern making can be of particular value for children with very limited motor control, for uncontrolled movements frequently result in more interesting and exciting patterns than controlled movements which become stilted and lacking in spontaneity.

Collage

Most children enjoy collecting material for collages as well as finding the work itself easy and rewarding. The child's task is extremely simple, requiring him to do no more than place or stick objects on to a piece of background material. Obviously planning and thought are involved in the placing of the objects, but even random placement frequently results in interesting end products. It may be helpful for the teacher to start the collage off, giving some guidelines and selecting materials. This need not detract from their creative effort. It may also be necessary to encourage the children

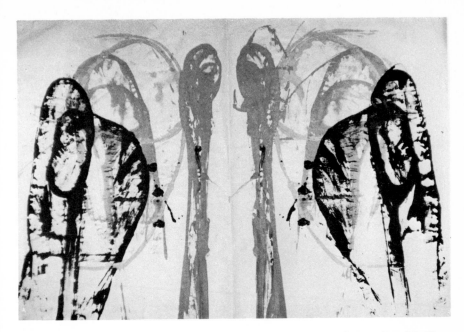

Fig. 7. String art. This was made by a fourteen-year-old boy, I.Q. less than 50. He is a brain-damaged child who was extremely withdrawn and nervous.

to be bold in their approach and to vary the textures and shapes of the materials that they have chosen. The use of staples or pins instead of glue may make the task simpler for some children.

The ram illustrated in fig. 8 was constructed using a stiff cardboard baseboard, artificial grass as the background, tweed material for the legs and face, leather for the horns, eyes, nose and feet, and waste man-made fibre for the body. Real wool could obviously have been used for the body but this would have been much more expensive. In this instance materials were glued on to the background cardboard.

The village scene shown in fig. 9 was made from assorted fabrics, with animal and human figures cut out of magazines. The base material in this case was cotton with dowelling strips attached to top and bottom through a hem. The collage is based on a magazine picture and the materials were chosen by the children to match its colours and main features. The materials were pinned or stapled on to the base fabric.

Silhouettes

Silhouettes add an element of personal involvement to picture making and can help with the development of body image and body awareness. There are many ways of making silhouettes. The most obvious involves standing the subject in front of a projector and using the shadow that is cast. In this way a faithful representation of

Fig. 8. Ram collage. This was group work from a mixed group of children of all ability levels in the thirteen to fifteen age group.

the person or object can be made, or unusual shapes created by using the compound silhouettes of several objects or people. Full-size body silhouettes can be made simply by drawing around the person while they lie on a large sheet of paper. Hands, feet and other large shapes are easy by this method, but it is harder to obtain fine shape variations such as occur on the silhouette of a person's face. Another method useful with objects, but of limited use with people, is to lay the subject on a sheet of paper and splash paint over it on to the paper, thus leaving the shape of the object as a clear area in the paint. There are also many different ways of finishing off silhouettes which can help add variety to the work. The silhouette can simply be cut out and pasted on to a contrasting background, especially if black or strong-coloured card has been used for the silhouette. Alternatively the silhouette can be painted, either within the shape or around the outside. Collage techniques can also be incorporated by using items such as foil, shells, coloured cellophane and paper to add distinctive features to the silhouette.

Three-dimensional activities

Three-dimensional work seems to add an element of reality to art and craft work for many children and provides extra motivation for them to develop painting skills and to complete work to a higher standard. Many art and craft activities can involve three-dimensional work but the following are particularly useful:

Fig. 9. Village collage. This was also group work by a mixed group of twelve- to sixteen-year-olds of all ability levels.

Decorating objects

Decorating objects is the most obvious and the simplest form of three-dimensional work. Many objects can be decorated to give interesting effects; the most appealing are those which can have some use afterwards. Tins, for example, can be decorated to make wastepaper bins, or magazine or telephone directory holders. Bottles can be decorated with shells, pebbles, pieces of glass or simply painted to make vases or candle holders. Plain white utensils, earthenware tiles, beakers, and plates can be painted and then varnished and used for their original purpose or as ornaments. Large stones can be painted and varnished for use as paperweights or door stops. Eggshells can be decorated with paint, sequins or ribbon to make Easter or Christmas decorations. The list of objects that can be decorated and serve some useful purpose is really endless.

Perhaps the greatest value of decorating objects such as these though lies not in immediate artistic considerations but in the fact that they can be taken home to be displayed and used. The benefits for the child's self-esteem and emotional well-being are obvious.

Construction

Constructional activities interest older and more capable children, even if they are generally beyond the scope of the very young and the multiply handicapped. Larger constructions are usually easier to manage. Most construction work can employ acquired materials. Basic frameworks can be made from boxes, wire, wood, tins, crumpled or rolled newspaper, pipes or other discarded building materials, and even old tights stuffed with paper. As long as it makes a firm foundation any material can be used for the framework. It is a good idea to vary the materials available so that the children experience a variety of materials and textures. Similarly, the outer materials can, and should, be varied too. The basic framework can be painted directly or covered in paper, card, cloth, carpet, lino or wood and then painted or decorated. Clay, plasticine or plaster can be used to good effect if shaped or rounded surfaces are required. The materials need not be permanent or durable. For example, food can add an exciting touch to a construction. Cake is ideal as it can be cooked or cut to shape, but biscuits, sweets, rock, icecream cones and wafers, and fruit can all be used – and eaten afterwards. Constructions made entirely of food can also be fun around Christmas time or when a birthday is coming up.

Construction work is an area of art and craft that can usually be linked directly with other school work. For example a visit to a fire station or railway museum can be followed up by making a fire engine out of boxes and cardboard tubes. Or unfamiliar objects, such as planes and rockets, can be made and explored.

Clay and plaster

Moulding materials such as clay and plaster are amongst the most rewarding of all materials to use. They are enjoyable to work with, are suitable for the most severely handicapped child, and can also be a good source of emotional release. They can also be worked and reworked if the finished product does not satisfy the child or teacher. A further advantage is that they tend to be familiar to children even before they start school since play dough and plasticine are so popular and widely used. However, time should be allowed for the children to experiment before expecting specific items to be produced. Allow plenty of time for banging, squeezing and squashing so that the children can experience texture and feel. Most importantly keep your aims realistic and appropriate to the children's ability level. While these materials can be used by almost all children, it would be unrealistic to expect a multiply handicapped child to produce a coffee mug or a vase; aim instead for a paper weight or an animal.

If you do wish to work with clay it is advisable to take a course yourself before attempting to teach children. Working with clay requires some expert knowledge and children's painstaking work can so easily be ruined by an inexperienced teacher firing the clay incorrectly. If you have no access to a course then books are available, but it is essential to practise first.

The difficulties of using clay are by no means insurmountable and should be confronted, but there are a number of materials on the market now which are easier to use than pottery clay, and some of these – such as plastone, sofenbak, barbola paste and some vinyl modelling compounds – have the advantage of not requiring kiln firing. An economic alternative to pottery clay and its commercial substitutes can be made from flour and water. Take nine cups of flour and mix it with three cups of water and half a cup of salt until it is soft and pliable. The resulting material can be used for making any sort of object and hardened by baking in an ordinary oven. When hard it can be painted with powder or gloss paint and varnished.

Plaster work is very much easier than clay work as there is very little that can go wrong. At the same time it is less creative as it usually involves a mould. It is, however, interesting to children and has the advantage of producing perfect items nearly every time. When models are set they can be painted or decorated, and this does allow for some individuality and creativity.

Model making

Another three-dimensional activity that has value for the mentally handicapped is model making. Apart from being fun and resulting in usable end products it has good experiential value. Models of many shapes and sizes can be made simply and easily by using materials of various textures and colours. Corrugated paper is one of the most useful materials. Because of its strength it can be used to make almost any shape yet it is very easy to work with. Also it is often available in abundance in schools since it is used in packaging of all kinds.

Balloons can be used to make a variety of shapes. If the balloon is inflated, lightly greased, and then covered with layers of thin paper pasted on to the surface, birds, animals, fish or anything similar can be made. Newspaper is as good a paper as any to use and usually three layers of paper are sufficient. Be sure to leave a small hole in the paper around the fastening end of the balloon because when the paper is dry the balloon has to be undone and removed. Before the balloon is removed, though, the paper should be covered with cold-water paste and allowed to dry for several days, depending on the thickness of the paper and the drying conditions of the room. When the model is dry it can be decorated in a variety of ways.

Papier-mâché is another medium for making models. Making the mâché is enjoyable in itself, is suitable work for even the most handicapped child and involves a variety of skills and experiences. The paper first has to be torn, mixed with warm water and made into pulp. In the final stages water has to be squeezed from the pulp; this can be linked with measurement work, for it is possible to chart how much water was added initially and how much is extracted at the end — assuming of course that not too much ends up on the floor. The final process of adding the cold-water paste is less interesting but does of course offer the possibility of experiencing another con-sistency. Less exciting than coarse mâché is papier-mâché made from tissue paper soaked in paste. This is ideal for finer work and shaping features on a larger object.

Actual construction using mâché is frequently not as easy as making the mâché itself and the children may need a lot of help at this stage, though simple objects and ornaments are well within the scope of most children. It is ideal for making parts of constructions which are difficult to make using other techniques — e.g. a head on a human figure. Articles made from papier-mâché can subsequently be painted or varnished to provide an attractive surface.

Woodwork

With older and more able children woodwork offers many possibilities. Good wood and an adequate supply of tools are essential and make the task easier and more satisfying for all concerned. All too often woodwork is attempted with odd bits of wood scrounged from here and there. Unless the school has the appropriate equipment to transform scrap wood into usable lengths and sizes the results can be disappointing; much of this sort of wood is hard and difficult to work with. Similarly good tools kept in good order are vital. A blunt saw makes sawing difficult even for a skilled craftsman, let alone a handicapped child. Obviously too, a woodwork bench complete with a vice and clamps is a must. Safety is, as always, a vital consideration.

Fabrics

Sewing

The extent to which this will be successful depends very much on the ability of the children involved. Some children never develop sufficient motor control even to weave in and out of open-meshed fabric, while others will be able to use a sewing machine with considerable skill and dexterity. The connection between needlework and visual motor development is obvious and the benefits beyond artistic development or interest can be considerable.

Tie and dye

This can be most exciting work and is suitable for a wide range of ages although perhaps most relevant to older children. A number of materials are suitable for this work, including paper, but unbleached calico is probably the cheapest and easiest to use. Exciting results, and very wearable clothes, can be produced from white tee-shirts. Here the benefits of personal involvement and motivation are obvious. There are many variations on tie and dye but the basic steps are simple.

It is best to begin by soaking, washing and ironing the fabric or garment so that any shrinkage occurs before dyeing. The dye also appears to be more easily absorbed when this is done. The fabric is simply tied with string, twisted or knotted, so that when it is immersed in a solution of cold-water dye, salt and soda only the free areas will absorb the colour. The process can be repeated any number of times to obtain different colours although the most interesting effects seem to be produced when you start with light shades and proceed to darker shades. When the item has been dyed it is finished by thoroughly rinsing it, drying it, and then washing it in hot water.

Thus while the end product is an attractive creation the work involved can be undertaken by anyone who can, with or without assistance, tie a knot and dip material in
and out of liquid. Perhaps the limiting age factor is the actual appeal of the finished
product, which seems to be basically to adolescents. One final note about this technique. Do encourage the children to think big. Working with small amounts of material is rarely exciting and the end product seldom very useful.

Batik

This is another fascinating way of producing patterns and designs which can be used
for making clothes or other items such as aprons, scarves, cushion covers or wall hangings. It requires more skill than tie and dye and involves the use of hot paraffin wax.
It is not therefore recommended for the very young or the multiply handicapped.

Unbleached calico makes an excellent base material. Finer materials such as cotton
and silk can be used but require more skill and should be left until the basic techniques
have been mastered with calico. Washing the material before use seems beneficial, as
it is with tie and dye. When the fabric has been prepared it should be placed on plain
paper — not newspaper as the print tends to transfer itself to the fabric — attached
to a flat board and securely anchored. Paraffin wax is then heated, preferably in a
double boiler, or in a can standing in a saucepan of water, until it has melted and
flows freely. Remove it from the heat and, using a brush, paint the wax over those
parts of the pattern on which you do not want the dye to appear. The pattern can
be created with the brush or drawn first on to the material with a soft lead pencil.
If a more exotic design is required try using templates, or stencils, or fruit and vegetable prints. Make sure the wax soaks through the material. If the wax cools during
application, return it to the heat or it will not penetrate the material sufficiently.
When the wax has dried, the material should be plunged in to a solution of cold-water
dye, salt and soda. Only the material which has not been coated with wax will absorb
the dye; the waxed areas will repel it. Rinse the fabric gently and dry. If further
colour is desired simply paint more wax over other sections of the material and repeat the dyeing process using another colour. This can be repeated as many times
as desired. Once the dyeing is complete place the material on a flat surface and scrape
off as much wax as possible. Then place the material between sheets of absorbent
paper and run a hot iron over it. The paper will absorb the remaining wax. Wash in
very hot soapy water, rinse well, dry and iron. The material is now ready for use.

Some special tools are available for this work. There is a 'tjanting' tool, a sort of
cup to hold the wax with a funnel for drawing with, but this is not of much use with
mentally handicapped children who generally find it easier to work with a brush.
Apart from the danger of the hot wax this whole process is well within the grasp of
many mentally handicapped children. Furthermore it requires little special equipment
and it costs very little to produce most interesting and exciting results. Rubber gloves
and laundry tongs are useful for the washing and hot water work.

Masks and puppets

Masks and puppets have a seemingly endless fascination for children. Behind masks
children can assume a certain anonymity, a new identity, and speak out in ways in
which they may hesitate to otherwise. Similarly puppets offer great opportunities
for emotional release and many avenues for the exploration of feelings and emotions.
Generally they prove extremely popular with the mentally handicapped, although
making them is perhaps limited to the older and more able.

In many ways making masks and puppets is an extension of model making. The
balloon technique and papier-mâché make excellent masks and can be used to make
heads or other body parts for puppets (as shown in fig.10). However there are many
ways of producing masks and puppets, many of them extremely simple and speedy.
Large lightweight boxes or corrugated paper tubes which fit over children's heads

Fig. 10. Puppet with a papier-mâché head.

and rest on their shoulders are excellent for masks. Decorated with paint or acquired materials they are easier to make than moulded masks and thus more suitable for younger age groups. Half masks can be made from cardboard, paper, cloth, or other materials, again with a minimum of complicated work. Apart from masks to wear, decorative masks can be made using dough, plasticine or clay fixed on to a background or placed on a pole and used for decoration or dramatic work.

Puppets can be made from a large variety of materials, ranging from clothes pegs, to paper bags, socks, paper plates — almost anything. Somewhat more complicated to use, marionettes are equally easy to make, especially large ones. The basic shape can be made from felt, cardboard tubes, tins, stuffed tights, or scraps of rag. Outer graments can be made easily. They need not be sewn but can be made from single pieces of cloth stapled or glued together. Joints need to be loose. Strings are attached just above the knees, at the wrists, and at each side of the head. These are then attached to two lengths of crossed dowelling so that the puppet can be manipulated. In most cases puppets and marionettes are easier to make than masks and therefore more suitable for younger and less able children.

An obvious extension of mask and puppet work is the construction of a puppet theatre. This need not be difficult and is an excellent project for a group of more able children. A three-sided clothes horse provides an excellent base as it is big enough to work behind and ideal for hanging curtains on.

EXTENSION ACTIVITIES

The activities above represent a basic core. There are, however, many other activities which the teacher of the mentally handicapped may wish to explore and which can be used to add variety to the art and craft programme. A few of these are described below.

Candle making

Candles are fun to make. They are also always welcome at home and consequently a source of increased self-esteem for the child. Furthermore they are relatively inexpensive to make, with the possibility of melting down any failures and using the wax again. But candle making involves the use of hot wax. An accident can be serious as the wax usually needs heating to around 82°C (180°F). This means restricting the activity to older and more able children. It is possible, though, to make candles using wax at a much lower temperature and then it can become an activity for younger children as well. The method involves whipping the wax. If it is whipped with a fork when it is just above melting point it can be handled quite easily and moulded by hand. At this temperature yoghurt cartons, margarine tubs and detergent containers can be used as moulds; at higher temperatures they melt as the wax is poured in. At Christmas white snowball candles can be made using this method. A point worth bearing in mind is that a thin household candle can be used in place of a standard wick, and this is much easier to handle. The end product is equally as efficient and effective and this puts the activity within the reach of many more children.

There are many candle making kits available and if you are not sure of the value of this activity for a group of children, a kit may be an economical way to investigate its potential, rather than investing in larger quantities of wax, dye and wick. There are many commercially prepared moulds available and most are quite cheap, but anything that will withstand heat can be used and can give an extra touch of individuality.

Pressed flowers

Flowers, leaves and grasses can be collected as part of nature study and then pressed in art and craft and used for decorations or card and picture making. A flower press makes pressing easier but obviously a stack of books can be effective. Placed under a piece of cellophane on a piece of card, pressed flowers and grasses can make beautiful greetings cards.

Brass rubbing

This can be fascinating work with enormous potential for incidental learning. Initially you can experiment by rubbing readily accessible surfaces such as coins, gratings and walls, and at this level rubbing can be an activity for quite young children. Church brasses, however, may be suitable only for older and more able children. Very few materials are needed — large sheets of paper, heelball or rubbing sticks, Sellotape, a soft brush and a duster — and the skill needed to obtain reasonable results is not great. Before undertaking a rubbing in a church be sure to make arrangements with the vicar first, and make it clear that children will be involved. Most vicars are helpful and co-operative. Frequently a fee is charged although this is often waived for a school party.

Felt work

Felt is an interesting and flexible material for art and craft work. Cutting can provide problems for younger and less able children, but in many activities an imperfect shape can add to, rather than detract from, the end product. If perfectly cut shapes are required they can be made by the teacher and simply stuck or sewn on by the child. Apart from its colour and durability, felt provides a good medium for tactile experiences. It is an excellent material for covering objects such as waste paper bins and for making tea- and egg-cosies, coal and oven gloves, dolls, and draught excluders. Felt can also be used for picture making, as a background material or in collage work. Fine hessian makes a good background material for felt pictures.

Stained glass windows

Realistic stained glass effects can be obtained relatively easily with readily available classroom materials. This is an activity more easily undertaken with older, more able children, but it can be suitable for younger children if designs are kept simple. Collect together greaseproof paper, Sellotape, templates, thick lead pencils, coloured inks, fine paint brushes, thick felt-tip pens (black), cold-water paste and a thick brush. Step one is to prepare a piece of greaseproof paper to fit the window you wish to decorate. If it is a large window you can join pieces of greaseproof with Sellotape. Remember that greaseproof paper will shrink slightly when wet and allow for this in your measurements. Draw a design on the paper using the lead pencil and templates such as dustbin lids, plates, rulers or whatever is handy. Keep the pattern simple and bold to begin with. Using the coloured inks and fine brushes, paint in the pattern areas and allow to dry. Now use the black felt-tip pen to go over the original pattern, applying pressure to ensure bold lines. When you are ready to put the 'stained glass' on the window, paste the wrong side of the paper, place it in position, pat it into place with a clean cloth, and smooth out any wrinkles.

CONCLUSION

The final choice of activities in any classroom must be based on a consideration of the teacher's and the children's interests and abilities. The teacher's enthusiasm for a particular activity is unlikely to produce results if the activity is not within the ability of the children or is of little interest to them. Similarly, enthusiastic children are unlikely to produce exciting results if the teacher is uninspired by, or ill-equipped to teach, a particular activity. Enough has been said in the previous chapter of the importance of adequate teacher preparation and experience, but perhaps enthusiasm tempered by common sense is the key to success. At this stage it is possibly worth suggesting that the children should be involved in course planning. Often children have to be guided to choose activities that are within their ability and yet which will at the same time extend them, but they can usually be relied upon for ideas and it is generally easy to determine their preferences. This helps enormously with motivation and interest.

Activities have been presented in this chapter in isolation and as independent activities. In the classroom it is obviously valuable if they can be related to other areas of the curriculum and treated within the framework of general curriculum themes. Themes can provide an excellent means of integrating art and craft activities with other areas of the curriculum yet seem to be so rarely used to the full by teachers. At Christmas and Easter many teachers become aware of this possibility but then fail to generalise its use at other times of the year. The co-operative group work component of theme work should also not be ignored.

Finally, it is perhaps worth repeating that art and craft should be fun. It is an area of school work that has enormous appeal for mentally handicapped children and one in which they are virtually assured of success. Nonetheless it is an area in which work should be carefully planned and programmed. If the teacher is willing to exercise some imagination in lesson planning and in developing ideas for motivation, then it can be among the most enjoyable activities the mentally handicapped child will experience. If the teacher treats the art and craft lesson as free time when she doesn't have to teach, then it can become boring and repetitive. Let us try to make it a rewarding experience for both teacher and pupil.

Further reading

General

Albrechtsen, L. (1972). *Wigwam and Moccasin.* Van Nostrand Reinhold, New York. An account of North American Indian art and suggestions for adapting Indian crafts – a tepee, costume moccasins, head bands and braids, work with beads, wood, leather and clay, feather head dresses, ornaments, and drama and dancing equipment. Illustrated.

Collins, J.B. (1969). *Starting Points in Art.* Ward Lock Educational, London. Chapters include picture-making, montage, collage, papier-mâché, constructions, mobiles, modelling, mosaics. Intended for the non-specialist art teacher. Well illustrated.

Glenister, S.H. (1953).*The Technique of Craft Teaching.* Harrap, London. A text aimed primarily at teaching wood and metal work, but with general principles applicable to the teaching of all crafts.

Hart, T. (1971). *Fun with Historical Projects.* Kaye and Ward, London. For general interest and ideas. Covers four projects – early British settlement, Roman villa, feudal village, and Norman castle. Well illustrated.

Holmes, K. and Collinson, H. (1952). *Child Art Grows Up.* The Studio Publications, London. Chapters include the appreciation of pattern, picture making, lettering, co-ordination of art and craft subjects, and art and our daily environment. Well illustrated.

Kramer, E. (1971). *Art as Therapy with Children.* Elek Books, London. Discusses work with disturbed and handicapped children. The author relates art work to specific psychological problems quoted in the book.

Norton, M. (1975). *Infant Crafts for School and Home.* Blandford Press, Poole, Dorset. Gives mass of information and ideas. Many illustrations and diagrams for patterns.

Peters, J. and Sutcliffe, A. (1970). *Making Costumes for School Plays.* Batsford, London. Discusses ways in which creative activity and improvisation can contribute towards costume for school plays for normal children, but many of the ideas do translate directly for use with the mentally handicapped.

Peter, J. (1968). *McCall's Golden Make-It Book.* Paul Hamlyn, Feltham, Middx. Contains many ideas and good detailed instructions for many topics. Many illustrations, all in colour.

Pickering, J.M. (1971). *Visual Education in the Primary School.* Batsford, London. Shows how to develop an awareness of tactile and visual experiences in children. Very good for general reading. Illustrations, some in colour.

Pownall, G. (1973). *Simple Crafts*. Allison and Busby, London.
Includes instructions for leaf printing, paste painting, spatter painting, shellcraft, soap carving, collage and papier-mâché.
Robertson, S.M. (1952). *Creative Crafts in Education*. Routledge and Kegan Paul, London.
Covers a wide field including clay work, booklet making, lino cuts, potato prints, masks and puppets. Few illustrations.
Stapleton, M. (1975). *Making Things Grandma Made*. Studio Vista, London.
Includes stained glass windows using such things as sweets and pastry, pressed flowers, clothes-peg dolls, sugar and fondant mice, and silhouettes.
Target, B.R.H. and Green, M.C. (1967). *Space Age Craft*. Harrap, London.
For information and interest. Provides general ideas which can be readily adapted. Illustrated.
Tilley, P. (1975). *Art in the Education of Subnormal Children*. Pitman Education Library, London.
Exceedingly interesting and useful. Includes chapters on art as a creative experience, the teacher's role, children's work, art for the severely subnormal, organisation and working in two and three dimensions. Illustrated.
Wood, D.N. (1975). *Starting Patterns with Thread*. Studio Vista, London.
Outlines basic requirements and procedures. Illustrated.

Decorations, gifts and toys

Keuhnemann, U. (1966). *Presents for Mother*. Mills and Boon, London.
Gives many ideas complete with detailed instructions, diagrams and photographs.
Lamarque, C. (1972). *Lots of Things to Make*. Collins, London.
Shows how to make things like a paper daisy, clothes-peg soldiers, rice lizard, furry egg-cosies, paper angels, hobby horse. Very colourful with clear illustrations.
Moloney, J. (1971). *Gifts and Games*. Ward Lock, London.
Ideas for making costumes and masks, games and small gifts. Well illustrated.
Skinner, M.K. (1974). *How to Make Decorations*. Studio Vista, London.
Includes party decorations, fruit and vegetable animals, candle holders, painted bottles, lanterns, wrapping paper, turnip table-lights, and window decorations. All are very simple and cheap to make. Illustrations, a few in colour.
Slade, R. (1968). *Toys from Balsa*. Faber and Faber, London.
Gives clear and detailed instructions for twenty models including a string puppet, totem pole and snake. Illustrated.
Strobl-Wohlschlager, I. (1969). *Make Your Own Party Decorations*. Batsford, London.
Includes items such as an Advent calendar, Christmas crib, sofa cushions, Christmas angel, kitchen gloves, wooden spoon figures and a sack for Father Christmas. Well illustrated.
Tyler, M. (1972). *Let's Make Soft Toys*. Evans Bros., London.
Each section describes the construction of a toy and provides a basic pattern for developing your own ideas. Illustrated.

Fabrics

Chappell, P. (1974). *Make it from Felt*. Evans Bros., London.
Patterns include ones for a wall hanging of The Owl and the Pussy Cat, a mouse string bag, a rabbit bag and a dachshund draught excluder, along with many other interesting and colourful items. Illustrated.
French, E. and Schrapel, S. (1972). *Tie-Dyeing and Fabric Printing*. Robert Hale, London.

Includes chapters on dyes and dyeing, batik, block printing, stencils, combined methods designs, and colour schemes. Illustrated.

Fressard, M.J. (1970). *Creating with Burlap*. Oak Tree Press, London.
Contents include painting on burlap, draping and shaping, burlap backgrounds, and embroidering burlap. Illustrated in black and white.

Haywood, H. (1974). *Enjoying Dyes: How to Pattern your own Clothes*. David and Charles, Newton Abbot, Devon.
Deals simply and clearly with the main methods of patterning fabrics with dyes. The practical uses as well as the sheer enjoyment of these crafts are explored. Illustrated in colour.

Holder, E. (1974). *Let's Decorate Fabric*. Evans Bros., London.
Very clear instructions and well illustrated.

Kuehnemann, U. (1976). *Textile Printing and Painting Made Easy*. Mills and Boon, London.
Contains mainly illustrations, but is most interesting and provides good stimulus material for the teacher.

Lammer, J. (1970). *Fun with Felt*. Batsford, London.
Clear and simple instructions for lots of basic activities. Illustrated.

Maile, A. (1971). *Tie and Dye Made Easy*. Mills and Boon, London.
A basic reference on tie and dye. Detailed instructions and illustrations for over 300 items.

Seyd, M. (1974). *Let's Use String*. Evans Bros., London.
Experimenting with and dyeing different types of string. Illustrated.

Timmins, A. (1970). *Making Fabric Wall Hangings*. Batsford, London.
Includes sections on collage, folded and rolled fabrics, machine and hand stitchery, and patchwork. A very interesting and stimulating book with lots of ideas. Many illustrations, some in colour.

Jewellery

Barber, J. (1975). *Nature Jewellery*. Chatto and Windus, London.
Jewellery made from objects found by the sea, in the countryside and in woods. Includes items made from seeds, nuts and pips, fur, feathers and bones, pebbles and stones. Illustrated.

Bennett, M., Capua, S. and McArthur, J. (1974). *Jewellery Anyone can Make*. Collins, London.
Media include plaster, buttons, clay, sequins, leather, foil, cork. Well illustrated in colour.

Finmark, S. and Whickers, D. (1975). *How to Make Jewellery from Junk*. Studio Vista, London.
Jewellery made from simple and easily obtainable materials — berries, seeds, pips, stones, pine cones, acorns, dried beans and peas, noodles, sweets, carrots, pebbles and shells. Illustrated.

Paper and card

Alkema, C.J. (1974). *Starting with Papier Mache*. Oak Tree Press, London.
Very useful with lots of practical suggestions. Lots of illustrations, some in colour.

D'Amato, J. and D'Amato, A. (1978). *Eighty Things to Make in Cardboard*. Odhams Books, London.
Many interesting ideas for making things with boxes and cartons. Well illustrated.

Hartung, R. (1966). *Creative Corrugated Paper Craft*. Batsford, London.
Mostly illustrations in black and white but a good source of ideas.
Law, F. (1974). *Things to Make from Card*. Collins, London.
Lots of good ideas and very colourfully illustrated.
Maile, A. (1975). *Tie-Dyed Paper*. Mills and Boon, London.
An excellent introduction to the use of tie-dye techniques with paper rather than
fabric. Many illustrations, some in colour.
Payne, G.C. (1966). *Fun with Paper Modelling*. Kaye and Ward, London.
Step by step instructions on how to make animal and bird models, paper masks and
decorated balloons from inexpensive materials. Includes photographs and numerous
drawings.

Picture making

Beaney, J. (1970). *Fun with Collage*. Kaye and Ward, London.
For general information and interest this is a most useful book. Plenty of photographs.
Bennett, M., Capua, S. and McArthur, J. (1974). *Crayon Craft*. Collins, London.
Includes the wet and dry processes of crayon etching, crayon on cloth, crayon batik.
Very colourfully illustrated.
Davies, R. (1971). *Let's Make A Picture*. Evans Bros., London.
Includes straw pictures, silhouettes, mosaic pictures and junk pictures. Illustrated.
Davies, R. (1971). *Let's Paint*. Evans Bros., London.
Explains in simple terms how to make pictures and experiment with paint. Illustrated.
Davies, R. (1972). *Let's Make Patterns*. Evans Bros., London.
Details how to create growth patterns, ink and splatter patterns, shape patterns, dis-
torted shapes, marbling, magazine collage, seed patterns, and pencil patterns. Illus-
trated.
Pluckrose, H. (1963). *Picture Making with Juniors*. Oldbourne, London.
Provides a practical guide to picture making with the emphasis on detailed practical
information. Some illustrations.
Scott, G. (1973). *Introducing Finger Painting*. Batsford, London.
Very helpful and full of interest. Nearly 150 illustrations.
Scott, G. (1971). *Let's Crayon*. Evans Bros., London.
Explains in simple terms how to make pictures and experiment with wax crayons in
conjunction with other materials – ink, powder paint, string, cardboard, detergent
and chalk. Illustrated.
Simms, C. and Simms, G. (1971). *Introducing Seed Collage*. Batsford, London.
For general interest and information. Very interesting. Illustrated.
Tingle, R. (1971). *Let's Print*. Evans Bros., London.
Includes finger painting, smudge printing, string and roller printing, junk and leaf
printing, vegetable and carbon paper printing. Illustrated.
Zaidenberg, A. (1963). *How to Draw Landscapes, Seascapes and Cityscapes*. Abelard-
    Schuman, London.
Good for general interest and information with lots of useful ideas.

Puppets and masks

Beresford, M. (1966). *How to Make Puppets and Teach Puppetry*. Mills and Boon,
    London.
Ways of introducing puppetry, making various types of puppets, notes on puppetry

in other countries, and puppet plays, are all topics that are explored in this most useful book. Some illustrations.
Law, F. (1975). *How to Make Puppets and Dolls.* Collins, London.
Ideas using all sorts of bits and pieces. Very well and colourfully illustrated.
Oppenheimer, L. and Lewis, S. (1964). *Folding Paper Puppets.* Frederick Muller, London.
Details how to make toys, puppets and party decorations by paper folding. Well illustrated.
Peters, J. and Sutcliffe, A. (1975). *Making a Mask.* Batsford, London.
Shows clearly the construction of masks from acquired materials. Nearly 200 pictures.
Philpott, A.R. (1974). *Let's Make Puppets.* Evans Bros., London.
Good ideas especially for the more able mentally handicapped child.

Three-dimensional work

Davies, R. (1974). *Let's Build.* Evans Bros., London.
Models and constructions requiring simple materials. Illustrated.
Farnworth, W. (1973). *Clay in the Primary School.* Batsford, London.
Full of sound advice and help. Illustrated.
Geipel, E. (1972). *Let's Model with Plaster.* Evans Bros., London.
Ideas for using plaster of Paris and Polyfilla. Illustrated.
Hartung, R. (1972). *Clay.* Batsford, London.
The objects described are mostly hand made with very few tools involved. Over 100 photographs show the methods involved together with the results.
Jackson, B. (1971). *Models from Junk.* Evans Bros., London.
Good ideas for using 'acquired materials'.
Lewis, A. (1974). *Let's Model.* Evans Bros., London.
Includes ideas for a flower tower, printing with clay, a night-light tree, and models with wire. Illustrated.
Payne, G.C. (1971). *Fun with Sculpture.* Kaye and Ward, London.
Suggestions for the use of many materials which can be used for sculpture work. Illustrated.
Pownall, G. (1973). *Pottery.* Allison and Busby, London.
Good book for general interest and basic information and ideas. Illustrated.
Schmitt-Menzel, I. (1969). *Fun with Clay.* Batsford, London.
Very interesting and useful, giving valuable basic information and instructions. Includes suggestions for candlesticks, tiles, masks, animals, vases, a decorative wall tile using machine and tool parts, and for firing finished work. Illustrated.
Weiss, H. (1960). *The Young Sculptor.* Nicholas and Kaye, London.
For general interest and information. A most valuable book. Includes information on use of wood, stone, clay, cardboard, plasticine and plaster. Illustrated.

Using acquired materials

Cutler, K.N. (1974). *Creative Shellcraft.* World's Work, London.
Includes an introduction to shells, collecting shells, shellcraft and gift work. Some illustrations.
Gilbert, D. (1970). *Can I Make One?* Faber and Faber, London.
Ideas for toys and models using mostly acquired materials — yoghurt tubs, egg boxes and cardboard tubes.

Griffin-King, J. (1969). *Making and Creating with Everyday Materials.* Blandford
    Press, Poole, Dorset.
Sections include picture work, decorating with stamps and shells, pressed flower
and leaf decoration, matchbox, cork and cotton reel toys, cards and calendars,
and mobiles. Illustrated.
Herder, K.G. (1970). *Working with Metal Foils.* Search Books, London.
Very interesting book with lots of good ideas, many of which translate easily for
use with mentally handicapped children.
Herder, K.G. (1971). *Things to Make from Odds and Ends.* Search Press, London.
Good for ideas. Covers use of scrap materials and remnants. Gives instructions for
oven gloves, beach towels, cosmetic bag, pin cushion, tool case, book covers, and
cosies. Well illustrated with some pictures in colour.
Hutchings, M. (1963). *What Shall I do with This?* Mills and Boon, London.
Describes and illustrates ways in which items from the kitchen, larder, garden shed,
bathroom, workbasket, etc., can be transformed into various decorative and useful
objects. Well illustrated.
Law, F. (1974). *Things to Make from Junk.* Collins, London.
Shows how to make a scrap metal man, a clockwork collage, models with wire and
wood shavings, egg shell pictures and a castle. Very well and carefully illustrated.
Moore, W. and Cynar, R. (1971). *Fun with Tools.* Kaye and Ward, London.
Gives instruction on essential tools for woodwork with instructions for many easy-
to-make objects.
Slade, R. (1965). *Take an Egg Box.* Faber and Faber, London.
Directions for making a variety of objects and shapes from egg boxes. Illustrated.

Miscellaneous

Gittings, C. (1970). *Brasses and Brass Rubbing.* Blandford Press, Poole, Dorset.
An interesting and informative book which covers actual brass rubbing techniques,
background information, and details of locations. Many illustrations.
Halsey, M. and Youngmark, L. (1975). *Foundations of Weaving.* David and Charles,
    Newton Abbot, Devon.
Provides all the relevant information and instruction for basic weaving and textile
design. Detailed and complete. Illustrated.
Kuehnemann, U. (1972). *Cold Enamelling.* Mills and Boon, London.
Good for general interest and detailed information. Illustrated.
Spencer, M. (1975). *Pressed Flower Decorations.* Collins, London.
Basic techniques illustrated with clear photographs.
Zechlin, K. (1971). *Setting in Clear Plastic.* Mills and Boon, London.
Good for general interest and specific instructions and techniques. Illustrated.
Znamierowski, N. (1973). *Weaving.* Pan Books, London.
Excellent brief introduction to the basics of weaving, with specific patterns for a
variety of objects. Illustrations, some in colour.

INDEX

adolescent, physical needs of, 36–8
apparatus, for movement
    large, 38–43
    playground, 46–7
    small, 43–4
art and craft
    classroom requirements, 145–8
    component skills, 152–4
    difficulties of, 136–7
    experimentation in, 137–9
    lesson preparation, 139–41
    materials for, 148–50
    and other subjects, 141–2
    see also display
art and craft activities
    core, 154–66
    extension, 167–9
autistic tendencies
    children with, 51–2

batik, 165
body awareness
    of the centre of the body, 27–9
    and drama, 119–21
    of ground, 26–7
    of hips, 30–1
    of knees, 29–30
    and locomotion, 29
    of other part of body, 31
    of stability, 31
brass rubbing, 168
brush work, 155

candle making, 167
clay, 162
collage, 158
construction, in art and craft, 161
creative activities
    research on, 4–6
    theoretical basis for, 6–8

value of, 4–6

decorating objects, 161
display of art and craft work,
    142–5
drama
    through constructive and creative
      play, 110–12
    in education, 113–15
    and experience, 108–110, 112–13,
      116–19
    and movement, 119–24
    and music, 84–5
    and oral skills, 126–8
    topics for, 130
    see also body awareness *and* move-
      ment

fabrics, 164–5
felt work, 168
finger and toe painting, 155
finger plays, 87–9

games, musical
    with instruments, 82–3
    listening, 80–2
    mystery sounds, 80–1
    sounds in space, 81–2

Heathcote, Dorothy, 108
hyperactive child, movement with,
    47–51

kits, art and craft, 149

marbling, 155
masks, 166
mobile cupboard for art and craft
    materials, 145–6
model making, 163

movement
  and drama, 119–24
  and music, 46, 85–7
  and relationships, 18–21
movement play, 21
multiply handicapped children
  movement with, 52–4
  art and craft with, 135
music
  attention to, 58–9
  and communication, 57–9
  and drama, 84–5
  and environmental sounds, 67–8
  and improvisation, 82–4
  and language development, 61–2
  and maturation, 64–5
  and movement, 46, 85–7
  programmes for, 71–5
  and social development, 62–3
  made by teacher, 68–70
  see also partner work *and* songs
music corners, 75–7
music groups, teacher-directed, 78
musical instruments
  to buy, 95–6
  games with, 82–3
  to make, 96–101
  playing, 73–5

paper
  cutting, 152
  folding, 153
  tearing, 152
partner work
  in movement, 21, 23, 32–3
  in music, 70, 77–8
pasting, 153
pattern making, 156, 157
physical activities
  research on, 4–6
  value of, 6–8
plaster, 162
play
  development of, in movement, 21
  and drama, 108–13
post-school-age mentally handicapped, 54
pressed flowers, 168
printing, 156
project method, 8–10
puppets, 166

rhythm
  consciousness of in music, 71–2
  development of in music, 72–3
  and drama, 121–4
  ostinato, 73–5
riding, horse, 45–6
rolling, art and craft, 154

sensory-motor development, 15–17
sewing, 164
silhouettes, 159
social development, and music, 62–3
songs, 87–95
sounds
  discrimination programme, 71
  environmental, 67
  and listening games, 80–2
special education, efficacy of, 2
stained glass windows, 169
stencils, 156
story telling, and music, 84
swimming, 44–5

terminology, 1
threading, 153
tie and dye, 164
tracing, 153

wax resist, 156
Way, Brian, 117
woodwork, 164